EARLY YEARS EDUCATION
AND CARE IN CANADA

EARLY YEARS EDUCATION AND CARE IN CANADA

A Historical and Philosophical Overview

EDITED BY

Susan Jagger

CANADIAN
SCHOLARS
Toronto | Vancouver

Early Years Education and Care in Canada: A Historical and Philosophical Overview
Edited by Susan Jagger

First published in 2019 by
Canadian Scholars, an imprint of CSP Books Inc.
425 Adelaide Street West, Suite 200
Toronto, Ontario
M5V 3C1

www.canadianscholars.ca

Library and Archives Canada Cataloguing in Publication

Title: Early years education and care in Canada : a historical and philosophical overview/
    edited by Susan Jagger.
Description: Includes bibliographical references.
Identifiers: Canadiana (print) 20190117443 | Canadiana (ebook) 20190117478 |
    ISBN 9781773381244 (softcover) | ISBN 9781773381268 (EPUB) | ISBN 9781773381251 (PDF)
Subjects: LCSH: Early childhood education—Canada. | LCSH: Child care—Canada.
Classification: LCC LB1139.3.C3 E34 2019 | DDC 372.210971—dc23

Page layout by S4Carlisle
Cover design by Ana Chabrand

Printed and bound in Ontario, Canada

Canadä

TABLE OF CONTENTS

LIST OF FIGURES, PHOTOS, AND TABLES

FIGURES AND PHOTOS

TABLES

PREFACE

Drawing Together Common Threads in the History and Philosophy of the Early Years

Susan Jagger

At the beginning of my History and Philosophy of Early Childhood Education class, I am often met by anxious looks, worried glances, and some glazed-over stares. I find that this course is one that students start with strongly held perceptions about the study of history and philosophy. It is dry. It is difficult. It is boring. It has nothing to do with the present.

I think quite the opposite. The study of the historical foundations and philosophical conceptions of early childhood education is an exploration of the ideas, themes, motivations, discoveries, challenges, questions, and tensions that have been theorized and practised. While the topics that we study and enact in early childhood education and care, such as play, development, and inclusion, can be rooted in past events and in the work of earlier scholars and practitioners, it is important to recognize the persistence of those discourses, and very often disagreements, in our current and future work with children and families.

Early Years Education and Care in Canada: A Historical and Philosophical Overview is a synoptic text that invites the reader to explore where we have been, where we are, and where we might go in our practice and research related to children and families. Early years scholars and educators, both beginning and established, from across Canada and across disciplines, including curriculum studies, philosophy, teacher education, early childhood education, sociology, and Indigenous studies, have contributed original chapters that share ideas, issues, and investigations into early years theory and practice that are widely relevant and also present uniquely Canadian narratives, perspectives, and histories.

This collection shares texts of ideas, experiences, and understandings of topics well studied throughout history and also "newer" theories, practices, and questions. Its chapters examine Indigenous knowledge and ways of knowing; play; the nature of children and childhood; education for all; the whole child; experience; developmental approaches to the early years as well as the reconceptualization of the early years; sociology of childhood; common worlding pedagogies; children's rights; equity, diversity, and inclusion; programs and practices supporting First Nations, Métis, and Inuit children and families; ecology and Nature Kindergarten; and multimodalities, media, and technology. Within these chapters, key theorists and philosophers, policies, programs, and practices are also discussed.

And while the chapters in this book are organized linearly, the themes presented and the ideas explored persist across places, spaces, and times. Common threads weave between and within its chapters that when pulled bring together differences in contents and contexts that create a complex patchwork of histories and philosophies, theories and practices, and policies and processes that inform and indeed define our conceptions and perceptions of the child, childhood, and early childhood education and care, and guide our actions with children and families.

Angelina Weenie reflects on her own experiences of childhood and education as both a learner and educator in the first chapter, "*Awāsisīwiwin*: Early Childhood Education and Indigenous Ways of Knowing." Weenie's text brings together the traditional and holistic teachings of the Seven Fires, the Circle of Life, and the Circle of Courage with the Western models of cognitive development, psychosocial theory, bioecology, and zones of proximal development, and realizes the complementary and connected nature of ways of learning, knowing, and being that have historically been viewed as separate and even binary. Her weaving together of both traditional knowledge and wisdom and Western approaches allows us to imagine an inclusive and holistic foundation for early childhood education and to guide educators in their practical realization of such an education.

Patrick J. Lewis similarly takes up the role of weaver in his chapter as he considers play, an acting and action well embraced in early years education and care, as a spiritual engagement and explores the spirituality of play. Lewis draws from multiple conceptions and perceptions of play, from Vygotsky's ideas to Sutton-Smith's rhetorics to Huizinga's philosophy, in his suggested re-interpretation of those theorists' notions of the ludic form, of play itself. He invites us to think about play as spiritual and as integral to the process of becoming human.

Margaret MacDonald examines through a diffractive lens the traces of the past that inform our practice in early childhood education and permeate our actions and engagements with early learners. Following Barad, MacDonald recognizes, as one method and practice, knowledge and knowing, and the learner and context. Her analysis explores our views of children and nature, the maternal role in early learning, and developmental approaches to pedagogy though the ideas asserted and propositions made by Jean-Jacques Rousseau in his treatise *Émile*. In particular, she examines Rousseau's ideas of "the expert," "readiness," and "vulnerability" of children in society.

Peter Pericles Trifonas also looks back as he looks forward in his exploration of the history of children's right to education. Central to Trifonas's examination is the life and philosophies of Comenius, both an idealist influenced by utopian visions of a free and equitable society and a pragmatic educator who created an early system of teaching or didactics with a view to learning by doing. Perhaps the most significant of Comenius's contributions was his belief that every child has the right to free education, an assertion taken up centuries later in the United Nations Convention on the Rights of the Child. Comenius's work influenced the development of early childhood education and the later theories and practices of Rousseau, Pestalozzi, Froebel, and Dewey, to name but a few.

Lovisa Fung's chapter realizes many themes and ideas explored in the preceding chapters as it presents holistic education and its key concepts and practices in early childhood learning. Fung delves into the historical background and origins of whole child education, the methods and practices of holistic teaching, and the role and preparation of the educator to actualize holistic teaching in the early years. Reflections from Fung's own experiences as an early years educator, current research in holistic education, and foundations of early childhood curriculum and pedagogy in Canada are woven throughout the chapter to provide unique insights into holistic education and its connection to the early years.

Susan Jagger explores the place of experience in early education and the educational places of experience. Following the articles of John Dewey's "My Pedagogic Creed," Jagger traces the theories and practices of Dewey, arguably the most influential educational theorist of the 20th century, and ideas and practices related to education, school, curriculum, pedagogy, and social progress. The chapter blurs the perceived binary oppositions of experience and education, child and curriculum, and teacher and student, and encourages an organic and contextual learning process that centres on the child and their experiential relationships with and in the home, school, and physical and social communities.

Developmentally appropriate practice (DAP) has been the standard approach of, and continues to be taken up by, many early learning centres and schools without question. In her chapter, Kristy Timmons provides an important critique of DAP as best practice in the early years. She details the historical perspectives of DAP, examines potential misunderstandings and misconceptions related to DAP, and considers implications of the philosophy for educators, parents, and children. Concluding the chapter are suggestions for the ongoing refinement in understanding best practices in the early years.

Children's rights, inclusive of their right to participate in community, society, and the environment, are examined in depth by Aurelia Di Santo and Bethany Robichaud in their chapter, "Children's Rights: Raising Awareness amongst Professionals Working with and for Children." The United Nations Convention on the Rights of the Child asserts that children have rights specific to their survival, development, protection, and participation in matters that affect them. Despite this declaration and despite the availability of related frameworks, Canadian early years education lags behind that of other nations. Di Santo and Robichaud explore why this is the case and identify strategies for moving our early years education and care forward and raising awareness in those working with and for children.

Following, and also guiding our work with children and families, is the sociology of childhood, which Noah Kenneally explores historically and contextually. "Children *in* Society—Thinking Sociologically about Children and Childhood in a Canadian Context" details the ideas foundational to this theoretical and practical approach that acknowledges the influence of children and their role in society. Kenneally notes the early stages of engagement of Canadian scholars and practitioners with the sociology of childhood and encourages our recognition and embrace of it as an important element for thinking about and working with young children, particularly in the field of Canadian early childhood studies and practice.

Rachel Berman and Zuhra Abawi's chapter, "Thinking and Doing Otherwise: Reconceptualist Contributions to Early Childhood Education and Care," marks a turn to "new" and contemporary ideas in early years theory and practice moving beyond developmental approaches. It introduces the reconceptualization of early childhood education through an exploration of the philosophical and theoretical foundations of this movement toward re-viewing and re-imagining the child, childhood, and early childhood education and care. Berman and Abawi invite our active questioning of the frameworks we adopt and how they impact how we research, plan for, work with, and respond to children and the knowledge that these engagements produce.

Next, Veronica Pacini-Ketchabaw, Randa Khattar, and Meagan Montpetit take up the invitation to reconceptualize early childhood education as they explore common worlding pedagogies beyond the space of developmental practice that respond to our current social and environmental situations. Through their personal narratives of reconnaissance, experimentation, and the more-than-human, they illuminate possibilities for acting, being, and thinking with and in the world in ways that challenge assumptions and relations in early childhood education and care that persist and perpetuate inequality and privilege and allow for children's participation in the world.

Kathryn Underwood focuses on equity, diversity, and inclusion as she explores their uptake in early childhood education and care programs. Her chapter considers capability theory and its focus on difference as catalyst both for human capability and also for oppression. Next, she examines the broader social context for equity, diversity, and inclusion, and the possibilities for early childhood education and care to foster and support meaningful social change.

Jessica Ball's chapter shares with us the promising programs and practices available to First Nations, Métis, and Inuit children and also the very significant gap in supports and opportunities for Indigenous children and families to establish in the early years a solid foundation for wellness, life-long learning, and contribution to society. Ball provides us with an overview of First Nations, Métis, and Inuit children's access to early childhood programs, including federally funded programs and provincial and territorial initiatives, and examples of promising practices. While these supports are encouraging, Canada has been very slow to honour its commitments related to the findings and calls to action of the Truth and Reconciliation Commission. Ball calls for access to high-quality early learning opportunities that are based on local cultural understandings, goals, and practices, and that afford opportunities to learn one's heritage language, and advocates for Indigenous community self-determination, supported by government resources, as one means toward cultural safety, cultural continuity, and decolonization in early education.

Enid Elliot states that "There Are Relationships beyond the Classroom" as she takes early years teaching and learning outdoors. The Nature Kindergarten situates early childhood education in the local natural landscape and focuses on sustainability though engagements with place, the life and natural materials that it affords, and opportunities for explorations of the world that we live with and in. Elliot shares her experiences in the founding of the Nature Kindergarten in Victoria, BC's Sooke School District on the traditional lands of the Coast Salish First Nations, the Kwsepsum

(Esquimalt), Lekwungen (Songhees), Scia'new (Beecher Bay), and T'Sou-ke (Sooke) peoples, and the creation of a community of young learners and educators that has come to know and care about the place that they live.

Finally, Laura Teichert looks at multimodality in relation to technology and digital media, and how their growing presence in our lives has redefined what it means to be literate. This is of particular importance for children who now live media-rich lives from birth and who engage with digital devices at home and in early learning environments. Through her study of Belle, Teichert describes how children use technology and digital media to entertain themselves, acquire knowledge, and transmediate from digital to non-digital modes.

The chapters of *Early Years Education and Care in Canada: A Historical and Philosophical Overview* invite you to engage with their content and, in doing so, explore and reflect on the historical and philosophical realizations, roles, and relations of the child, childhood, and early childhood education and care. They encourage you to consider and critique your current understandings and experiences with children and families and will hopefully motivate you to continue writing, through your own theoretical and practical work, the evolving stories of early years that support and nurture children, families, communities, societies, and environments.

CHAPTER 1

Awāsisīwiwin: Early Childhood Education and Indigenous Ways of Knowing

Angelina Weenie

GUIDING QUESTIONS:

1. How might Indigenous knowledge and ways of knowing inform early years theory and practice?
2. How do Indigenous knowledges compare with Western theories?

The purpose of this chapter is to discuss how Indigenous knowledge and ways of knowing can be used to convey an important historical and philosophical underpinning to early childhood education. It is proposed that the traditional teachings of *kēhtē-aya* (Elders) and knowledge keepers can contribute to a foundational understanding of early childhood education, one that can guide early childhood educators.

Concepts from First Nations languages and cultures can serve to enrich our knowledge of early childhood education. The teachings of the Seven Fires (Knight, 2011), the Circle of Life teachings as conceptualized by *kēhtē-aya*, and the Circle of Courage model (Brendtro, Brokenleg, & Van Bockern, 2009) will be considered as to how they inform early childhood education. It is proposed that these Indigenous knowledges are analogous to Western theories such as Piaget's (1970) theory of cognitive development, Erikson's (1980) psychosocial theory, Bronfenbrenner's Bioecological Model (1989), and Vygotsky's (1986, 1993) zone of proximal development. Western and Indigenous perspectives on childhood development will be discussed and analyzed in order to create a deeper understanding of appropriate teaching practice in early childhood education.

INTRODUCTION

First Nations perspectives about the history and philosophy of early years education are not widely written about. This became apparent to me when I was teaching a class on human development. By comparing Western and Indigenous perspectives it is clear how there are similarities and common ground for strengthening approaches to early childhood education. A theoretical model that conveys First Nations perspectives on human development is discussed. *Awāsisīwiwin* means childhood in the Plains Cree language. What has shaped my ideas on *awāsisīwiwin* in relation to early childhood education and Indigenous ways of knowing? What has informed how I think about and apply First Nations pedagogy? These guiding questions form the essence of this chapter on *awāsisīwiwin*.

The perspectives I am putting forth are shaped by my history, identity, language, and lived experience as an Aboriginal woman and educator. I use the terms *First Nations*, *Cree*, and *Indigenous* interchangeably. According to the Canadian Constitution of 1982, *Aboriginal* refers to First Nations, Métis, and Inuit. The term *Indigenous* is used to refer to those "people or communities who have a historical continuity with pre-invasion and pre-colonial societies that developed on their territories" (United Nations, 2004, p. 2). I am Indigenous to Canada and I am a First Nations Cree woman, *nehiyawiskwew*. I am from Sweetgrass First Nation, Saskatchewan, Canada. I am a Plains Cree "y" dialect speaker. I am currently a faculty member at First Nations University of Canada, Regina, Saskatchewan, Canada. I teach undergraduate and graduate courses in the Indigenous Education program.

READINESS TEACHER

My teaching background includes being an early childhood educator for nine years at the Prince Albert Indian Student Education Centre, in the 1980s. Band-controlled schools had come into existence after Indian Control of

Indian Education was introduced (National Indian Brotherhood, 1972). The chiefs from the twelve bands within the Prince Albert Grand Council controlled this residential school. While I was teaching at the student residence, I taught students who were designated at the Readiness level. It was more of a pre–grade one class. This was in my first years of teaching. My class included six- to eight-year-olds who were fluent Cree or Dene speakers. They came from northern Saskatchewan. They did not speak English, and because I was a fluent Cree speaker, I was assigned to teach them how to speak English and to prepare them for reading. It was an introduction to school for them. I was told that these early years were the most important years of their education and I needed to provide a good foundation in literacy learning.

We were required to use the provincial curriculum, and much of my work was focused on adapting the resources and making them more meaningful to my students. I often felt I was failing my students because what I was teaching them was not related to their lived reality. They lived in the far north, where hunting, fishing, trapping, and other traditional practices were part of their lives.

I had been educated in the Western educational theoretical notions of Piaget on child development. Knowledge of developmentally appropriate practice was beneficial, but for the most part, this educational theory was forgotten in the everyday busyness of classroom routines and rituals. I felt that the university education I had received was disconnected to my teaching practice, and I felt ill-prepared. In those days, I believe that First Nations educators were primarily being trained to follow the Western curriculum as part of the whole assimilative process for First Nations people. The need to include First Nations pedagogy was not discussed or taught. There was a lack of meaningful engagement with the language and cultural background of First Nations students and their lived experiences.

TOWARD A DECOLONIZING APPROACH IN INDIGENOUS EDUCATION

Historically, First Nations people were subjected to a rigorous process of colonization and assimilation. We were part of a colonial project that was intended to erase our languages and cultural identity. As a First Nations educator I felt somewhat complicit in this process. My early teaching practice and my role seemed to be about paving the way for my students to assimilate into white culture and society. I often asked myself what was First Nations about my teaching and how I was helping my students. The difference in my approach was that I talked to the children in their language, and I did not, in any way, think that their language was holding them back from being successful learners. I encouraged them to speak their language. Despite these efforts, I felt that I needed to learn more in order to teach more effectively. For this reason I started graduate studies.

During graduate studies I was drawn to the ideas of postcolonial theorists like Edward Said (1979), who wrote about how the East was permeated by "the web of racism, cultural stereotypes, political imperialism, dehumanizing ideology" (p. 27). Although he was writing about the East, his ideas helped me to see the racism and cultural imperialism experienced by Canadian First Nations people in the same light. Rigney (2006) expressed how "we must first immerse ourselves in and understand the very systems of thought and ideas and knowledges that have been instrumental in producing our position" (p. 39). This was the process of how I came to recognize how deeply embedded colonialism was in our education system. A colonized approach to education subverted alternate ways of knowing. This awareness influenced me to work toward privileging First Nations content and perspectives. This became the focus of my work.

For my doctoral dissertation, I wrote that "as an Aboriginal educator, my work is focused on how to develop greater insight into Aboriginal thought" (Weenie, 2010, p. 27). Jones Royster (1996) maintained how marginalized people have the capacity to "move with dexterity across cultural boundaries, to make themselves comfortable, and to make sense amid the chaos of difference" (p. 37). This notion also shaped my purpose and intent as an Indigenous educator. One can come to profound understandings of our knowledge systems through *miskâsowin*. *Miskâsowin* is about "finding one's sense of origin and belonging, finding one's self or finding one's centre" (Cardinal & Hildebrandt, 2000). This has been my process of knowing. I started to remember what I had learned as a child. What had been disregarded, ignored, and devalued in my educational experience became my most valuable source of knowing. I learned to value my own knowledge and language as a Cree person. I started to understand that I had knowledge that I could use to teach First Nations children. Courses on Aboriginal epistemology and pedagogy, in particular, supported my work as an Indigenous educator. These courses helped me to think about what I knew and how I had come to know things in order to pass along this kind of knowledge in my teaching practice. I started to work and learn from *kêhtê-aya* and knowledge keepers as a way of developing a decolonized approach in education. Their knowledge helped me to bring a spiritual and cultural aspect to my teaching as informed by First Nations epistemology and pedagogy.

EARLY FORMATIVE UNDERSTANDINGS

The courses I teach include First Nations and non-First Nations students. Even though First Nations content and perspectives are, increasingly, a regular part of our work in Indigenous education we cannot assume that all students have foundational knowledge of our culture. Due to colonization, cultural transmission has been disrupted, and much of our work is about restoring and revitalizing First Nations ways of knowing and being. I often rely on early childhood experiences to teach about culture and worldview. I feel that it is necessary to begin with a clear articulation of what culture is. Culture is defined as "the social framework for participating in and understanding the world" (Alberta Education, 2005, p. 10). We come to know our culture by experiencing the practices of our communities. Culture is how we live our lives on a daily basis.

Current Indigenous educational practice is, most often, focused on the circle. Talking circles, sharing circles, and reading and writing circles are most common in utilizing First Nations pedagogy. However, as part of using this strategy, it is important to understand why the circle is powerful in our culture. As a child, I remember the ceremonies that were held in my home reserve of Sweetgrass First Nation. There were protocols that we had to follow, and spiritual ceremonies were conducted in a circle. For the feasts, we all sat in a circle. The men and boys sat on one side and the women and girls sat on one side. The head Elder would sit in the north. The food was passed in a clockwise manner. The sundance ceremony was similar, in that the lodge was constructed in a circular manner. Round dances were also in a circle. These practices showed us about the power of the circle. Although, as a child, I did not understand the deeper meaning of the circle, I have come to understand the significance it has in our worldview. Garrett, Bellon-Harn, Torres-Rivera, Garrett, and Roberts (2003) write the following:

> The Circle is a symbol of power, relation, peace and unity. It serves as a reminder of the sacred relationship we share with all living beings in this world and of our responsibility as a helper and contributor to the Circle of Life by living in harmony and balance with all our relations. (p. 227)

These cultural beliefs lead to other representations of circle teachings. The teachings of the Seven Fires (Knight, 2011), the Circle of Life teachings as conceptualized by *kêhtê-aya* (Four Worlds Development, 2012), and the Circle of Courage model (Brendtro, Brokenleg, & Van Bockern, 2009) are part of using circle pedagogy. When I was teaching a course on understanding and enhancing human development, it became evident that these models could be associated with the learning theories that were being used in the field of educational psychology. It seemed that a closer examination of the correlations of these theoretical models could serve to enrich our knowledge of early childhood education.

The medicine wheel represents our journey through life and our "capacity to grow and change" (Four Worlds Development, 2012, p. 16). The medicine wheel is also referred to as *nêhiýaw pimâtisowin*, or Cree way of life. It is a holistic model that informs the teachings of the Seven Fires as presented by Elder Danny Musqua (Knight, 2011). *Awāsisīwiwin* is the first and most important stage in our development as human beings. These are the ideas that formulated the approach I took in teaching an educational psychology class on human development. These cultural ways of knowing were considered in relation to Western theories of learning and child development.

WESTERN AND FIRST NATIONS PERSPECTIVES ON CHILD DEVELOPMENT

Educational psychology is "a distinct discipline with its own theories, research methods, problems, and techniques" (Woolfolk, Winne, & Perry, 2016, p. 11). It is related how the historical context of these theories goes back to Plato and Aristotle; so how does this vast area of knowledge compare to First Nations ways of knowing? How do we make a place for First Nations perspectives? The more that I listened to Elders and knowledge keepers, the more it became apparent how traditional knowledge is equally valid and relevant to teaching and learning. I created a visual representation of each of the Western theories we were reading and learning about in educational psychology and how they were connected to First Nations perspectives. The model is titled "Theorizing from the Periphery on Human Development," and it follows, in part, the work of Knight (2011) in the "translation of foundational traditional education principles into a contemporary frame of thought and description" (p. 15). What follows is a discussion of Western and First Nations perspectives on child development.

Table 1.1: Theorizing from the Periphery on Human Development

WESTERN PERSPECTIVE	INDIGENOUS PERSPECTIVE
Piaget's Theory of Cognitive Development Four stages: sensorimotor, preoperational, concrete operational, formal operational	Medicine Wheel: Four aspects of self; includes spiritual development The Circle of Courage is attuned to the science of "positive youth development"
Erikson's Psychosocial Theory Eight stages: trust, autonomy, initiative, industry, identity, relationships, parenting, reflection and acceptance of life	The Seven Fires Finding oneself Circle of Courage: developing a sense of mastery, a sense of belonging, independence, generosity
Bronfenbrenner's Bioecological Model "Every person develops within a microsystem (family, community), inside a mesosystem (social settings)"	Circle of Life teachings Finding one's origin; *miskasowin*.
Vygotsky's Zone of Proximal Development Emphasis on language and learning "Recognizes that culture shapes cognitive development"	The importance of language and culture "Knowledge is enshrined in your language" (Musqua, in Knight, 2011 p. 49)
Gardner's Theory of Multiple Intelligences Eight intelligences	*miykosowin*: giftedness; we all have been gifted in ways to help us in our journey
Kohlberg's Theory of Moral Development Developing a sense of right and wrong Preconventional—determined by personal needs and wants Conventional—laws and authorities must be obeyed Post-conventional—universal principles of human rights, human dignity, and social justice	*pastahowin*: crossing the boundaries of what is right and proper The Seven Disciplines (Musqua)
Maslow's Theory of Motivation Self-actualization	Blackfoot Model Self-actualization leads to community actualization and cultural perpetuity

Jean Piaget, a Swiss psychologist, conceptualized the four stages of cognitive development, and these included the sensorimotor, the preoperational, the concrete operational, and the formal operational. These stages prompted the development and advancement of concrete ideas and principles to help us understand appropriate developmental practice. In comparison to these stages, First Nations perspectives have an added component. The Medicine

Wheel, or Circle of Life, is constituted by mental, emotional, physical, and spiritual aspects of self (Four Worlds Development, 2012). Elder Danny Musqua states, "Babies are extremely aware and, inherently, have strong spiritual awareness" (Knight, 2011, p. 62). For development of each of these aspects, the old ones provide children opportunities to learn discipline and responsibility (Knight, 2011). The milestones of child development are marked by ceremony and celebration. Naming ceremonies are held to provide guidance to the child. The name that a person is given has spiritual significance, and it means that they have to live up to their name. These cultural practices strengthen identity and a sense of self, and these are all critical elements to mental, emotional, and spiritual growth. They are not stages, but they are to be looked at as part of the lifelong process of learning and being. As we work toward decolonizing ourselves and our communities, these kinds of practices are increasingly important and worthy in early childhood education practices.

The Circle of Courage model (Brendtro et al., 2009) is "based in four universal growth needs of all children: belonging, mastery, independence, and generosity" (Manitoba Ministry of Education and Training, 2017, p. 2). This model brings in another aspect to youth development, namely, that children need to have a sense of belonging. Elder Danny Musqua states, "When a child was born there was an immediate sense of belonging" (Knight, 2011, p. 59). Children need to feel competent, and this is done by giving them responsibilities. They are taught independence and they are taught values. These values are part of the Seven Fires, or the seven disciplines, which Elder Danny Musqua shares (Knight, 2011). Elder Danny Musqua states, "The seven disciplines that have been established to facilitate learning are: prayer, meditation, fasting, benevolence, parenting, learning and teaching" (Knight, 2011, p. 51). These cultural teachings are part of the whole process of educating children, and they bring in another dynamic to appropriate developmental practice.

Erik Erikson developed the eight stages of psychosocial development, and these included: trust, autonomy, initiative, industry, identity, relationships, parenting, reflection, and acceptance of life. These stages are similar to what is learned and taught in First Nations culture. The life process includes having a sense of purpose and knowing that the journey is part of what the Creator has intended for our lives (Knight, 2011).

Vygotsky was a Russian psychologist who developed the sociocultural theory, and he "believed that human activities take place in cultural settings and cannot be understood apart from the settings" (Woolfolk et al., 2016, p. 50). This theory follows what First Nations people believe also, given the holistic and cultural teachings that are central to human development. The significance of Vygotsky's work is that he believed that language, culture, and social interaction played a part in cognitive development (Woolfolk et al., 2016). Similarly, Elder Danny Musqua maintains that "The tools for learning include the ceremonies, the rituals, and the language" (Knight, 2011, p. 53). He also states that "knowledge is enshrined in your language" (Knight, 2011, p. 49).

Another parallel that can be drawn in relation to First Nations ways of knowing is to Bronfenbrenner's bioecological model of human development. His model "refers to the total situation that surrounds and interacts with an individual's thoughts, feelings, and actions and shapes development and learning" (Woolfolk et al., 2016, p. 70). His model includes the microsystem, mesosystem, exosystem, and macrosystem of an individual (Woolfolk et al., 2016). This would include the family, community, and society within which an individual lives. This can be seen as being the same as the Circle of Life teachings, wherein the social context and environment are considered in child development.

Howard Gardner developed a new theory of intelligence, which he referred to as multiple intelligences (Woolfolk et al., 2016). These intelligences included the linguistic, musical, spatial, logical-mathematical, bodily-kinesthetic, interpersonal, intrapersonal, and naturalist abilities of an individual (Woolfolk et al., 2016). In First Nations view, we have *miýikosowin*, or giftedness. The Elders tell us that we have all been gifted in ways to help us in our journey. Some people are also gifted with spiritual power and talent, and this is called *mamâhtâwisin* (Wolvengrey, 2001).

Kohlberg's theory of moral development brings in another dimension to child development. He conceptualized that there were three levels of moral reasoning in children: preconventional, conventional, and postconventional. In First Nations culture we are taught about *pâstâhowin*, which is defined as "transgression, breach of natural order" (Wolvengrey, 2001, p. 176). As children we are taught that when we do wrong, there will be consequences for us. Our wrongdoings can also affect family members. For this reason, we are careful not to do harm to others. *Pâstâhowin* means crossing the boundaries of what is proper and good. The seven disciplines that Elder Danny Musqua shares are part of moral development. It is by practising and following spiritual principles that we can be good people. This is the relevance and applicability of First Nations cultural teachings.

Maslow developed a theory of motivation in 1970 in which he lists a hierarchy of needs "ranging from lower-level needs for survival and safety ... to higher level needs for intellectual achievement and finally self-actualization" (Woolfolk et al., 2016, p. 404). The similarities between Maslow's motivational theory and the beliefs of Blackfoot people are noteworthy. Michel (2014) compared the two models, and the difference with the Blackfoot model is that it shows self-actualization as the base from which community actualization and cultural perpetuity develop. This is an example of how First Nations perspectives have been used to inform or influence educational theory and practice.

DISCUSSION

First Nations views of human development are not clearly defined or acknowledged in current research and literature on humanistic educational psychology. More work on relating cultural teachings, as shared by Indigenous scholars, elders, and knowledge keepers, for use and consideration in the field of early childhood education, is needed. It is proposed that First Nations cultural teachings proffer a depth of knowledge to early childhood educators. The theoretical model presented in this chapter, which juxtaposes First Nations and Western perspectives, is a beginning to broadening perspectives on human development, and it invites further thought, insight, and discussion.

REFERENCES

Alberta Education. (2005). *Our words, our ways. Teaching First Nations, Metis and Inuit learners*. Retrieved from https://education.alberta.ca/media/3615876/our-words-our-ways.pdf

Brendtro, L. K., Brokenleg, M., & Van Bockern, S. (2009). *Reclaiming youth at risk. Our hope for the future*. Bloomington, IN: Solution Tree Press.

Bronfenbrenner, U. (1989). Ecological systems theory. In R. Vasta (Ed.), *Annals of child development* (Vol. 6, pp. 187–249). Boston, MA: JAI Press.

Cardinal, H., & Hildebrandt, W. (2000). *Treaty elders of Saskatchewan: Our dream is that our peoples will one day be recognized as nations*. Calgary, AB: University of Calgary Press.

Erikson, E. H. (1980). *Identity and the life cycle* (2nd ed.). New York, NY: Norton.

Four Worlds Development. (2012). *The sacred tree*. Twin Lakes, WI: Lotus.

Garrett, M. T., Bellon-Harn, M. L., Torres-Rivera, E., Garrett, J. T., & Roberts, L. C. (2003). Open hearts, open minds: Working with native youth in the schools. *Intervention in School and Clinic, 38*(4), 225–235.

Jones Royster, J. (1996). When the first voice you hear is not your own. *College Composition and Communication, 47*(1), 29–40.

Knight, D. (2011). *The seven fires. Teachings of the bear clan. As told by Dr. Danny Musqua*. Muskoday First Nation: Many Worlds.

Manitoba Ministry of Education and Training. (2017). *Circle of courage poster*. Retrieved from https://www.edu.gov.ca/k12/cur/cardev/gr9_found/courage.pdf

Michel, K. L. (2014). *Maslow's hierarchy connected to Blackfoot beliefs*. April 19, 2014. Retrieved from https://lincolnmichel.wordpress.com/...Maslow's hierarchy-connected-to-blackfoot-belief

National Indian Brotherhood/Assembly of First Nations. (1972). *Indian control of Indian education*. Ottawa, ON: Assembly of First Nations. Retrieved from http://www.oneca.com/IndianControlofIndianEducation.pdf

Piaget, J. (1970). Piaget's theory. In P. Mussen (Ed.), *Handbook of child psychology* (3rd ed., Vol. 1, pp. 703–732). New York, NY: Wiley.

Rigney, L. I. (2006). Indigenous research and aboriginal Australia. In J. E. Kunnie & N. Goduka (Eds.), *Indigenous people's wisdom and power. Affirming our knowledge through narratives* (pp. 32–48). Burlington, VT: Ashgate.

Said, E. W. (1979). *Orientalism*. New York, NY: Vintage Books.

United Nations. (2004). *The concept of Indigenous peoples*. New York, NY: Author. Retrieved from www.un.org/esa/socdev/unpfii/documents/workshop_data_background.doc

Vygotsky, L. S. (1986). *Thought and language*. Cambridge, MA: MIT Press.

Vygotsky, L. S. (1993). *The collected works of L. S. Vygotsky* (Vol. 2, J. Knox & C. Stevens, Trans.). New York, NY: Plenum.

Weenie, A. (2010). *Self-study: The inbetween space of an aboriginal academic* (Unpublished doctoral dissertation). University of Regina, Saskatchewan.

Wolvengrey, A. (2001). *Nêhiyawêwin: itwêwina*. Volume 1. Regina, SK: University of Regina.

Woolfolk, A. H., Winne, P. H., & Perry, N. (2016). *Educational psychology* (6th Canadian ed.). Don Mills, ON: Pearson Canada.

CHAPTER 2

Spirituality of Play

Patrick J. Lewis

GUIDING QUESTIONS:

1. What are your beliefs about play, and where do they originate?
2. How might early childhood play contribute to the idea of spirituality, and how might they be realized in practice?

> Play has features that are likely to make it especially suitable for finding the best way forward in a world of conflicting demands.
>
> —*Bateson, 2014, p. 104*

Play is often said to be universal; children everywhere are said to engage in some form of play. However, even though play is said to be universal and widely recognizable, play is also very difficult to explicate. That is because play is not an object, an action, or a place. Play is abstract, a dynamic and fluid process. Further complicating the idea of play is the plethora of meanings, so together the fluidity of play and the multiplicity of meanings make it impossible to adequately define play; almost any pursuit or act could be play simply by how we frame it (Johnson, Christie, & Wardle, 2005). Nevertheless, many people have expounded multiple theories of play and how it may or may not function.

In Euro-Western thought, it is generally accepted that play contributes to development and development can be seen in play. From infancy, a child begins to play into the world through what Piaget called the sensorimotor stage (birth to two years). Children develop an understanding of their own physical being and then expand that and engage with the object world, all through play. Children, through play in early life, learn about their world and their immediate environment and then explore what effect their play may have on their environment, so that their play becomes more systematic over time. But it is vital to understand that development does not happen in a straight, sequentially linear route, where a child simply adds on new behaviours, skills, or abilities cumulatively over time. What is most important to understand is that a child's development is more about transformation—a qualitative change of ability and skills and increased sophistication of play behaviours over a sustained period of time. Play researchers and theorists have created categories of play for the purpose of study. However, keep in mind that no child has ever entered into play thinking of how to learn something or what kind of play they are going to take up—they enter into play with only play and the pleasure that comes from that play in mind!

Play researchers tend to categorize play into four broad categories: motor, object, social, and symbolic play. From there, researchers have delineated a hierarchical set of stages of play development through cognitive stages (practice/functional play, constructive play, dramatic/symbolic play, games) and social stages (independent play, parallel play, cooperative play, observer, non-play) (Smith & Pellegrini, 2013). In early childhood and young childhood, children tend to move back and forth through these levels of play, building upon the skills and abilities developed in the so-called earlier stage of play. However, it is very common to observe children engaged in several of the levels of play development in any one play episode. Play and development are a complex, if not complicated, process that should not be seen as sequential step-by-step growth and development. Rather, play should be seen as a complicated aggregation of seemingly disparate experiences and explorations of children.

The landscape of play is littered with theories from the ancients through to current times. In fact, almost everyone seems to have some kind of theory of play, as well as some belief about how important it may or may not be in the lives of not just children, but adults too. However, as Gwen Gordon (2009) noted, "For a single definition to meet the challenge of encompassing the full trans-rational paradox and variability of play, it must be as protean and flexible as play itself" (p. 3). More recently, Gordon Burghardt (2014) offers that "Play is repeated, seemingly non-functional behavior differing from more adaptive versions structurally, contextually, or developmentally, and initiated when the animal is in a relaxed, unstimulating, or low stress setting" (p. 91). He then goes on to admit that even this definition is not meant to be definitive, nor does it capture all the possible nuances; however, it does cast the net further to include more animal play beyond mammals and anthropomorphic tendencies.

It is important to note that I am not trying to articulate a new or particular theory of play. I think, at best, we can say that play, like theory of mind or narrative mind, is an abstraction, a fluid and dynamic process of ongoing interpretive cycles that generates and regenerates experience. "Play is an elusive term which defies all conceptualization, in part because we are already so familiar with it" (Nagel, 2002, p. 1).

Nevertheless, I do want to try to transcend Brian Sutton-Smith's rhetorics of play, or at the very least add to or maybe even pull them together. And in that aim, I begin by suggesting that play is a spiritual process; from the moment we are born we are in the midst of play and move through it our entire lived experience up to and including the moment of our death; one might say we play at or toward our own death, both imagining how it might be and playing toward the actual clinical moment. In attempting to delineate the idea of play as spiritual I am both liberated and restrained by language. Heidegger (1962) said that "language is the house of being" and all we need is within that house; however, even he had to make up new words because, as he noted, the existing lexicon was worn out from overuse. Moreover, how do I avoid what Sutton-Smith said was almost impossible not to do when drawing upon persuasive narrative writing when exploring play: that it is essentially a declaration of my own rhetoric/ideology? Perhaps "in travelling across several of the rhetorics … we can see the many benefits of play regardless of biases and although our understanding of play remains ambiguous perhaps our appreciation of play deepens" (Lewis, 2017, p. 21). Needless to say, in what follows is my playing with/toward the idea of the spirituality of play, the play of spirituality.

PHILOSOPHICAL PLAY

Johan Huizinga (1950) reminds us that "Play is older than culture, for culture, however inadequately defined, always presupposes human society, and animals have not waited for man to teach them their playing" (p. 1). In his work *Homo Ludens* (man the player or playing man), he argued that play is a fundamental human function that permeates all cultures from the be-ginning. Indeed, he argues that "human civilization has added no essential feature to the general idea of play" (p. 1). Play is not a by-product or con-sequence of culture—rather play exists before culture. More recently, Brian Boyd (2009), in his work *On the Origins of Stories*, argues that those things we so easily associate with culture and its development, like the arts and stories, actually emerge from/through play. As Huizinga said,

> [Play] is a *significant* function—that is to say, there is some sense to it. In play there is something "at play" which transcends the immediate needs of life and imparts meaning to the action. All play means something. If we call the active principle that makes up the essence of play, "instinct," we explain nothing; if we call it "mind" or "will" we say too much. However we may regard it, the very fact that play has a meaning implies a non-materialistic quality in the nature of the thing itself. (1950, p. 1)

Brian Sutton-Smith began his lifelong study of play with Huizinga's work and at the end of the 20th century pondered,

> Maybe the function of play is quite different from the kinds of things we have been looking at, or perhaps we have been looking at the wrong kinds of function. Perhaps we need another kind of rhetoric for human beings and their play than the one that focuses always on some kind of skill—physical, cognitive, or emotional. (1995, p. 282)

Then, at the dawn of the 21st century, he asks if a theory of play is even possible, finding only "the ambiguity of play" (2001) through his seven rhet-orics of play.

SPIRITUALITY AND PLAY

To pick up with Sutton-Smith's ambiguity of play is to transcend his rhetorics in that to propose the spirituality of play is to suggest a way of augmenting and deepening our *appreciation*, rather than our understanding, of play. The word *spirit* itself is possessed with several meanings and/or senses, which may assist an exploration of the spirituality of play. Spirit comes from the Latin root *spiritus*, "breath" or "spirit," from the root *spirare*, "breathe," which sug-gests life itself. We need only look to everyday uses of the term/word *spirit* to

Box 2.1: Brian Sutton-Smith's Seven Rhetorics of Play

Progress: Argues that play is a developmental process of children and animals, but not adults. It has dominated Euro-American thinking more as a belief than a demonstrated fact that children's play is about development and learning rather than enjoyment.

Fate: One of the oldest rhetorics, which sees human lives and play controlled by the gods, Fortuna, luck or destiny with only those skillful in magic or reading the stars able to influence things.

Power: An ancient rhetoric exemplified through sports, athletics, and contests that very much persists today. It is a representation of conflict to consolidate the status of those who control the play or those who are its heroes. It rises out of warfare and the patriarchy and is anathema to modern play theory of progress.

Identity: Refers to cultural and community identity when such play in the form of festivals, traditions, and celebrations reaffirmed and/or maintained the community's identity.

Imaginary: Argues the importance of play as integral to imagination, flexibility, and creativity and is sustained by modern positive attitudes toward creativity and imagination.

Self: Emphasizes the desirable experiences of players—the fun, enjoyment, pleasure, joy—and the intrinsic or aesthetic satisfactions of the play performances.

Frivolous: Historically applied to the trickster or fool characters that were at the heart of carnival, enacting playful protest against the authorities of the day. More recently applied to the idle or foolish, but inverts the "work ethic" view of play, against which all the other rhetorics exist as rhetorics of rebuttal. (Sutton-Smith, 2001, pp. 9–12)

get a sense of its multidimensionality: a harmony between body and spirit; that's the spirit; a spirit haunts the home; she was in good spirits; she died last spring, but her spirit lingers; team spirit; the spirit of the age; her spirit did not falter; she played with great spirit; the spirit of the law; they were drinking spirits; and she was spirited away. The idea or sense of meaning of play and spirit are both possessed with a fluid dynamism that creates multiple understandings, or rather what Sutton-Smith (2001) called *ambiguity*. Spirit, like play, tends to elude a definitive meaning.

Environment and context through sociocultural perspectives are often purported to shape and influence play, and indeed they do, but not in the way that most adults observe or intend. Rather, it is the environment that facilitates children's nature of play in the way that it will determine what they need to do to transcend the boundaries of that environment in order to pursue their *desires* (long for); exert their *intentions* (attention to and sense of the world—real or imagined); and fulfill their *beliefs* (to hold dear). As Nancy King noted, play "is about deconstruction of context, the escape from contexts; in fact, one of play's major purposes is to make context irrelevant" (King, 1992, p. 58). I think it is here that we may attend to the "spirituality of play." Play is simultaneously of the material world and our inner world; the play happens in the immediate place, yet the play itself transforms the place into a new space, both in our exterior and interior realities. It is the *what-if* attitude of play that simply allows us to imagine the self, the other, and the world as otherwise. It is to see that how the world is at present need not remain so, and in that, I need not remain as I am. Story or narrative imagining, like play, is also of this world and of endless possible other worlds. Similarly, spirit is of the world and of us, that is, the spirit of *life*, our immediate quotidian existence, is entwined with the *life* of the world. Dwayne Huebner (1999a) offered that to talk about the spiritual is to "talk about lived reality, about experience and the possibility of experience. Another sphere of being is not being referred to. The 'spiritual' is of this world, not of another world; of this life, not another life" (p. 344).

Desire is entangled with spirit, as are human intention and belief. Arguably, it is desire that impels us to play and not necessarily freedom, choice, or an intrinsic pleasure motivation, although all those characteristics may have a secondary or tertiary influence on play. There is research evidence showing that we have a fundamental brain system that is responsible for the play drive (Panksepp & Biven, 2012). Vygotsky said it is only through play that we develop, and it is in this sense that he referred to play as the leading activity—leading a child's development. He used the term *perezhivanie*—the unity of affect and intellect, the mastering of imagination through play. It is a unified process of making meaning that integrates the *affect and the intellect*, a mastering of imagination in the sense of *process* rather than mastering as a form of *control*. Vygotsky shows us that imagination through play is active, a directed process woven through the development of cultural cognitive tools, in particular language and story. Story is an integral part of play, but it is also integral to any notion of spirituality. Play, spirituality, and story are very much of this world; however, all three work together to enable us to re-imagine this world and to imagine other possible worlds.

Consequently, Vygotsky asserted that "before play there is no imagination" (as cited in El'konin, 2005, p. 14). But Vygotsky was very careful to also caution that to

> refuse to approach the problem of play from the standpoint of fulfillment of the child's needs, his [*sic*] incentives to act, and his affective aspirations would result in a terrible intellectualization of play.... I think that an analysis of play should start with an examination of these particular aspects.... a child satisfies certain needs and incentives in play; and without understanding the special nature of these incentives, we cannot imagine the uniqueness of that type of activity we call play. (1933/2002)

Although Vygotsky's ideas are often considered central to constructivist theory and his ideas about play are often aligned with Sutton-Smith's "play as progress" rhetoric, I want to suggest a re-interpretation, hermeneutics if I may, of Vygotsky's, Huizinga's, and Sutton-Smith's ideas, to cast play as a spiritual activity/process.

Similar to Vygotsky, Huizinga (1950) articulated the difficulties and dangers of trying to impose some demarcation upon play and takes us toward the notion that play is "outside" our usual axiology.

> The more we try to mark off the form we call "play" from other forms apparently related to it, the more the absolute independence of the play-concept stands out. And the segregation of play from the domain of the great categorical antitheses does not stop there. Play lies outside the antithesis of wisdom and folly, and equally outside those of truth and falsehood, good and evil. Although it is a non-material activity it has no moral function. The valuations of vice and virtue do not apply here. (1950, p. 6)

It has been suggested that the "play drive" is similar to the "sleep drive" in humans; just as we have to sleep, we also have to play. However, without sleep we become ill and sometimes die; the same cannot be said about play. Nevertheless, play deprivation has been shown to have severe and long-lasting debilitating effects. Gray (2011) makes a connection between the decline of children's play and the rise of children's rates of anxiety, depression, suicide, helplessness, and narcissism (p. 447). And Stuart Brown's (2014) study of play also provides evidence of the long-term dysfunctional effects of play deprivation. Through his 45-plus years of study, Brown has provided evidence to suggest that "prolonged sustained play deprivation has major dire consequences for human competency and well-being," not the least of which are potential causal links to individuals hav'ng a "predilection for violent antisocial criminal activities." Play study ___ arch across multiple disciplines with human and non-human pl___ ___ rive at the intersection of agreement that we play and w___ ___ Panksepp and Lucy Biven (2012) note that, throug___ ___ rigorous scientific approach to play reveal___ ___ mental brain system, PLAY, which a___ ___ ___. Current research suggests th___ ___ ___ in the epigenetic develo___ ___

If, as Hu___ theories/rhe___ then we canno___ tainty. Perhaps we___ ___tly observed when he sai___ ___ ie that satisfies the adult desire t___ ___' (p. 271). If you ask children abou play___ ___ it is fun, but if you interrogate further, you ___ ___ standpoint play tends to occur outside the gaze and ___ ___ (unless the adult is a genuine player in the context). The few ___ ___ ave looked at play from a child's perspective found that children ca___ ___ play differently than adults do. Children sort play by activity type, nam___y role play, construction activities, and outdoor play; the level of control they have of the play; and finally, whether an adult is present or not (Howard, 2014). Here lies the difference between so-called good play and bad play, what Sutton-Smith (1988) called sacred and festival play (p. 45) and what Kuschner (2012) terms "good play and illicit play": an adult-manufactured binary between play for/with a learning purpose and play that derives from children's interests, needs, and desires. It is the illicit play that children want to engage with, but they often have to do so outside the gaze of the teacher or the parent. In the words of Sutton-Smith, "I am rather skeptical of any purely rationalistic interpretation of *ludic* phenomena. I do not share the linear view that evolution is at work singly and solely within an individual to create play as a form of learning" (Brown, 1995).

What do I mean when I talk about the spirituality of play? Johan Huizinga said, "we play and we know that we play, so we must be more than merely rational beings, for play is irrational" (Huizinga, 1950, p. 4). However, most significant is that "the whole point is the *playing*.... Child-play possesses the play-form in its veriest essence, and most purely" (p. 17). Well, if we talk about the psyche, the mind, or the soul being that which is the idea of self, who we are as individual beings, then when I talk of spirit, *pneuma*, that which is breathed or blown or a creative force, I am speaking of *life*, the persistence of it. And in my notion of the spirituality of play, perhaps it is in our play that we interact with and move in and out of spirit, the exterior and interior realities of being, the real and the imaginary, what might have been referred to in the past as the sacred and the profane. Jaak Panksepp has argued "play is quintessentially capable of activating the very best that the cortex is capable of" (as cited in Smith, 2010, p. 217). Here is where spirit and play are so entwined because they both exist before and outside any notions of culture, civilization, theories, or rhetorics. Spirit is that which is within us but also transcends us: the spirit of the lived-world, the life force of the world, what Jung called the collective unconscious, and what some Indigenous people call the ancestors. Winnicott (1991) offered that there is something between our psychic reality and our external reality in which we actually spend most of our time, and he asks the question not "what are we doing" in this space, but rather "where are we (if anywhere at all)" (p. 105)? He notes that the first two realities are fixed (acknowledging the variabilities within that fixedness), but the third reality, in which he states "creative playing" happens, is not fixed; it is variable because it "is a product of the *experiences of the individual person* in the environment" (p. 107). Winnicott called this in-between "a potential space" where play and cultural experience are located, and the special feature of this place "is that it *depends for its existence on living experiences*, not on inherited tendencies" (p. 108). The spiritual is not accessed, rather it is experienced, and it is through play that the spiritual may be experienced. It is not a thing, a body of knowledge; it is an experience, a process that is in "relationship to all modes of knowing" (Huebner, 1999a, p. 346). We know that "everyone experiences, and continues to have the possibility of experiencing the transcending of present forms of life, of finding that life is more than is presently known or lived" (p. 345), and that is the spirituality of play.

In his closing of *The Ambiguity of Play*, Sutton-Smith says, "it is also interesting to think of play as a lifelong simulation of the key neonatal characteristics of unrealistic optimism, egocentricity, and reactivity, all of which are guarantors of persistence in the face of adversity" (2001, p. 213). I ask, is this not an allusion to spirituality, the human journey of living into being human and human being? It is very difficult to articulate this idea of the spirituality of play. I am beginning to think that this is at best a formidable task and at worst ineffable. Or perhaps it is in fact the opposite—at worst it is a formidable task and at best it is ineffable. Nevertheless, such binary thinking does not speak to what I set out to try to articulate, so we need to see that "spirit is that which transcends the known, the expected, even the ego and the self. It is a source of hope" (Huebner, 1999b, p. 403). That is what I mean by the spirituality of play, that play is a source of hope; it is that "persistence in the face of adversity." The human species began with play, and we have been playing toward becoming human for millennia.

Brian Sutton-Smith suggests that we need to think about play as mythology and explore the links between play and narrative (Brown & Patte, 2013, p. 17). I think that it is not so much a link, but rather an integration, a coalescence of play and narrative that transcends a symbiotic relationship. It is an integration that emerged through the process of mythological constructs across human cultures over time and that gave birth to spirituality and grew and flourished through story and play, really creating a triad— story, play, spirituality. However, we have been engaged with play, story, and spirituality for so long that they have receded far into the background of our consciousness; we no longer easily perceive or are necessarily aware of them; they are just there, like the air. As Fagan (1981) commented, "play taunts us with its inaccessibility[;] we feel that something is behind it all (play), but we do not know, or have forgotten how to see it" (p. 493). More recently, through the intersection of multidisciplinary approaches to the study of play across humans and non-humans, science and social science have still not come up with a satisfactory *function* of play. However, as Burghardt (2014) notes, "if any general theory of play function is emerging, the role of play in regulating emotion and stress may be very promising, as it can be involved in many diverse types of play and various contexts" (p. 96). Yet others, in answering the question *what is play for?* have suggested "this question is not directed at the individual's motivation. It is concerned with how the various aspects of play increase the individual's chances of survival and reproducing itself" (Bateson, 2014, p. 104). That being said, perhaps we can transcend that difficulty if we turn our attention to ritual and mythology and see how play and spirit figure into that context.

We can begin with Johan Huizinga (1950), who said, "just as there is no formal difference between play and ritual, so the 'consecrated spot' cannot be formally distinguished from the play-ground" (p. 10). He was pointing out that whatever and wherever the play or the ritual, it takes place in a temporary world that is created within the real world; the creation of that temporary world is to perform the act (play or ritual) outside the real world. As mentioned earlier, play is of this immediate world and our inner world; play transforms spaces into places similar to the way rituals do. Play, just like ritual, simply allows us to imagine the self, the other, and the world as otherwise. It is seeing that how the world is at present need not remain so and, in that, we need not remain as we are.

Huizinga (1950) noted that there is a spiritual aspect to play in that the player must follow the rules despite the overwhelming desire to win, which requires the player to draw upon the energy of their "spiritual powers—'fairness'" (p. 11) to maintain not just self-control but the illusion of the play world and the engagement with the play and other players. Vygotsky articulated a similar idea but framed it through his theory of cultural constructivism, whereby the cultural practices compel the child to "follow the rules" of whatever the play may be, because not following disrupts and destroys the shared reality of the play, while following the rules provides the promise of reward, "a greater pleasure," as he called it.

> To carry out the rule is a source of pleasure. The rule wins because it is the strongest impulse.... Hence it follows that such a rule is an internal rule, i.e., a rule of inner self-restraint and self-determination, ... and not a rule the child obeys as a physical law. In short, play gives the child a new form of desires, i.e., teaches him to desire by relating his desires to a fictitious "I"—to his role in the game and its rules. Therefore, a child's greatest achievements are possible in play—achievements that tomorrow will become his average level of real action and his morality. (Vygotsky, 1933/2002)

Both Vygotsky and Huizinga were writing toward notions of the development of conscience and moral character that are often associated with spirituality and being and give birth to empathy. It may well be significant to remind ourselves that the opposite of play is not work or seriousness; rather, the opposite of play is depression (Sutton-Smith, 2001, p. 198).

Perhaps we might think of the seven rhetorics of play as a braid so that we travel through and with them all simultaneously and separately. Yet all seven rhetorics of play work together through multiple ludic forms, with spirituality and story woven through the braid, having merged and receded into the background. Or we can recall the beginning of the chapter and the so-called forms of play and stages of play and how they work together over time, propelling us through story into more complicated and sophisticated forms and functions of play, so that play becomes simultaneously the pull of the future, the press of the moment, and the force from the past (Johnson, Christie, & Wardle, 2005, p. 86) in our life journey. We can then imagine that play is what impels and pulls us into the human story; that is to say, we play at our existence and our becoming human. In our play we transcend the known, the expected, and the self and become other than who we have been and are now; we become more than who we are through the spirituality of play.

REFERENCES

Bateson, P. (2014). Play, playfulness, creativity and innovation. *Animal Behavior and Cognition, 1*(2), 99–112. doi: 10.12966/abc.05.02.2014

Beckett, C., Lynch, S., & Pike, D. (2017). Playing with theory. In S. Lynch, D. Pike, & C. Beckett (Eds.), *Multidisciplinary perspectives on play from birth and beyond: International perspectives on early childhood education and development, 18,* 1–24. doi: 10.1007/978-981-10-2643-0_1

Boyd, B. (2009). *On the origin of stories: Evolution, cognition and fiction.* Cambridge, MA: Harvard University Press.

Brown, F., & Patte, M. (2013). *Rethinking children's play.* London, UK: Bloomsbury Publishing.

Brown, S. (1995). Concepts of childhood and play: An interview with Brian Sutton-Smith. *Revision, 17.*

Brown, S. (2014). *Consequences of play deprivation.* Retrieved from http://www .scholarpedia.org/article/Consequences_of_Play_Deprivation

Burghardt, G. M. (2014). A brief glimpse at the long evolutionary history of play. *Animal Behavior and Cognition, 1*(2), 90–98. doi: 10.12966/abc.05.01.2014

El'konin, D. B. (2005). The psychology of play. *Journal of Russian and East European Psychology, 43*(1), 11–97.

Fagan, R. (1981). *Animal play behavior.* Oxford, UK: Oxford University Press.

Gordon, G. (2009). What is play? In search of a universal definition. In D. Kuschner (Ed.), *From children to red hatters: Diverse images and issues of play. Play and cultures studies* (Vol. 8, pp. 1–13). Lanham, MD: University Press of America.

Gray, P. (2011). The decline of play and the rise of psychopathology in children and adolescents. *American Journal of Play, 3*(4), 443–463.

Heidegger, M. (1962). *Being and time.* (J. Macquarrie & E. Robinson, Trans.). London, UK: SCM.

Howard, J. (2014). Play and development in early childhood. In T. Maynard & S. Powell (Eds.), *An introduction to early childhood studies* (pp. 115–126). Thousand Oaks, CA: Sage.

Huebner, D. (1999a). Spirituality and knowing. (1985). In V. Hillis (Ed.), *The lure of the transcendent: Collected essays by Dwayne E. Huebner* (pp. 340–352). Mahwah, NJ: Lawrence Erlbaum Associates.

Huebner, D. (1999b). Education and spirituality. (1985). In V. Hillis (Ed.), *The lure of the transcendent: Collected essays by Dwayne E. Huebner* (pp. 401–416). Mahwah, NJ: Lawrence Erlbaum Associates.

Huizinga, J. (1950). *Homo ludens: A study of the play-element in culture.* London, UK: Roy.

Johnson, J., Christie, J., & Wardle, F. (2005). *Play, development, and early education.* New York, NY: Pearson.

King, N. (1992). The impact of content on the play of young children. In S. Kessler & B. Swadener (Eds.), *Reconceptualizing the early childhood curriculum: Beginning the dialogue* (pp. 43–61). New York, NY: Teachers College Press.

Kuschner, D. (2001). The dangerously radical concept of free play. In S. Reifel & M. Brown (Eds.), *Early education and care and reconceptualizing play* (pp. 275–293). Oxford, UK: Elsevier.

Kuschner, D. (2012). Play in new developmentally appropriate practice: Analysis and critique. In L. E. Cohen & S. Waite-Stupiansky, *Play: A polyphony of research, theories, and issues (Play & culture studies)* (Vol. 12, pp. 191–205). Lanham, MD: University Press of America.

Lewis, P. (2007). *How we think but not in school: A storied approach to teaching.* Rotterdam, Netherlands: Sense.

Lewis, P. (2017). The erosion of play. *International Journal of Play, 6*(1), 10–23. doi: 10.1080/21594937.2017.1288391

Mergen, B. (1995). Past play: Relics, memory, and history. In A. D. Pellegrini (Ed.), *The future of play theory: A multidisciplinary inquiry into the contributions of Brian Sutton-Smith* (pp. 257–274). Albany, NY: SUNY.

Nagel, M. (2002). *Masking the abject: A genealogy of play.* Lanham, MD: Lexington Books.

Panksepp, J., & Biven, L. (2012). *The archaeology of mind.* New York, NY: W. W. Norton.

Smith, P. K. (2010). *Children and play.* Meldon, MA: Wiley-Blackwell.

Smith, P. K., & Pellegrini, A. (2013). Learning through play. In R. E. Tremblay, M. Boivin, & R. Peters (Eds.), *Encyclopaedia on early childhood development.*

Retrieved from: http://www.child-encyclopedia.com/play/according-experts/learning-through-play

Sutton-Smith, B. (1986). The spirit of play. In G. Fein & M. Rivkin (Eds.), *The young child at play: Review of research* (pp. 3–15). Washington, DC: NAEYC.

Sutton-Smith, B. (1988). The struggle between sacred play and festival play. In D. Bergen (Ed.), *Play as a medium for learning and development: A handbook of theory and practice* (pp. 45–47). Portsmouth, NH: Heinemann.

Sutton-Smith, B. (1995). The persuasive rhetorics of play. In A. D. Pellegrini (Ed), *The future of play theory: A multidisciplinary inquiry into the contributions of Brian Sutton-Smith*. Albany, NY: SUNY.

Sutton-Smith, B. (2001). *The ambiguity of play*. Cambridge, MA: Harvard University Press.

Vygotsky, L. (2002). Play and its role in the mental development of the child. (C. Mulholland, Trans.). In *Psychology and Marxism Internet Archive (marxists.org) 2002*. Retrieved from http://www.marxists.org/archive/vygotsky/works/1933/play.htm. (Original work published in 1933).

Vygotsky, L. (1987). *The collected works of L. S. Vygotsky, Problems of general psychology* (Vol. 1). (R. W. Rieber & A. S. Carton, Eds.). New York, NY: Plenum Press.

Vygotsky, L. (2003). Imagination and creativity in childhood. *Journal of Russian and East European Psychology, 42*(1), 7–97.

Winnicott, D. W. (1991). *Playing and reality*. London, UK: Routledge.

CHAPTER 3

A Diffractive Analysis of Early Childhood Education in Canada through Jean-Jacques Rousseau's *Émile*

Margaret MacDonald

GUIDING QUESTIONS:

1. Who was Jean-Jacques Rousseau, and what were his central ideas about early years education and care?
2. How does Rousseau's work continue to inform early years education and care?

INTRODUCTION

In 2013 I wrote, along with my graduate students Magdalena Rudkowski and Janine Hostettler-Schärer, a critical discourse analysis of Jean-Jacques Rousseau's treatise *Émile* to examine the "lingering discourses" that continue in the field of early childhood education (ECE) in Canada and elsewhere. A critical examination of Rousseau's teaching propositions and his methods seemed valuable at the time to trace back some of the advice literature to mothers and to identify the power and dangers of expert advice. It seemed important to identify ways that advice replicates and perpetuates stereotypes and myths about good mothers and what "best practices" and standard ways of viewing young children can and do leave out. Given the invitation to contribute a chapter to this book and to move my earlier work forward, I have chosen to approach Jean-Jacques Rousseau's treatise *Émile* again using a *diffractive* analysis that can be put into dialogue with the earlier critical account of his work. The purpose of this will be to try to attend to the differences that have resulted both despite and because of Rousseau's writing, rather than the similarities. In this work, I am re-imagining memory and time as time-space-matterings (Barad, 2007) so that this view or memory of Rousseau's work is not as something that can be written over, recovered, or erased from creases in an individual's mind (mine or another's) but is held in "the folded articulation of the universe in its mattering" (Kindle location [KL] 89–90). This can help to re-imagine this work not as a critique but a diffraction to see the influences or traces of Rousseau's work as an "entanglement and [the] responsibilities of which we are a part" (KL 94). I am also taking up Iris van der Tuin's suggestion to look at the *potentia*; that is, to see what is generative of/from Rousseau and, in important ways, to see how over time different material approaches to Rousseau's ideas and methods create resistance and differentiate sameness when we attend to, observe/notice, and map the impossibilities.

I would also like to acknowledge the difficulty of complexifying this work. Introducing diffractive analysis to the earlier analysis of Rousseau's work has been disruptive to me because of our scholarly habits of reducing, simplifying, reflecting or critiquing, and moving on. These practices are rarely placed in dialogue with what is left out or what has changed for us in space-time-matterings. Here I try to fold into my method and analysis the fact that this process of re-examining my critique of Rousseau has been influenced also by my intra-actions with new materiality theory to allow me to better consider non-traditional ways of seeing and re-imagining this work. This includes thinking and acting both consciously and subconsciously and recognizing that this diffractive act of "pulling through" has been aided by conversations with G7, a research group I belong to in the Faculty of Education at Simon Fraser University (including Drs. Diane Dagenais, Cher Hill, Nathalie Sinclair, Suzanne Smythe, and Kelleen Toohey), and also recent conversations we have had with Iris van der Tuin, who has encouraged us to see diffractively by attending to aspects that are counterintuitive but generative. As I worked through this analysis, reading and re-reading diffractive theory with Rousseau's writing, I also had a dream that I was in conversation with Nathalie Sinclair and Karen Barad, and when I awoke from this dream I realized that my consideration of this method and my understandings have also been aided by my subconscious dialogue and our continued practice of "staying with the trouble" (Haraway, 2016). Ultimately, this also rests upon a re-imagining of ECE through our past and, in particular, our call to attend to the impossibilities.

In her discussions of diffraction, Karen Barad (2007, 2014) draws on her background in quantum field physics and the work of physicist Niels Bohr (1937) to highlight the relationship between our being~becoming and our ways of knowing. Here she proposes that the two are one, namely that method and practice, knowledge and knowing are combined if we attend to the apparatus and observer as part of the deep situational context that creates a "cutting together apart" of the very patterns that we set out to observe and understand. Barad uses the methodological device of diffraction in her thought experiments to avoid the mirroring and sameness that come about when using reflection or even critical reflection. Using diffraction, she is able to stress that difference is heterogeneous; it is not an absolute boundary between object and subject, past and present, here and there and can be understood as having ontological implications if we attend simultaneously to the device and method. When we examine our so-called seminal ideas diffractively through our worldviews and the "pedagogical methods" used in Canadian early childhood education, we can begin to attend to the entanglement of methods and approaches to parenting through time to understand how our teaching and learning propositions shape us, young children, parents, and other educators. Here, we can better see how "vestiges" from the past, including the ways that we generate and transmit knowledge, have created old~new patterns that intra-act to dominate how we imagine the maternal role in families and what matter has mattered in and defines Canadian *early childhood education*. In this chapter, I place diffractive analysis in dialogue with a critical discussion of Rousseau's propositions in *Émile* to understand how our views of expertise, vulnerability, development, and location have been diffracted (pulled) through the lingering methods and material practices of Jean-Jacques Rousseau and his treatise on Émile. In this work, I am primarily diffracting teaching or pedagogical methods through Rousseau's advice about how to "guide, raise, or train" Émile, but I have also diffracted Rousseau's advice to mothers and tutors through location, both in his way of locating expertise as in an individual body or person and in his romantic notion of exposing Émile to nature and the outdoors.

TEACHER EDUCATION: WHAT DOES IT REALLY INVOLVE?

In teacher preparation (i.e., teacher training) instructors often remark on the challenges of breaking through the past attitudes and experiences of students, given the many years of mentorship, instruction, and training we have all received by the time we embark on our own "formal" or "professional" teaching careers. The same is true for our approaches to parenting and grandparenting and the "tools of the trade" we use to instruct or guide children. Are screens and devices bad for children? Should we be spending more time outdoors with our children? What are the benefits of reading to children or telling them stories? What limits and routines are best for children? What programs or schools should they be going to, and what child cares or preschools should they attend? We often answer these questions without too much consideration of where our values, approaches, materials, and methods come from and what has been obscured when we look toward standards of care and so-called best practices to guide our decision-making. Yet we also find ourselves making use of distinct ways of talking to, telling stories to, and reading with children or adopting phrases, material practices, or routines that we once lived through (and endured or enjoyed) ourselves. It should also be said that many parents are in survival mode, and these questions cannot even be entertained when options are non-existent. Trying to see generative ways of approaching this dialogue is essential to fold others into the conversation about ECE and being~becoming with our children and grandchildren and to take up thinking about the entanglement and responsibilities that we are all a part of.

DIFFRACTION

In an interview with Rick Dolphijn and Iris van der Tuin (2012), Karen Barad discusses her concern with the abundant use of "critique" in scholarly discourse, suggesting that critique has become so ubiquitous that the effect has become limited to an exercise in distancing and othering. For many, critique is merely used to "turn aside, to put someone or something down" (p. 49). In this chapter, my intention is not to perform a critique of Rousseau's writing, as has been done in the past, as a way to distance our practice in ECE from the past or to identify a "best practice" but, instead, to follow Barad's advice to attend to both apparatus and object and the suggestion proposed by Donna Haraway (1992, 1997) to use "diffraction" as a way to understand and attend to the effects that the differences create and to set this in motion with a past critique of Rousseau's methods and advice to mothers.

In this way, the use of diffraction goes beyond reflexivity and critical reflection. In reflexivity, we attend to ourselves and our subjectivity while examining the educational experience of the child and the education context (Johansson & White, 2011). Using critical reflection (Anderson, 2014), we view our practice critically by examining our actions as part of an understanding of the experience of the child and the phenomenon in question. Both of these techniques of reflexivity and critical reflection can be powerful methodological tools, but, as pointed out by Vivienne Bozalek and Michalinos Zembylas (2017), "much work has yet to be done conceptually to put these two practices—reflection and diffraction—in conversation with each other" (p. 111). As noted by Barad (in Dolphijn & van der Tuin, 2012), in diffraction,

> instead of there being a separation of subject and object, there is an entanglement of subject and object, which is called the "phenomenon." Objectivity instead of being about offering an undistorted mirror image of the world, is about accountability to marks on bodies, and responsibility to the entanglements of which we are a part. (p. 52)

Rousseau's eminence as a French philosopher, writer, and composer can be traced back to the 18th century, making this engagement with diffractive analysis particularly apt, given the impossibility of making meaning of Rousseau's intentions or the precise pedagogical outcome of his advice. Forgoing interpretation is important in this type of analysis so we can avoid attending to representation or meaning and more easily focus on the methods that Rousseau employs to raise and guide Émile. General advice about how to rear children and educational methods can be traced back to key philosophers such as Socrates, Plato, Aristotle, Comenius, and Locke. However, as discussed in the *Encyclopedia of Motherhood* (Esterberg, 2010), advice literature on parenting prior to that of Jean-Jacques Rousseau is fairly scant and typically includes advice directed to fathers, given their positions as patriarchs of the family (pp. 27–30). Among the first books of advice written to mothers and tutors of young children was Jean-Jacques Rousseau's treatise on Émile (1762).

FOLDS IN TIME: WHO WAS/IS ROUSSEAU?

Jean-Jacques Rousseau was born in Geneva, Switzerland, in 1712. The time of his birth coincided with what Fernand Braudel (1982) describes as a tumultuous period, where the countryside was being transformed through territorial wealth and power, and consolidations of merchant capitalism in Europe. This historic period was marked by commerce born and broken through conquests and clashing civilizations and a growing division of labour, alongside a complex gendering of roles and relationships within and outside the family system. Heightened fears of God, punishment, death, the power of government structures, and the church also marked the human experience. Life as described by Braudel (1982) was cruel, and children were often ignored until they survived infancy and were able to contribute to the family or the economy. During this era, a small number of privileged families were hierarchically positioned at the top of an entangled assemblage of the human and the material as capitalism took hold and where "everything invariably falls into the lap of this tiny group: power, wealth, a large share of surplus production" (p. 466). Rousseau himself was born into a family of relative wealth on his mother's side, but events shifted almost immediately when his mother died nine days later. The death of Suzanne Bernard Rousseau left Jean-Jacques's father responsible for his education and care and resulted in their fall in social position as his nuclear family adjusted to diminished means without Suzanne's family income. With his experience of loss (both human and material) his veneration of the ideal was born (Ballinger, 1965).

His climb politically and within the scholarly community began in 1749, when Rousseau won a contest for the best essay written on the topic "Has the progress of the arts and sciences contributed more to the corruption or purification of morals?" Here Rousseau argued that civilization had essentially created evil among men, a critique that in many ways provided a foundation for Rousseau's continued thesis on the purity of nature and the corruption of humankind. His perspectives were timely, emerging when the inequalities of power and privilege and the shifts from local feudal systems to political nationalism were assembling. This critique was also introduced during heightened fragmentation in the Christian church and a concomitant rise in humanism and empirical science (Braudel, 1982). Here "truth" emerges as tangible, rational, and objective, an important factor in Rousseau's position as an eminent expert in both social criticisms and new ways of thinking and approaching human relationships, including, as we see in *Émile*, parenting and pedagogy.

Rousseau's essay on the corruption of civilization was later published as the "Discourse on Political Economy" and appeared in the *Encyclopédie* in 1755. It found an audience among the industrious active class, who were critical of those born into wealth and power rather than earning their privilege. Following the success of this exposé, Rousseau worked concurrently on *The New Héloïse* and *The Social Contract*, both published in 1762. Stanley Ballinger (1965) describes these books by Rousseau as addressing his many contradictory ideas with a passionate rhetoric that fuelled many revolutionary ideas.

The contradictory and often utopian ideals that Rousseau puts forth also extend to optimum methods of rearing children in his book *Émile*, where he directs his advice to citizens who were intent on taking up positions in a reformed and ideal society (Duff, 2010). For Rousseau to have these opportunities to think deeply about what it might be like to have the ideal upbringing with a loving and devoted mother is testament to the fact that he remained relatively privileged, as a man with the means of acquiring patrons for support and education, and had the time to consider how to raise and care for a child. In this, he should be credited with an ability to theorize about "the possible." This he demonstrates in his writing on the topic of parenthood, something he had only scant personal experience with. In fact, his treatise on Émile was the antithesis of Rousseau's own lived experience and the unlikely result of his personal situation. Through *Émile*, Rousseau was able to write about what a child, mother, father, or tutor should be and do.

Although Rousseau did have brief direct experience tutoring two young boys, by his own admission, his tutoring/teaching experience was unsatisfactory, and he considered himself a failure. Rousseau also fathered five children, whom he may have drawn experience from but whom he chose not to have contact with. Instead, he sent them off to the foundling hospital, where, undoubtedly, their lives would be far from the ideal guidance and tutelage he described for Émile. He writes the following in *Confessions*:

> My third child was therefore carried to the foundling hospital as well as the two former, and the next two were disposed of in the same manner; for I have had five children in all. This arrangement seemed to me to be so good, reasonable and lawful, that if I did not publicly boast of it, the motive by which I was withheld was merely my regard for their mother.[1]
> (Rousseau, 2009, KL 7225)

Despite his admission to failure as a tutor and his practice of abandonment as a father, Rousseau provided theoretical advice with authority using a method that might best be called didactic. The book *Émile* is filled with rhetorical quandary after quandary answered by proposition after proposition driven home in the voice and tone of "the expert." Rousseau raises questions related to swaddling, nursing, and attending to children and admonishes mothers of privilege for their practice of using nannies and retaining wet nurses rather than "loving their own children." Here, Rousseau states the following:

> Does not the child need a mother's care as much as her milk? Other women, or even other animals, may give him the milk she denies him, but there is no substitute for a mother's love. The woman who nurses another's child in place of her own is a bad mother; how can she be a good nurse? She may become one in time; use will overcome nature, but the child may perish a hundred times before the nurse has developed a mother's affection for him. (Rousseau, 2009, p. 10)

Here in particular we see Rousseau's judgment around the mother's body and the practice of breastfeeding and the assertion that feeding should be done through her body alone. With a delivery style that gives no room for thought or reflection, his tonality entangled with his words creates an assemblage of rational persuasion and a god-like judgment, all of which linger today in many forms of "advice to parents." Diffracted through method, this notion of the expert patriarch who disseminates his advice through the written word has been replicated in the form of medical advice to mothers found in books such as Benjamin Spock's pediatric guides to mothers and other medical and sage advice disseminated and accessed digitally. However, digital methods have also created other "possibilities" for parents who have taken up the qualities of expertise in diffractive ways.

Today, through the device of the digital world, expertise has morphed into parent blogs and Facebook groups where bloggers provide solutions and resources to common dilemmas encountered by parents who are seeking answers and share solutions through a form of crowd-sourcing. As proposed by Alicia Blum-Ross and Sonia Livingstone (2017), this form of shared parenting, or what the authors term "sharenting," has become a new path to self-representation and identity formation:

> Bloggers grapple with profound ethical dilemmas, as representing their identities as parents inevitably makes public aspects of their children's

lives, introducing risks that they are, paradoxically, responsible for safe-guarding against. Parents thus evaluate what to share by juggling multiple obligations—to themselves, their children in the present and imagined into the future, and to their physical and virtual communities. (p. 110)

If we look at the written word in its assemblage with the global digital community, bloggers are able to draw on their unique experiences through networks that reach across spatial and temporal boundaries. This is discussed by May Friedman (in O'Reilly, 2010):

> Mommy blogs are sites of *both homogeneity and diversity*: while the majority of mommy blogs are written by white, middle-class, partnered women in heterosexual relationships, there are nonetheless a smaller number of blogs that represent a much wider range of maternal experience, in terms of both social location and other aspects of maternity, than are found elsewhere within narrative accounts of motherhood. Mommy blogs, like other Web logs, are usually written by a single person, with frequency of posting vary-ing considerably across blogs. The majority of blogs have open comments through which readers may respond to posts. In addition, the majority of mommy bloggers routinely link to other bloggers (through imbedded links within posts, or through a blog roll that collects the Web addresses of a number of others to whom the blogger is connected). It is these links and the comments that tend to create dialogue within all blogs, but most espe-cially among mommy bloggers. (p. 785, emphasis mine)

The entanglement of parenting with technology in this case allows us to diffract the notion of expert as detached. Here multiple sites of advice are possible, creating the potential to find diverse opinions and multiple voices and move closer to a dialogic encounter. To attend to the effects created through the blogosphere, we still see an isolated mother blogging advice to other isolated mothers or fathers. However, in the blogosphere, unlike parent magazines, advice manuals to mothers, or books on developmental mile-stones, the potential exists to reduce the isolation of mothering and the re-sponsibility of "getting it right" or "making it better," as advice is increasingly complexified in a now global world and where context is both here and there and culture is both local and global.

The notion of getting it right or making it better as an assumed qual-ity of the tutor and mother features strongly in Rousseau's writing. This is one among the many objective and ultimately unobtainable dispositions that mothers and early childhood educators are intended to possess. Through time we see ourselves set up in what Avital Nathman (2014) refers to as "the good mother myth," where archetypes of what and who good mothers are and can be are juxtaposed almost immediately with the reality of our lived experience. As described in *The Good Mother Myth* by the 36 bloggers, writers, scholars, artists, filmmakers, and feminists who contributed to this collection, this archetype simply doesn't exist. The diffracted effect of contrasting our lived practice with these archetypes of the good mother results in the impossibility of seeing mothers and fathers as beyond "good" by being authentic and real.

VULNERABILITY AND DEVELOPMENT

Characterization and a developmental profile are also produced by Rousseau through his fictitious child, Émile, who grows up through the nominal stages of infancy, childhood (boyhood), preadolescence, adolescence, and young manhood. As irony and the device of reductionism again would have it, Émile is filled with potential *if* he (and parenthetically all children his age) can be provided with gentle and optimal guidance and direction. Here the reader is set up for a trepidatious journey into ways to instruct a child who is in need of selective adult cueing and support at various life stages.

This developmental perspective on how to raise and educate young children has since been presented over and over as the orthodox approach to early childhood education. We see these ideas pulled through space-time-matterings into Piaget's stages of development, Maria Montessori's sensitive periods of instruction, and more recently, the National Association for the Education of Young Children's "developmentally appropriate practice." In these cases, the conceptualization of development requires us to agree with a normative psychological profile and trajectory or developmental milestone and work with this as if it exists (Petty, 2016; Younger, Adler, & Vasta, 2012) as the child moves from stage to stage to attain completion. In Canada, we have been influenced by the discourse of the normative child and at times have used it to protect and prevent children from rigid instruction that is considered developmentally "inappropriate" and hampers children's freedom and right to play (another strong early childhood discourse). We have also used this discourse to promote early intervention for children who are delayed or not "neuro-typical." Across time, these practices have perpetuated a standardization and the aspiration among parents that their children be "normal." We rarely question *what is normal, how has normal come to be,* and moreover, *why does normal matter, what does normal yield*, and *what materials create or detract from normal?* By way of disembodiment, we also see the child in isolation and often also see the child in parts as we focus on brain, body, and senses as sites of normativity and, overall, an assumption that we are working toward normative outcomes (see discussion by Colebrook, 2014).

Rousseau's thoughts on human development in education also demonstrate how stages of development become compartments and dictate our educational goals. Do we really enter and exit these discrete categories and domains, and how does the child's becoming congeal with their senses, personal interests, and material intra-actions? The methods that Rousseau describes set out to deliberately isolate one sense from another to avoid errors:

> We must learn to confirm the experiences of each sense by itself, without recourse to any other, though we have been in the habit of verifying the experience of one sense by that of another. Then each of our sensations will become an idea, and this idea will always correspond to the truth. This is the sort of knowledge I have tried to accumulate during this third phase of man's life. (Rousseau, 2009, KL 15467–15469)

Rousseau suggests this practice of isolating different sensory experiences so that young Émile isn't so easily fooled by tricks of perception where he might imagine movement in the wrong direction or optics that distort size and shape. This speaks to the need Rousseau sees of using a measured pseudo-scientific method in approaching instruction to young children, as opposed to holistic approaches where the child is immersed in reality and sees self in connection and relation with other. Here the Rousseauian assumption is that re-integration of these parts will happen (the work of the child?) and that the child is too delicate or deficit to handle the gestalt experiences of reality or holistic practices. When this happens, learning is not situated in the context of a need, problem, or curiosity, but is prescribed—taught and evaluated. The other effect of isolating our senses in learning so as "not to be fooled" in our perception is a concomitant assumption that this can and should be done by children and that there is an objective truth or correct way to perceive and discern, regardless of other (things, persons, goals). If we examine this practice diffractively, the heightened fragmentation of the curriculum has created the impossibility of a re-turn to embodied ways of knowing, as we see the potential we can gain from sensory tactile activities and finding ways to understand through touching, observing, and exploring (de Freitas & Sinclair, 2013), and embodied ways to know. Here, although Rousseau and others have set out to isolate (in this case) senses pulled through space-time-matterings, the effect has been a reestablishment of new~old ways of knowing through haptic encounters with materials and a re-turning to experiences that involve sensory explorations and ways of knowing that are embodied. Different than the suggestion given by Katz, Chard, and Kogan (2014) to analyze projects as a form of scientific method, Merleau-Ponty (2012) saw the basis of cognition as embodiment and was concerned about the ways that the procedures in scientific method could be harmful to learners, as they move us too far away from our natural embodied ways of knowing, while forcing us to engage deductively. The ideas proposed by Merleau-Ponty are not new ones; here we might turn to the earlier interpretations of Baruch Spinoza to help deepen our philosophical understandings around embodied engagement in experiential learning and the idea that understandings are not limited to our minds alone but are intimately connected to our bodies. Spinoza, born in 1632, provided an early proposition about this mind-body connection. As Deleuze (1988) explains, Spinoza proposed that "each thing is at once body and mind, thing and idea; it is in this sense that all individuals are *animata*" (p. 86). Deleuze goes on to explain that "all that is action in the body is also action in the mind, and all that is passion in the mind is also passion in the body" (p. 88). The image of individuals as animate is a powerful one. The Latin word *animata* is more familiar in its modern form, *animate*. The root or origin of the word *animata* is *soul* or *life*. It also can be thought of as something that is filled with life or animated to come alive. In Spinoza's use of *animata*, there is no distinction between ontology and epistemology, in that our being is our knowing and vice versa. As Deleuze explains, in Spinoza's conceptualization, "the body is a mode of extension; and the mind a mode of thinking" (p. 86). In this way, the mind is an idea of the body and cannot be separated.

Rousseauian discourse also extends the image of vulnerability and development of the child to all of humanity. Rousseau's solution is in education, seen here as a method of salvation:

> We are born weak, we need strength; we are born totally unprovided, we need aid; we are born stupid, we need judgement. Everything we do not have at our birth and which we need when we are grown is given us by education. (1979, p. 38)

In this writing, Rousseau poses both a problem and, true to his didactic form, provides the reader with an embedded solution and advice valorizing the role of education. For educators and teacher educators, in this discourse we ordinarily see a progressive statement, but when looking at both the device and the object using a diffractive view of this statement, we see education taking the material form of books and direct instruction of the type that is broken down, fed to the passive learner in parts, and is carefully controlled and evaluated by the teacher. As I have suggested elsewhere, Rousseau's message on education can be looked at as constituting education in a particular fashion and form that strips power from holistic, embedded, and relational approaches. As we stated in our critique of *Émile*,

> Although the message that education is a gift that can fulfil us is a powerful and hopeful one, it is also a message conceptually that implies education can somehow be separated from other holistic and embedded practices such as nurturing children and engaging them relationally. Several conceptual metaphors follow from this. Conceptually, as we strengthen the value and power of "education" to see it as something beyond ourselves i.e. as something that can only be given to us formally by tutors or teachers, we lessen the active role and our ownership of learning through individual action, reflection, modelling, peer learning or learning from extended family members. Young children are learning all the time, but Rousseau asks us to see "education" as something that should be delivered. This begs the question of the time and location of learning and the "curriculum" that is to be taught, and if, when and why we should see learning as separate from other experiences. (MacDonald, Rudkowski, & Hostettler-Schärer, 2013, p. 24)

Here, again, locating education as a thing that requires a shelf to put it on distracts us from the possibility to see learning as woven throughout our relationships with young children, where the responsibility for "getting it right" is concentrated among a few chosen "credentialed" persons who are vested in the structure and system or "business" of education. This viewpoint is divisive when we separate curriculum from child, child from adult, preschool from child care, teacher from parent and grandparent, school environment from home and community, and of course, human from non-human. And while the African proverb "it takes a village to raise a child" is often mouthed among members of early childhood communities, our pattern is to work in isolation from others in systems that divide duties and responsibilities. Setting this critique in dialogue with diffraction, we can, however, move beyond these boundaries to see the *potentia* to view education in community when we re-imagine the boundaries as connections. Preschool to child care, teacher to parent to grandparent, school environment to home and community, and human to non-human. The divisions are made conceptually and can be unmade conceptually.

Vulnerability and development are also taken up by Rousseau: as Émile is developing, it is not by his own construction of understandings but by the wisdom and guidance of his mother and later his tutor. This image of a passive, vulnerable learner who is only guaranteed success through the strength, wisdom, and protection of the adults who surround him pays no attention to the other influences in a child's education (e.g., siblings, other children, other extended family members, the community, and the non-human elements that make up the child's environment). It is important to note here that Rousseau has also highlighted the innocence of Émile as a vulnerable boy who must be kept away from the corrupting influences of society and, ironically, the corrupting influences of privilege among royalty and high class (Duff, 2010). Rousseau notes the following:

> This is one reason why I want to bring up Émile in the country, far from those miserable lacqueys, the most degraded of men except their masters; far from the vile morals of the town, whose gilded surface makes them seductive and contagious to children; while the vices of peasants, unadorned and in their naked grossness, are more fitted to repel than to seduce, when there is no motive for imitating them. (Rousseau, 2011, KL 13208–13210)

What does this yield ontologically? The image of the child in nature is a compelling one, often bringing us back to Rousseau's romantic view that nature and the garden are sources of re-birth and provide a fortification (purity) against the avarice, influences, and excesses of society. This reading of Rousseau, if diffracted through time, can be seen in the appeal of many of the current and fashionable "forest preschool programs," where parents are placing their children on waitlists so that they can attend forest programs. In the views of the parents, seeing their children outside in nature is understood as an antidote to life in the city. In the forest programs, parents feel their children have opportunities to commune with nature or experience the freedom of the outdoor environment (Rudkowski, 2015). As pointed out by Claire Colebrook (2014), however, this image of child in nature is still based firmly on a human-centric desire to consume nature for the good of humankind, as opposed to a true communing in nature, where reciprocity between human and non-human exists. Here the duty of making correct parental choices and finding ways to advantage and educate children and fortify them from societal avarice becomes antidote. In this movement toward nature, parents embody protection as they remove their children from traffic, concrete, and screens for a few hours from Monday to Friday. In this becoming, however, when viewed diffractively, even against this critique of the embedded human-centrism as we return children to nature, children do experience a closer connection to the rain, wind, and expanse of nature, and the ontological effects are pulled through as children will now be taught by the wind, rain, snow, sun, and the forest in all its complexity.

LOCATION

In *Émile*, Rousseau also uses a tone of responsibility and an appeal to the mother to attend with care in her devotion, coupled with the threat that if she fails at this endeavour, she alone is responsible:

> Tender, anxious mother, I appeal to you. You can remove this young tree from the highway and shield it from the crushing force of social conventions. Tend and water it ere it dies. One day its fruit will reward your care. From the outset raise a wall round your child's soul; another may sketch the plan, you alone should carry it into execution. Plants are fashioned by cultivation, man by education. (1979, p. 6)

This image of duty is embedded with the message that if the mother is successful in the care of her children she will be rewarded in her old age: "One day its fruit will reward your care." Rousseau furthers this point:

> The earliest education is most important and it undoubtedly is woman's work. If the author of nature had meant to assign it to men he would have given them milk to nurse the child. Always speak, then, preferably to women in your treatises on education; for, beyond the fact that they are in the position to watch over it more closely than are men and always have greater influence on it, they also have much more interest in its success, since most widows find themselves almost at the mercy of their children; then their children make mothers keenly aware, for good or ill, of the effect of the way they raised their children. (p. 37)

The entanglement of mothering with duty along with Rousseau's earlier message about love and tenderness is now met with the idea that *what* we contribute through our maternal practices will become an outcome or reward (in our old age over time—a temporal component). Here we (as mothers) are to be selfless but later will be rewarded for that selflessness by our children's care of us. This action of "now for later," when pulled through space-time-matterings and Rousseau's device of admonishment, can "mark" us with guilt and promise as we parent. It can also mark us with a conflicted sense of devotion and purpose. Do our roles, responsibilities, relationships, and the entanglement of the material rewards in old age become what matters in parenting? It is no wonder that many parents turn away from "expert" advice and turn to love and intuition as guiding forces in parenting practice or simply choose not to have children, given the weight of the responsibilities. In Rousseau's treatise, the present becomes later (old age) and love entangles with security and mercy. In this assemblage, he also distances the role of the fathers to locate parenting solely with mothering and to locate paternal responsibility with instruction and a dissemination of the correct truth or approach to educative practices.

Rousseau's location of nurturing and early education with the biological mother as a method of successful child-rearing also employs the device of isolation. We see in *Émile* a child raised first with his mother and later guided in early childhood by the careful, measured developmental approaches of the tutor. The lingering effects of being raised in isolation from community and having methods imposed on the mother and tutor still haunt us in Canadian early childhood education. If we look at the holistic practices of Indigenous communities in Canada, we can see how our Eurocentric traditions of isolating the child within a "family," assigning the responsibility of childrearing to the mother, and medicalizing practices like childbirth have disrupted Indigenous communities and the traditional role of fathers in their families and kin networks. According to Jaime Cidro, Elisabeth Dolin, and Christina Queskekapow (2017), dislocation and a re-location of the birth experience have been as disruptive to Canadian Indigenous communities as residential schooling. Tulugak, a 53-year-old Inuk man from Nunavut, recalls that members of his generation were born in igloos but that his own five children were delivered in Weeneebayko General Hospital in Moose Factory, Ontario, where, Tulugak states, "My kids were born to strangers," adding, "I feel a bit angry about not being there" (Cidro, Dolin, & Queskekapow, 2017, p. 76). Who is there, who is absent, and the experience of birth that separates the mother and child from their community can be seen as the effects of different worldviews where expert advice, method, and physicality are differently situated through different material traces.

The effect of locating early childhood education in a person or site of practice diminishes family and community ties and the role of the non-human (environment and material). If we pull this practice of expert methods taught or delivered by a specialist through the device of location, we also begin to notice the ways we have separated education from everyday life. Child care centres and schools as "locations of expert education" rarely make it a practice to mix with the elderly (unless they happened to be trained early childhood educators) or mix with the community (unless community members have "expert" knowledge, e.g., a music specialist, a storyteller). From a First Nations perspective and others with a holistic worldview, the work of education is collaborative and located on the land, in the longhouse, and in the home, and is ubiquitous. Moreover, the Elders in these communities are knowledge and cultural carriers who have earned their place through experience and knowledge-making practices. In this holistic view of being~becoming, we understand that we can never really locate sites of learning but understand learning as omnipresence. To put this critique in dialogue with diffraction is the work of our future, as we still grapple with what has been distorted or misappropriated in Canadian early childhood education. Generative models like those developed by Alan Pence and Jessica Ball show promise as we try to understand the *potentia* of pulling the past through the present. With work that has been done on reconciliation (also seen by some as a discourse of appropriation) in British Columbia, we have begun to look at curriculum more holistically through the First Peoples Principles of Learning and Indigenous practices and have begun the important epistemological~ontological~ethical work of indigenizing our "curriculum" (British Columbia Ministry of Education, n.d.; First Nations Education Steering Committee and Government of British Columbia, 2006).

CONCLUSIONS

The ways we connect with children, share joint attention, tease, cajole, nag, teach, or over-teach and how we choose to direct children's behaviours are all influenced by our own unique engagement with resources, materials, interests, and temperament and the past parenting styles in space-time-matterings. In many cases, these ways and things we have been exposed to in our methods and practices keep recreating Émile or images of Émile if we reduce mothering and pedagogy to something told to us by outside experts and approach mothering and pedagogy reductively and in isolation. Instead, if we can engage diffractively and understand also the role of the material within the family and in early childhood education to better understand our potential ways of establishing what and who constitutes a family and an understanding of "all our relations" and the practices that are educative, we may be able to see in the complex entanglement that we are of and are creating something new~old.

As Donna Haraway (1997) reminds us, "whereas reflection is bound to 'repeating the Sacred Image of the Same,' 'diffraction patterns record the history of interaction, interference, reinforcement, difference'" (p. 273). In our Eurocentric traditions, as illustrated through Jean-Jacques's treatise on Émile, I have used critique to draw attention to the creation of maternal guilt; normative practices; standardization; role differentiation; the isolation of the child within the family; and the concomitant separation of family from their community. I have also used a diffractive analysis to see the *potentia* and what has been produced through this, noting the ways that some ideas pulled through the past have become different and are setting our practices in motion in new ways through their entanglement.

This diffractive account of the present through the past in time-space-matterings creates sites of possibility where we can observe an entanglement of time and materials (methods) and heterogeneous difference. In this chapter, I am not setting out to establish a proof of the causality of these outcomes but am searching for diffractive ways to understand and disrupt boundaries in early childhood education and begin to offer an invitation to re-see, re-invent, and re-integrate truncated ways of approaching early childhood education in Canada and to provide alternative or different ways of knowing~doing~being~becoming.

NOTE

1. Their "mother" refers to a woman Rousseau was intimate with but chose not to marry, given her lower position in society.

REFERENCES

Anderson, E. (2014). Transforming early childhood education through critical reflection. *Contemporary Issues in Early Childhood Education, 15*(1), 81–82.

Ballinger, S. E. (1965). The natural man: Rousseau. In P. Nash, A. M. Kazamias, and H. J. Perkinson (Eds.), *The educated man: Studies in the history of educational thought.* New York, NY: John Wiley & Sons.

Barad, K. (2007). *Meeting the universe halfway: Quantum physics and the entanglement of matter and meaning* (Kindle Ed.). Durham: Duke University Press.

Barad, K. (2014). Diffracting diffraction: Cutting together-apart. *Parallax, 20,* 168–187.

Blum-Ross, A., & Livingstone, S. (2017). "Sharenting," parent blogging, and the boundaries of the digital self. *Popular Communication, 15*(2), 110–125. doi: 10.1080/15405702.2016.1223300

Bohr, N. (1937). Causality and complementarity. *Philosophy of Science, 4,* 289–298.

Bozalek, V., & Zembylas, M. (2017). Diffraction or reflection? Sketching the contours of two methodologies in educational research. *International Journal of Qualitative Studies in Education, 30*(2), 111–127.

Braudel, F. (1982). *Civilization and capitalism: 15th–18th century: The wheels of commerce* (Vol. II). London, UK: Collins.

British Columbia Ministry of Education. (n.d.). *First People's principles of learning.* Retrieved from https://www2.gov.bc.ca/assets/gov/education/kindergarten-to-grade-12/teach/teaching-tools/aboriginal-education/principles_of_learning.pdf

Cidro, J., Dolin, E., & Queskekapow, C. (2017). Bored, broke, and alone: Experiences of pregnant and expectant First Nations mothers birthing in and out of the community. In H. T. Neufeld & J. Cidro, *Indigenous experiences of pregnancy and birth* (pp. 73–90). Bradford, ON: Demeter Press.

Colebrook, C. (2014). *Death of the post-human: Essays on extinction* (Vol. 1). Ann Arbor, MI: Open University Press.

Deleuze, G. (1988). *Spinoza: Practical philosophy.* San Francisco, CA: City Lights Books.

Dolphijn, R., & van der Tuin, I. (2012). *New materialism: Interviews and cartographies.* Ann Arbor, MI: Open University Press.

de Freitas, E., & Sinclair, N. (2013). New materialist ontologies in mathematics education: The body in/of mathematics. *Educational Studies in Mathematics, 83*(3), 452–470.

Duff, P. (2010). *The parent as citizen: A democratic dilemma.* Minneapolis, MN: University of Minnesota Press.

Esterberg, K. (2010). Advice literature to mothers. In A. O'Reilly, *Encyclopedia of motherhood* (pp. 27–30). Thousand Oaks, CA: Sage.

First Nations Education Steering Committee and Government of British Columbia. (2006). B.C. and First Nations sign education agreement. Retrieved from https://archive.news.gov.bc.ca/releases/news_releases_2005-2009/2006OTP0117-000907.htm

Haraway, D. (1992). The promises of monsters: A regenerative politics for inappropriate/d others. In L. Grossberg, C. Nelson, & P. Treichler (Eds.), *Cultural studies* (pp. 295–337). London, UK, and New York, NY: Routledge.

Haraway, D. (1997). *Modest witness@second millenium: Femaleman meets onco-mouse: Feminism and technoscience*. New York, NY: Routledge.

Haraway, D. (2016). *Staying with the trouble* (Kindle ed.). Durham, UK: Duke University Press.

Johansson, E., & White, J. E. (Eds.). (2011). *Educational research with our youngest voices of infants and toddlers*. New York, NY: Springer.

Katz, L., Chard, S., & Kogan, Y. (2014). *Engaging children's minds: The project approach*. Santa Barbara, CA: Praeger.

MacDonald, M., Rudkowski, M., & Hostettler-Schärer, J. (2013). Lingering discourses: Jean-Jacques Rousseau's 18th-century images of mothers, fathers, and children. *Canadian Children, 38*(1), 21–28.

Merleau-Ponty, M. (2012). *Phenomenology of perception*. London, UK: Routledge.

Nathman, A. N. (2014). *The good mother myth: Redefining motherhood to fit reality*. Berkeley, CA: Seal Press.

O'Reilly, A. (2010). *Encyclopedia of motherhood*. Thousand Oaks, CA: Sage.

Petty, K. (2016). *Developmental milestones of young children* (Rev. ed.). St. Paul, MN: Redleaf Press.

Rousseau, J. J. (2009). *The works of Jean-Jacques Rousseau: The social contract, confessions, Émile, and other essays* (Kindle ed., Kindle locations 7225–7227). Halcyon Press.

Rousseau, J. J. (1979). *Émile or on education* (Trans. Allan Bloom). New York, NY: Basic Books.

Rousseau, J. J. (2011). *Émile* (Kindle ed., Trans. Barbara Foxley).

Rudkowski, M. (2015). *The complexity of understanding: Young children's experiences in a forest program* (Unpublished doctoral dissertation). Simon Fraser University, Burnaby, BC.

Younger, A., Adler, S., & Vasta, R. (2012). *Child psychology: A Canadian perspective* (3rd ed.). Mississauga, ON: John Wiley & Sons.

CHAPTER 4

The Right to Education and the Child

Peter Pericles Trifonas

GUIDING QUESTIONS:

1. Compare and contrast the philosophies, ideas, and approaches of Rousseau (covered in chapter 3) and Comenius with respect to children and their education. In what ways are they similar and dissimilar?

2. Review the Dakar Framework in light of the ideas and approaches of Comenius. Where and how are his ideas included in the document?

Jan Amos Komenský or "Comenius" is as applicable to early childhood education today as four hundred years ago. On the one hand, he was an idealist influenced by utopian visions of a free and equitable society and, on the other, a pragmatic educator who developed a teaching system or "didactics" with a view to learning by doing, long before John Dewey. Perhaps Comenius's most significant contribution to educational theory was the belief that every child has the right to education, a claim endorsed by Maria Montessori in the creation of the Social Party of the Child (1937) that has been ingrained in Article 28 of the United Nations Convention on the Rights of the Child (1989). The chapter will discuss Comenius's influence on the development of early childhood education.

WHO WAS JOHN AMOS COMENIUS?

John Amos Comenius (born Jan Amos Komenský on March 28, 1592, in Nivnice, Moravia; died November 14, 1670, in Amsterdam, Netherlands) was a pivotal figure in educational thought. At 10 years old, he lived with an aunt in Strážnice for four years after the death of his parents and two sisters from the plague. Comenius then moved to attend school at Přerov. It was quickly realized that his great intellectual gifts would be well served in preparation for the ministry. Comenius later attended the Herborn Gymnasium in Nassau (Bavaria) and was tutored by the prominent theologians Johann Piscator, Heinrich Gutberleth, and Heinrich Alsted. The school curriculum promoted the practical uses of theory for moral didactic purposes, and he learned about the educational reforms of Wolfgang Ratke on the teaching of language. Reading the texts of Sir Francis Bacon nurtured and solidified Comenius's faith in the power of scientific inquiry, despite a worldview entrenched in Early Modern thought inflected with religious mysticism and doctrine. In 1616, he was ordained a minister of the Moravian Brethren and was appointed rector of a gymnasium in Přerov.

The Thirty Years' War in 1618 forced Comenius and other Protestant ministers to escape Bohemia under the Catholic persecution of Ferdinand II. He left behind his wife, Magdelena, and his infant sons, all of whom later died of the plague in 1622 during his absence. Comenius lost his property, and his writings were seized and burned in the town square. Two years later, he became pastor and rector of a notable church in Fulnek, a town in the Moravian-Silesian Region. Comenius wrote a description of the physical and spiritual suffering of this period in *The Labyrinth of the World and the Paradise of the Heart* (in 1623). He eventually fled, in 1627, to Leszno, Poland, where he married Jana Gajusova and joined the Moravian Brethren, in exile from the Habsburg Counter-Reformation of Bohemia, and where he assumed the role of bishop and rector of the local gymnasium from 1628 until 1641.

Comenius nurtured the dream of rebuilding society through educational reform and wrote a "brief proposal" (in 1627) delineating a full-time program of schooling for all youth to be taught both their "native" and European culture. The idea was progressive at the time but in line with his moral convictions. It was during this period that Comenius began to work on expounding his theory of knowledge and pedagogy in *The School of Infancy* (1630/1896), writing his first major work, the *Didactica Magna* (in 1638), in Czech. The treatise was published in Latin as part of the *Opera Didactica*

Omnia (in 1657), which contained most of the texts he had written since 1627. Comenius wrote *Janua Linguarum Reserata* (in 1633) in Latin and Czech, revolutionizing language teaching at the time to make learning easier. The book brought him pan-European fame, eventually being translated into 14 languages, including an English version, *The Gate of Tongues Unlocked*.

In 1638, Comenius was requested by the Swedish government to create a plan for the school reorganization and in 1641 was commissioned by the English parliament to reform the system of public education. After the publication, in London, of *Pansophiae Prodromus* as *A Reformation of Schools* (in 1639), he was recognized as a primary figure in the "pansophic movement" of the 17th century. Putting practical educational interests aside, he wanted to further Bacon's attempt to move forward the organization of all human knowledge. Although the original manuscript of *Pansophiae Prodromos* was destroyed in the burning of his Leszno home in 1657, pansophic ideas are expressed in the series of textbooks on didactics that circulated Europe. In these texts, Comenius attempts to arrange the entire field of knowledge within the comprehension of every child. The English Civil War (1642) forced his return to Sweden.

In 1650, Prince Sigismund Rákóczy of Transylvania invited Comenius to Sárospatak to give advice on school reform and pansophy. He remained there as a professor at the first Hungarian Protestant College, but, having little success due to the feudal administration of the region, he left for Leszno around 1654. Soon after, war broke out between Poland and Sweden. Leszno was completely destroyed. Comenius, having declared support for the Protestant Swedish side, had his house and manuscripts burned by the Polish Catholic troops, and again he was forced into exile. Destitute and desperate, he was invited to settle in Amsterdam at the house of Lawrence de Geer, the son of his former patron. During the next few years, Comenius wrote his most identifiable and significant work, the *Orbis Sensualium Pictus* (in 1658), with Latin and German text. It was the first school book to use pictures in the learning of languages. It put into practice a fundamental principle of language and pedagogy for Comenius: words must go with visual representations and cannot be learned without them. From the earliest period of infancy, the child must learn to join things and words because speech is the first introduction to the external world. Comenius believed the mind must not be distracted by meaningless words and vague concepts. His method of language learning prioritized a pedagogy linked to the "mother tongue," and the school books were organized according to sophistication and difficulty, following the pansophic method of graded instruction, dealing only with what is already a part of the child's experience. Comenius felt Latin was the language most appropriate for the purpose of wider communication. Charles Hoole brought out an English version, *Comenius's Visible World, Or a Picture and Nomenclature of All the Chief Things That Are in the World, and of Men's Employments Therein,* in 1659. Through his interest in pansophy, Comenius developed a profound interest in language and in education.

Comenius's concern with "didactics" was directed not only toward primary and formal schooling but to aspects of existence, resting on the principle that every aspect of life involves learning. Girls and boys were to be educated together in a creative and playful manner since all human beings are curious and have an innate desire for knowledge and goodness. Corporal punishment was to be avoided. Failure in learning was not the fault of the learner, but evidence of an inadequate teacher. Didactics or pedagogy is perhaps Comenius's most lasting contribution to educational theory and practice, and it has generally been considered his primary concern.

Comenius died in Amsterdam in 1670. He was buried in Naarden in a mausoleum devoted to him.

ON THE EDUCATION OF YOUNG CHILDREN

Comenius lived in a time of tremendous upheaval and dehumanization in Europe during the Thirty Years' War. His view on the education of young children grew out of experience as well as an innate desire to respect human dignity and freedom. Morality and truth were the foundation of pedagogy upon which to build a free spirit. Continuing the tradition of education for democratic emancipation after the Czech theologian, philosopher, and teacher John Hus, Comenius posited an educational system without any distinction for race, social origin, sex, nationality, or ability that would hamper the development of human potential to achieve an ideal state of knowing and being. He believed that schooling was the backbone of cultural perfectibility and that a nation could be improved by better teaching its citizens from a very young age. During his lifetime, Comenius fought for the independence of the Czech state, and this drive to protect the cultural foundations of his people informed his educational texts, as did his religious affiliation with the Unity of Brethren, a persecuted sect that was often denied the right to run its own schools. A system of pedagogy developed around the family, stressing the importance of teaching children from a very young age to be active and useful participants in society. The idea was derived from theories of Hus around a doctrine of human perfectability that could nurture the child's God-given gifts and natural capabilities in a lifelong pursuit of achieving an ideal state of being. Comenius advocated a system of universal education from birth to death as a way to reform society, based on the dictum that "it is easier to educate than to re-educate."

For Comenius, the growth of knowledge seen during the 17th century necessitated a view toward lifelong education. It was purposeful to live meaningfully and morally for the salvation of the body and the soul. He introduced the idea of concrete goals and objectives for pedagogy toward knowing the truth, which was good and could provide a moral compass for the benefit of the child and society. Comenius's innovations called for specialized education, taking into consideration the stage of growth, constitution or demeanour, and individual abilities to improve pedagogy. He placed priority on early childhood as the fundamental period of development that would form the foundations of future learning and social life. This perspective relegated Comenius at the periphery of educational thought at the time because the idea of a universal and lifelong learning from birth to the grave for the betterment of society was considered beyond the reach of ordinary minds and perhaps was not even desirable if it upset the status quo. He set out to enrich the learning experience and supplement, if not supplant, a curriculum rooted in memorization and far away from reality, to make the immediate world of the child the subject of inquiry and knowledge. Observations of life and nature at an early age would distinguish the core of teaching and learning from which to abstract larger principles later on that could be applied to parallel situations. For Comenius, the goal of education was to work from infancy toward a "universal life wisdom" to achieve a good and just relation with oneself, others, and God through a training of body and senses, language and action, reason and morality. Like Bacon, he believed in the value of empiricism and that the scientific inquiry of nature was a primary means to integrate all knowledge of the world.

The content of education for young children centred around family life, which was like a "little school" for Comenius. The parents were considered not only caregivers but teachers, ready to accept their duty to nurture the development of their offspring with love and respect. There are no boundaries placed on learning in this space. When the child asks, the parents are obliged to answer to the best of their abilities in order for the child to form good habits of mind and soul. Correcting errors of judgment or behaviour is done by "gentle discipline" and not corporal or harsh punishment. Words must be associated with things in the child's world to make familiar the home and external environment, which will motivate interest and engagement of thought. Comenius urged activity and play around engaging toys or games, not only for the development of body and sense but also mind and speech, especially in the early years up to age six, which he called the "School of Infancy," followed by the "School of Childhood" from six to eleven. The aim was to allow for interactive experience to help with the future development of reasoning and morality. Introducing the child to natural phenomena before the age of six establishes patterns of recognition that can be built upon as forms of learning: for example, discussing differences between plants or animals in relation to horticulture and biology.

Comenius called for universal education of all children between the ages of six and eleven, given that there was adequate mental and psychological preparation from the early ages. He expected a positive attitude toward schooling would be instilled by the parents so that there would not be resistance to teaching, and learning could be a pleasurable journey toward knowledge and understanding of the self and the world. Comenius believed rational thought grew from training observation and perception through play, and experience with reality to integrate reason with language. He produced textbooks for the young that contained pictures to illustrate human experience and knowledge in an elementary yet progressive way. Things depicted in the books were given a name, and ideas moved from very simple forms of representation and understanding to more complex types of expression that called for advanced reasoning skills.

TEACHING METHODS

Comenius was reactionary to the curricula and arcane methods of teaching and administration that formed the medieval scholastic school system. Education was based not in the vernacular language but in the scholasticism of an elitist knowledge base—for example, Greek and Latin—following the rise of humanist philosophy and dogma. He envisioned schooling as a democratic process, until at least age eleven, in which students were treated equally, for the betterment of the child and society. Instruction would be rooted in the spoken language of the young to break down resistance and enhance comprehensibility to stimulate interest. The content of the curriculum would be practical, with an emphasis on scientific knowledge rooted in the study of nature. With the demise of feudalism and the rise of the entrepreneurial economy that marked the beginning of capitalism, Comenius saw the importance of educating the so-called masses for a life of potential upward mobility by attempting to re-envision schooling to overcome the divisions between intellectual and manual labour that marked the division between the cultural elite and the working classes. He defended the right of each man to realize a full development and thus to be offered an opportunity to gain full knowledge about the world besides versatility in practical affairs.

Comenius hoped educational reform would bring about social change. This utopian viewpoint that envisioned "common good" for all rested on the new didactics he was developing to alter pedagogy so that there should be less ignorance and confusion, more enlightenment and peace. Comenius expounded on the social advantages of a democratic educational system and its significance to the state and humanity. He stressed that "enlightened" nations base their economic successes on the well-being of society by protecting the rights of each citizen and sustaining progress through equitable human relations. Comenius believed that government has the responsibility to safeguard the public welfare and maintain an abiding peace through education. In *Didactica Magna*, he wrote the following:

> It is time to ring the bell of awakening, to push the people out of their indifference and torpidity, in which they remain, neglecting the dangers threatening themselves and their relatives. It is the Europeans who ought to wake up first, to make the other nations follow them and unite together. (cited in Suchodolski, 1970, p. 35)

Looking beyond Europe toward a cosmopolitan and multicultural integration of human knowledge, Comenius wanted the study of pedagogy to move beyond the boundaries of national borders. He proposed a united college of education, very much like UNESCO today, that would be poised toward the research of teaching and learning from a non-Eurocentric perspective to enrich knowledge and promote academic exchange. Such an institution would demand us to inquire about the nature of curriculum and schooling from another, more global and multicultural, point of view. For example, UNESCO is a worldwide organization whose structure comprises many parts and partners, nations, states, and peoples. Comenius predicted the necessity of establishing filiations, friendships, and institutional interconnections among academics from different cultures to expand the archives of accepted knowledge. UNESCO, for example, could be viewed simply as a political organization that represents and wields the interests and power of a Western intellectual history at the expense of another because its constitution contains, and therefore appropriates, what is epistemologically different from its intellectual history as part of its governing charter. This negative aspect of its institutional lineage cannot be denied, given its origins as a union of nations, states, and peoples of "equal partnership" but of unequal participation, voice, power, and representation. Yet, for Comenius, the institution he calls for begs the question of why an international research community on education is important and how the question of schooling and pedagogy is a universal and moral imperative to maintain human rights and freedoms for "the greater good." It is not a matter of instilling and practising a homogeneous concept of a collective and general culture, but promoting common points of identification in the name of community by not effacing subjective or historical differences.

Comenius was critical of the school system because the methods of instruction in use were not relevant to the way a child learned, and the structure of the institution was alienating and not inclusive. Based in lectures and verbal exchanges that were hypothetical and ungrounded, the pedagogy of the time was less effective than practical training received though life experiences. Comenius regarded the everyday world as the great school of human character and reason. The first aspect of a young child's education was in the objects close at hand that leave sense impressions:

> Listening must be constantly supplemented by seeing, and the work of the tongue with that of the hands; what they are supposed to learn, must be not only told them, so that it slips through their ears, but it should be painted as well, so as to influence imagination through the eyes. And let them learn intermittently to speak up about it in words and then to express it by hand, so that they do not give up anything until it has sufficiently imbued their ears, eyes, reason, and memory. (cited in Suchodolski, 1970, p. 37)

Comenius established a linking of sense, speech, and action as the child's process of understanding achieved through interacting with things in the real world. The process is practical, empirical, and experimental. Suchodolski (1970) writes the following:

> In "*Ex Scholasticis Labyrinthis Exitus in Planum*" Comenius put forward ten principles for the training of the powers of reasoning and established three important objectives of this work. Firstly, reason ought to be able

to ascertain what exists; this is the level of cognition. Secondly, it ought to answer the question, why whatever exists, does so; this is the level of understanding. Thirdly, it ought to be able to find practical applications for what it has learned; this is the level of utility. (p. 37)

These coincide with the reason, will, and action in any effective learning situation. The internalization of external stimuli imprints images in the human mind as it tries to possess this aspect of knowledge in order to use it as a later time. Everything is filtered through the senses, and its willful use in the practice of life is creatively deducted according to three degrees of wisdom, theory, practice, and *chresis,* or application. The confirmation of knowledge in practical activity moves from recognition to use. The process of cognition and training is connected to speech and action. There is no right understanding without words. Actions bear out the perfection of cognition and reason to mirror what is in the mind. The universe of things is tied to the understanding expressed through speech and doing. Human progress is marked by such a pattern of teaching and learning.

A system of didactics was created by Comenius, adjusting teaching to the ability of the child and according to the type and difficulty of knowledge and its relation to practice. Even though pedagogy had to take into account the psychological demeanour and cognitive capacity, there were objectives to be met through play to reduce boredom and indifference in the teaching of foreign languages, specifically Latin, which was taught through grammar and repetition without reference to a student's native tongue. Such a pedagogy was anathema to Comenius because it did not begin with the world of "things." Abstracting language in use to grammatical laws without practice defeated the application and use of language that was its pleasure. Teaching was considered by Comenius to be an integral part of the school. He was also concerned with its administrative organization and created a system of rules and principles for how it was supposed to operate and how students should comport themselves for the most favourable educational results, helping to make the possibility of an effective teaching more attainable.

The didactics of Comenius were rooted in three great "books": God, nature, and art. In itself, this focus was nothing new at the time. But Comenius focused on the universal and useful wisdom of each in the form of *pansophia,* that is, the construction and reconstruction of the world built by human endeavours of understanding or reason and action. The practical application of knowledge was considered synthetic and tied together theory and practice through reason and ideas. For Comenius, schooling was supposed to achieve a "way to light" by bringing to the surface universal notions of understandings hidden beneath human consciousness. Teaching had to work toward revealing the ends of things clearly, "and the means to these ends, as well as the proper ways of employing them, are henceforth capable of directing all things in their possession towards good ends, and able to pursue such ends without any risk of error, by means which are good and valid" (Suchodolski, 1970, p. 42). It was a new form of rationalism, but the faith placed by Comenius in teaching the way to reason was quite different from that of René Descartes because it entailed a form of empiricism that put the child into a relation with nature. *Pansophia* reflected the ingenuity of human action in the consummation of the world of God, transformed through science. Comenius looked upon the task of education as much more than the training of children to read and write. It was a sacred obligation to actualize the goodness of the human spirit and restore being to a purity of form in childhood. The "rebirth" happened through proper teaching that would realize potential in the child and activate their social agency from within. The idea sounds like a product of contemporary educational theories seeking to empower and emancipate marginalized individuals and groups. Comenius valued the creative manifestation of human being in the universe as a supplement to divine creation and expression of the latent potential to improve the social condition. The utopian thrust of his ideas predicted the reconceptualization of curriculum for a more empowering and equitable education, initiated in later centuries by John Dewey and others.

THE FUTURE OF THE CHILD AND EDUCATION FOR ALL

After the end of the industrial revolution and the widespread introduction of public schooling, the 20th century was welcomed as the age of the child. Education once again became a paramount concern for social transformation because of advancements in developmental psychology, and the question of the future of human being in a modern world quickly formed discussion around the purpose of education. Comenius loomed large once again. The technological explosion had mechanized mass production and reduced the need for child labour but not the need for economically productive workers. Schooling was made compulsory to ensure the future of the state through education. But was the child an object to be moulded or a self-actualizing subject? The dichotomy represents the tensions Comenius had identified between an imposed education directed toward achieving curricular objectives to achieve predetermined standards of excellence, and a transformational learning that was based in the learning discoveries made through the child's natural curiosity about the external world.

The argument still exists today, even though there have been countless projects of educational reform. Curricula have been deconstructed and reorganized to satisfy either one or both sides of these hypotheses. Unfortunately, educational research has reinforced the confusion, and there has been a merry-go-round of pedagogical approaches and methods that are rooted in ideology and the politics of knowledge rather than epistemology and the welfare of the child. Whether it be "flipped classrooms," "multiple intelligence theory," "backwards planning," "learning circles," "blogs," or any other teaching innovation, the point is to stimulate and encourage intellectual and moral growth and development, although in ways that are appropriate or "natural" to the child and not the ideals imposed by the process of education. This caveat, after Comenius, has been a premise of progressive educators in order to make pedagogy a child-centred activity, to individualize learning for all. Safeguarding educational opportunities does not mean making schooling compulsory but allowing all children to participate and guide their own learning. The idea is radical for some, who see the child as an empty vessel to be filled with knowledge or a mound of formless clay to be shaped into a learned subject. There is little consideration for the rights of the child in the educational process and disregard for education as an outgrowth of the child's life. The child is, in effect, dehumanized and perceived to be a cog in the machine of schooling that spits out finished products that are exactly the same. Suchodolski (1970) explains the following:

> Indeed, significant progress has been attained in understanding the psychology of children and the basic principles of the process of education, particularly in its early stages, as well as in understanding the process of individuation and its difficulties and obstacles. However, this understanding has had but limited social significance. Education has been conceived as an expression of juvenile life and its cultivation. But then, what has been the concept of the transition from the child's universe to the adult one, or from novelty, curiosity, creativeness into routine, into fixed patterns of behaviour and imposed obligations? (p. 48)

Learning in the post-industrial age promotes the development of skills for competence and productivity, not the value of invention and discovery. Little interest is taken in the value of learning for its own sake. The principles of "liberal humanism" no longer ground the model of an emancipatory education through which autonomous self-actualization is attainable. Occupational horizons and careerism do. Consequently, schooling is informed by the economic imperative of gathering the situational knowledge needed to perform and excel at a job skill, as opposed to engaging in general inquiry. Functionalism overtakes learning. Didactics takes over learning. Method becomes a form of the cultural reproduction, not to mention the cognitive and affective preconditions, of teaching and learning. And yet, teaching and learning require creativity and imagination. They are moved forward by curiosity and not procedural outcomes that produce an educational subject as the product of specific teaching and learning instructions. How could such an educational result lead to a happy life if the identity of the child is suppressed or denied? How can this be called an education for all? UNESCO has spearheaded the global movement for equal access to education. The main thrust follows Comenius's notion that teaching and learning should be responsive to individual needs and preferences without regard to gender, age, socio-economic status, or physical ability. The object is to transform existing society through creative and active participation in life and looks toward the future of humanity. The World Education Forum in 2000 yielded the Dakar Framework for Action and "Education for All" (United Nations, 2015):

- Goal 1: Expand early childhood care and education
- Goal 2: Provide free and compulsory primary education for all
- Goal 3: Promote learning and life skills for young people and adults
- Goal 4: Increase adult literacy by 50 percent
- Goal 5: Achieve gender parity by 2005, gender equality by 2015
- Goal 6: Improve the quality of education

Although the goals of the Dakar summit have yet to be achieved fully around the world, mainly because of geo-political upheaval and conflict, there is a hope the framework will provide a call for action that will form the foundation for a more socially just and equitable existence.

ENDNOTE

In the 17th century, John Amos Comenius realized that there was a crisis in education and that the key to improving schooling was acknowledging the role of the child in it. He fought tirelessly and at great personal cost to overcome the basic contradictions of a pedagogical system designed to support the privileged and maintain the status quo. Comenius refused to accept educational inequality and recognized a new republic of childhood that had always been at the centre of what it means to teach and learn but was forgotten in plain sight. It is a lesson we should keep in mind today.

REFERENCES

Comenius, J. A. (1673). *The gate of languages unlocked, or, a seed-plot of all arts and tongues: Containing a ready way to learn the Latine and English tongue.* London, UK: T. R. and N. T. for the Company of Stationers.

Comenius, J. A. (1896). *Comenius' school of infancy: An essay on the education of youth during the first six years* (W. S. Monroe, Ed.). Boston, MA: Heath. (Original work published in 1630).

Comenius, J. A. (1967). *The great didactic of John Amos Comenius: Now for the first time* (M. W. Keatinge, Ed. and Trans.). New York, NY: Russell and Russell.

Comenius, J. A. (1968). *The orbis pictus of John Amos Comenius.* Detroit, MI: Singing Tree.

Suchodolski, B. (1970). Comenius and teaching methods. In C. H. Dobinson (Ed.), *Comenius and contemporary education: An international symposium.* Hamburg, Germany: UNESCO.

United Nations Educational, Scientific and Cultural Organization. (2015). *Education for all 2000–2015: Achievements and challenges.* Paris, France: UNESCO.

CHAPTER 5

Holistic Education: Teaching and Learning, Planning and Reflecting with the Whole Child in Mind

Lovisa Fung

GUIDING QUESTIONS:

1. What are the central tenets and who are the significant figures of holistic education in the early years?
2. Imagine that you are starting an early years learning centre that follows a holistic approach to teaching and learning. What would its curriculum, pedagogy, and day-to-day learning be like?

INTRODUCTION

In today's technologically advanced society, everything that we do is geared toward efficiency, speed, and a focus on materialistic pursuits. Holistic education offers an alternative approach to teaching and learning that engages the intellect, hands-on experiential learning experiences, and the wisdom of the heart. Its goal is to develop a connection with and respect for our surroundings and to fulfill the learner's potential. Teachers of all levels are well aware of the expectations and standards required of them to teach a standardized curriculum and to make sure students perform successfully for standardized testing. It is these pressures placed on teachers that sometimes make it difficult for them to readily follow children's natural interests, curiosities, and passions. Holistic education is, in a direct and clear way, the antithesis of mainstream schooling, which is focused on the attainment of grades as the be-all and end-all and schooling as preparing children for the workforce to compete in a consumerist world for individualistic gains.

Holistic education as a teaching philosophy and movement has various subdivisions of alternative schooling approaches, but shared overarching perspectives, beliefs, and goals about education hold them together. These include the importance of teaching that meets all domains of children's development (social, emotional, intellectual, psychological, physical, and spiritual), meeting and fulfilling each child's unique potentials and possibilities, and recognizing the interconnectedness that we have with each other and the earth. There is an emphasis on contribution to one's social surroundings that comes from a balanced and healthy inner consciousness of the individual.

To attain these goals and to put these perspectives into action in learning settings, holistic educators are intentional with how they plan their program, the resources they use, the learning environments they create, and the relationships they build with the children. A critical practice that stands out from mainstream schooling is the focus on nurturing teachers' inner lives with reflective and contemplative practices such as meditation, mindfulness, and personal reflections.

This chapter focuses on providing a snapshot of the central tenets of holistic education, the historical background of influential figures, alternative schooling approaches associated with holistic education, and the teacher's role and preparation needed to create an effective holistic teaching program in the early years setting.

CENTRAL TENETS OF HOLISTIC EDUCATION: CONNECTION, INTEGRATION, AND BALANCE

Approach the child as an "indivisible whole."
—*J. P. Miller, 2012, p. 9*

Regardless of the various teaching pedagogies in holistic education and its supporters, there are universal central tenets of holistic education that all practitioners agree on. According to scholars J. P. Miller (2012) and

R. Miller (1990), all holistic practitioners share these central beliefs: a spiritual worldview with a deep reverence for life; the importance of supporting the unfolding of each child's unique inherent potential; educating for connection instead of fragmentation; and a view of human nature as inherently good, with a striving for the good.

Spiritual Worldview

Holistic education is anchored with a spiritual worldview that is not religious but is based on what J. P. Miller (2008) describes as "a sense of the awe and reverence for life that arises from our relatedness to something both wonderful and mysterious" (p. 4). This perspective of seeing, interpreting, and living in the world allows us to experience the interconnectedness we have with each other, regardless of race, religion, gender, socio-economic status, and culture. It also helps us recognize our sacred relationship to the earth and our responsibility to it, to each other, and to ourselves.

Unfolding the Inherent Potential of Each Child

Holistic practitioners all agree that children have inherent potential and possibilities within them that are unique to their own soul's calling. According to J. P. Miller (2012), "Educating the whole child is to acknowledge that each person also has something of the mysterious within. We sometimes call this the soul, the inner life, or the creative spark" (p. 8). Teachers have the responsibility to create and provide the conditions and environment that can foster the child's natural process of unfolding.

Holistic education goes in direct opposition to the banking model of schooling stemming from the industrial revolution, which is still prevalent in today's schools. Freire (2000), in *Pedagogy of the Oppressed*, describes this banking model of education as treating children like consumers who are to be taught and assessed in a standardized way, much like a factory assembly line, to serve the needs and demands of the state. Consequently, it leaves no room for students to explore their interests, abilities, and passions. Up until now, holistic practitioners and various holistic teaching approaches throughout history have come up with alternative teaching methods and perspectives to implement in the learning environment for combating this approach to schooling, and to ultimately nourish the child's natural curiosities and unique potential. They are discussed in a later section of this chapter.

Connection Instead of Fragmentation

When we look at mainstream schooling throughout the 20th and 21st century and even further back in time, we can see that education is derived from and propelled by a sense of disconnection and fragmentation. For instance, if you take a look at a timetable in a typical classroom, you will see that learning is divided into subjects, the teaching of subjects is divided into separate time slots, and subjects such as math and literacy are valued more than others. This hierarchy of subjects gives children a view and experience that subjects are separated from each other with no relationship to one another and particular capacities are valued over others, which promotes fragmented learning.

Robinson and Aronica (2009), in *The Element*, provide a powerful example of the negative impact and consequences of valuing particular capacities over others when they share the story of a little girl, Gillian Flynn, who was told by her teachers that she was too active and needed to calm down. Her psychiatrist recognized that there was nothing wrong with Gillian, and in fact, she just needed to move her body in order to think. Her mother enrolled her in a dance school, and since then she has grown up to become one of the most successful producers of dance productions, including *Cats*. This example shows the potential pitfalls that come with mainstream schooling in its valuing of particular capacities and aptitudes over others, and its lack of attention, appreciation, and reverence for the child's innate potentials, possibilities, and interests. Holistic education, then, offers a viable alternative because it strives to meet the child with where they are at, what they are called to do, explore, and learn, by bringing balance, connection, and appreciation for all domains of development, capacities, and aptitudes.

Jill Bolte Taylor's (2008) TED Talk, *My Stroke of Insight*, supports educating the child from a holistic standpoint, where the interconnectedness of life and the intuitive are revered. As a brain researcher, she shares her story of experiencing a stroke that left her with the left hemisphere of her brain completely shut down, leading her to rely on living and experiencing the world through the right hemisphere of her brain. The right side of the brain is associated with the emotional and intuitive, the connection with oneself and its surroundings as blended into one, and the focus on the here and now. Although we use both hemispheres of our brain, her experience of fully functioning using only the right hemisphere helped her to understand the interconnectedness and oneness with all beings and her surroundings.

Taylor's (2008) message relates to the importance of meeting and understanding the interconnectedness that we have with each other:

> So, who are we? We are the life-force power of the universe, with manual dexterity and two cognitive minds. And we have the power to choose, moment by moment, who and how we want to be in the world.... I believe that the more time we spend choosing to run the deep inner-peace circuitry of our right hemispheres, the more peace we will project into the world, and the more peaceful our planet will be.

Basic Human Nature as Good

Contrary to mainstream American culture's influence from centuries-ago belief in Protestant Christianity's viewpoint of humans as fundamentally flawed with original sin, holistic practitioners see people as inherently good: we aim for and have a natural inclination toward goodness and harmony (R. Miller, 1990). The belief in people's inherent goodness contributes to holistic practitioners' focus and intentionality in supporting children's natural desire and longing for reaching their own potential.

THE HOLISTIC EDUCATION MOVEMENT: KEY INFLUENTIAL FIGURES

As far back as several centuries ago, some scholars and educators who were not part of one educational movement could be seen as loosely connected to holistic education for their perspective and approach to learning. They focused on the whole child, with an emphasis on each child's inner unfolding. These pioneers of holistic education also viewed the intrinsic nature of children and people as good and as having inclinations toward growth and social harmony. These views developed by holistic practitioners were influenced by perennial philosophy, which originated from ancient history (J. P. Miller, 2008). Prominent figures that had a holistic view of education in their approach and philosophy include Johann Heinrich Pestalozzi, Jean-Jacques Rousseau, Friedrich Froebel, Ralph Emerson, and David Henry Thoreau, to name a few. The humanistic movement in the 1960s was also a part of the holistic education movement, with figures such as Carl Rogers, who focused on the psychological growth of individuals rather than exclusively focusing on the spiritual. The difference amongst educators in their holistic paradigm comes down to two essential camps. One camp is more tolerant and supportive of mainstream Western culture when nurturing children's unfolding potential, and the other camp views mainstream-society values as a significant contributing factor in disrupting an individual's ability and opportunity for self-actualizing their inherent possibilities (J. P. Miller, 2008; R. Miller, 1990). Regardless of specifics within a particular strand of holistic tradition, the emphasis is ultimately on cultivating, nurturing, exploring, and revering the inner consciousness and growth of the individual (whether psychological or spiritual or both) and translating that to the outer knowledge of the individual through their words and actions.

Rousseau

In the 18th century, a French philosopher, Jean-Jacques Rousseau, went against the grain of scientific and materialist worldviews by encouraging the importance of nurturing children. He saw that this process should be organic and meet the needs of the natural goodness that comes with the child's soul (J. P. Miller, 2008; R. Miller, 1990). Children are not meant to be born and inhabit the earth for the sole purpose of serving the needs of the state and becoming labourers of the workforce. Children, Rousseau argued, should be given the freedom to explore and participate in the natural unfolding of their inherent potential and possibilities. This view has sparked debate amongst educators about where the boundaries are drawn between freedom for children to explore, make decisions, and lead their own life and learning versus the role of the teacher in deciding and providing learning experiences that adults perceive as pertinent to a child's education and development. Nevertheless, Rousseau's ideas of child-rearing and his unconventional resistance to the overreliance on the scientific and materialist worldview inspired other philosophers, scholars, and educators to adopt his views into their philosophy toward teaching and educating the child with a holistic perspective.

Pestalozzi

Johann Heinrich Pestalozzi was a Swiss educational reformer in the 18th and 19th centuries who was influenced by Rousseau's ideas. He wrote about parenting, mothering, child-rearing, and educational pedagogy. In his lifetime, he ran several schools, including a children's institute in Stanz and Yverdon, with his philosophical approach, which was different from what was in mainstream culture at the time. His philosophy included developing and cultivating emotionally sensitive relationships with students; family as having a role in learning; the importance of providing a variety of learning experiences that contain hands-on child-centred approaches; and the integration of the mind, hands, and heart in teaching and learning (McKenna, 2010).

As with many other educators, philosophers, and pedagogues who are advocates of holistic education, he also believed in the innate goodness of human beings: that children are born with inherent potential, which should be nurtured and respected. In supporting the child's natural unfolding, Pestalozzi urges that it is our responsibility as educators to provide the resources and environment, coupled with our caring nature, to bring forth human beings who grow up to experience personal fulfillment and a desire for social harmony (McKenna, 2010; R. Miller, 1990).

A. S. Neill

Alexander Sutherland Neill (1883–1973) was an English educational reformer who founded Summerhill in the 1920s. His school and philosophy were unconventional during that time and can still be said to be so compared to today's mainstream schooling standards: students get to choose whether or not to attend classes, and teachers have no official curriculum or instructional methods they need to follow. He believed that when children are given the freedom to explore and learn through their choosing, it will help to foster an organic and natural process of learning (J. P. Miller, 2008).

As an example, according to Cahn (1997), students who go to Summerhill "do not have to stand room inspection and no one picks up after them. They are left free. No one tells them what to wear: they put on any costume they want to at any time" (p. 9). This idea of freedom to choose and the opportunity to follow one's desires, impulses, and inclinations is central to Summerhill's teaching philosophy and practices. Neill's idea required that "the school fit the child—instead of making the child fit the school" (Neill in Cahn, 1997, p. 10). Neill, like other practitioners and advocates of holistic education, believed that children are born fundamentally good. He believed in the natural capacities and possibilities of each child and that adults should not force their preconceptions of what the student should become onto the child but honour the child's preordained destiny instead.

There are many more educators and educational reformers who fall under the holistic education's paradigm throughout the centuries, including Ralph Emerson, Henry David Thoreau, Leo Tolstoy, and Bronson Alcott, to name a few. Under the scope of this chapter, it is impossible to cover all the contributions that they have made to the realm of holistic education. However, they shared a belief that propelled them in their life's work: to resist mainstream schooling's exclusive focus on the intellect and instead focus on nurturing students' inherent potential by educating students' minds and hearts.

MODERN-DAY HOLISTIC ALTERNATIVE APPROACHES TO SCHOOLING: MONTESSORI, WALDORF, AND EQUINOX HOLISTIC ALTERNATIVE SCHOOL

Montessori: Following the Child

Dr. Maria Montessori developed the Montessori teaching method in around 1899 through her work with developmentally delayed children in Italy. She then transferred what she learned from her experiences there to work with children of all abilities in mainstream school settings in Rome. Her method complements other holistic schooling approaches that are prevalent in the world today. The overarching philosophy in her teaching method is what she calls "follow the child": "The teacher, said Montessori, must follow the child, for the direction of its life is contained within its soul" (R. Miller, 1990, p. 127). Montessori stresses that teachers need to engage in spiritual preparation to order to facilitate, to lead, and to inspire in the classroom. The spiritual preparation of the teacher involves understanding that teaching is not about "train[ing] a child to use the [learning] materials correctly. This would put our material in competition with that of others" (Montessori, 1967, p. 149). Rather, it is about being astutely aware through observation of the child and having the self-awareness that the teacher is not the authoritarian who determines and drives the student's learning journey. Teachers' focus should be on developing their virtues of "tranquillity, patience, charity, and humility" (Montessori, 1967, p. 15). By doing so, it will help teachers to create an environment where children can thrive, learn, and develop of their own accord.

What makes her teaching method distinct from other holistic pedagogies is her focus on teaching that is sensorially based. Children learn by using concrete materials and by engaging all their senses. There are designated and specifically designed teaching materials that teachers are to introduce to each child sequentially, always moving from what is concrete to the more complex and abstract. The key is to follow the child's developmental readiness and not to force or pressure children to learn what they are not mentally, intellectually, and emotionally ready for (Edwards, 2002; Shell, 1992).

Montessori was ahead of her time because of her understanding that children develop in set stages (with variations in between). She believed that children in their early years grow in stages in what she described as "sensitive periods" (Montessori, 1995). Sensitive periods refer to a child's absorbent inclination toward various sensory experiences depending on their age and stage of development (e.g., language, movement, music). It is up to the teacher to take advantage of these opportune sensitive periods that are occurring in children to provide them with learning opportunities that meet these stages of development.

When introducing and teaching materials to children, children can have the freedom to select learning materials that they have been presented by

Photo 5.1: Holistic Teaching Approaches Are Child-Centred with a Goal of Nurturing the Child's Inherent Potential

Source: FreeImages.com/Jeremy Brown

the teacher. Teachers can also choose learning equipment that they know the child is developmentally ready for. There are designated shelves for each subject area (language, math, science/history, practical life, sensorial) filled with learning equipment that corresponds to the subject. Unlike traditional classroom settings, where the schedule of the day is divided into learning different subjects within a designated time slot (e.g., a period for art, a period for language, etc.), each child in a Montessori setting is completing their own chosen work. Some children may be painting on a canvas or conducting a science experiment, while others may be reading a book or solving a math problem. Although there are different areas of shelves for different subjects, they are integrated. All learning materials are designed with an intentional

Box 5.1: Crumpled Paper Orchid: A Lesson on Aesthetics, Interconnection, and Reverence for Our Surroundings

Currently, in the field of early years learning in Canada, there is a shift toward the holistic development of children. In the Ontarian early years pedagogical document *How Does Learning Happen?* there is a focus on creating a curriculum program with a prepared environment that supports play, inquiry, and exploration and encourages learning to occur in natural surroundings to foster an appreciation for the outdoors. Early on in my career as a Montessori early childhood educator, I encountered experiences in my classroom that correlate to this focus. Back in 2010, I was leading a typical everyday read-aloud circle in my class. We were reading a book about plants, and when we came to the section about orchids, I remembered that I had a white orchid in my classroom. I instinctively took the orchid from the windowsill and passed the plant around for the children to look at. I remember a child said, "If I put my eye close to it, I can see the lines on the orchid!" Hearing her say this, I quickly went to get several magnifying glasses and passed them around for the children to look at the petals. Another child said, "The white petals look like the lines when you crumple paper." It then led to a spur-of-the-moment activity where we crumpled up some paper to create paper orchids and then attached a straw to each of them as its stem.

By following the children's interests, remarks, and curiosities, this read-aloud circle turned into a creative and aesthetic activity that connected the children to their reverence and awe for nature and conjured appreciation for their natural surroundings.

and specific rationale in mind to bring together all aspects of children's development. For instance, when laying out learning materials to teach children, regardless of the subject area of focus, there is a general expectation that the teacher will lay out the materials in an orderly fashion starting from left to right. The rationale is that this helps to facilitate and prepare the child for learning to read print, which goes from the direction of left to right, later on.

Much of the learning equipment is designed with a self-correcting component in mind. This means that after the child completes exploring and working with the specific learning equipment in front of them, they can then check whether or not they have completed the task successfully, all on their own. All of the intentionality and specificity of the design of the learning materials ultimately helps children to develop accountability, responsibility, independence, and autonomy, which is what supporting the whole child is all about.

Photo 5.2: Holistic Teaching Approaches Encourage and Value Children's Experience and Connection with Nature

Source: FreeImages.com/Ilona Jedrusiak

Waldorf: The Importance of Thinking, Feeling, and Willing

Another holistic teaching method that was developed in Europe and has continued to grow and flourish around the world is Rudolf Steiner's teaching method of Waldorf education. Steiner (1861–1925) was a scientist and philosopher. Initially, he developed the Waldorf educational method for the children of his employees at the Waldorf-Astoria Cigarette factory in Germany in the 1920s (Edwards, 2002; R. Miller 1990; Petrash, 2002). Since then, this teaching approach has been adopted by various alternative schools that are specially certified Waldorf schools, and in schools that are influenced by the Waldorf philosophy, such as the Da Vinci School and Equinox Holistic Alternative School in Toronto, Ontario. Complementary to other holistic teaching approaches, Waldorf teaching also focuses on children's inherent goodness, that they are born with unique innate capacities and potentialities. The primary goal of education is to bring forth children's natural capabilities and to lead them to self-actualization (Edwards, 2002; R. Miller, 1990; Petrash, 2002).

According to Rudolf Steiner, children grow through various stages of development. Steiner sees that child development occurs in "three cycles of seven-year stages, each with its own distinctive needs for learning" (Edwards, 2002, p. 2). The three stages are willing, feeling, and thinking. Willing is the stage that the preschool age group up to age seven are in; feeling is the stage that young children in grade school, from age seven to fourteen, are in; and thinking is the stage that adolescents are in (Edwards, 2002; Petrash, 2002). Simply put, the capacity to develop willing is the ability to set one's actions with intention and purpose. The capacity to build feeling is being able to engage with one's emotions and go inward as one learns. The capacity for thinking is the ability to engage in critical thought and dialogue as one learns and perceives their surroundings. These three capacities, willing, feeling, and thinking, are seen as soul forces by Steiner. Creating a balance of all three soul forces will help to produce well-rounded individuals in society (R. Miller, 1990; Sobo, 2014).

Similar to other holistic teaching approaches, the Waldorf teaching approach also emphasizes the prepared environment. Natural materials made of wood with a curvilinear structure are used to create flow in the classroom and appreciation for nature. Learning materials are intentionally chosen and utilized in an open-ended way. For instance, dolls are blank-faced, and mass-produced plastic toys are not present (Sobo, 2014). The intentionality of using open-ended learning materials in the classroom directly connects with the core of Waldorf's teaching methods in the preschool years: the importance of imagination, fantasy, and play-based learning.

Within the curriculum, play-based learning is encouraged, sometimes with prompts from the teacher. For instance, a teacher may put tables and chairs with blankets in the middle of the room to pretend that it is an igloo and invite children to enter the igloo as an animal of their choice (Sobo, 2014). The same materials can be used for other imaginative play as well. The key is to provide opportunities for children to "play with the same object in a number of different ways [to] develop the kind of flexible thinking that can [encourage them] to consider a problem from a number of different perspectives" (Petrash, 2002, p. 42). Essentially, play is viewed as a child's work: they are not dichotomous from one another.

In addition to encouraging play inside the classroom and in the outdoors, art is infused throughout the curriculum. Dance and movement, painting, drama, narratives, and storytelling are all examples of how Waldorf education uses art to enhance student learning. For example, when learning the alphabet, children will learn each letter with stories, songs, and dance movements that accompany the letter (Petrash, 2002). The letter *S*, for example, can be seen as a snake; students can make hissing noises as they try to mimic the snake's slithering motions with their bodies. Art is recognized as having the ability to engage with one's emotions and intuition, and that is precisely the rationale behind why art is woven into all parts of the Waldorf curriculum.

Whole Child Education: Equinox Holistic Alternative School in Toronto

In 2009, Equinox Holistic Alternative School (formerly known as the Whole Child School) was established within the Toronto District School Board with the assistance of Jack Miller, a renowned scholar and academic in holistic education from the Ontario Institute for Studies in Education of the University of Toronto. He served as part of the committee to begin this holistic school within a public school board.

Equinox Holistic Alternative School was unique in its conception from the beginning, as it is housed within a public school board, with the goal of providing a well-rounded and deeply informed holistic curriculum.

Box 5.2: Connecting Holistic Teaching Approaches to Early Years Learning in Canada

In the Ontarian early years pedagogical document *How Does Learning Happen?* some of the main features of holistic education are highlighted:

1. Educating the whole child with equal attention paid to all domains of development: "Research tells us that high-quality programs are those that integrate all areas of development in a holistic manner, with no greater emphasis on one area over another" (Ontario Ministry of Education, 2014, p. 17).

2. Creating opportunities to help children foster a reverence for and a connection to their surroundings, with being in nature a crucial component: "Through opportunities to engage with and make contributions to the world around them, children develop a sense of belonging and connectedness to their local community, the natural environment, and the larger universe of living things" (Ontario Ministry of Education, 2014, p. 25).

3. Children have their potential, interests, and points of view and can contribute and co-construct knowledge with educators (Ontario Ministry of Education, 2014).

4. The educator's role is to provide a warm, inviting, and inclusive environment for the children, where educators and the children are both learning from and with each other. An emphasis on the educator as a reflective practitioner also contributes to the continued overall growth of the educator (Ontario Ministry of Education, 2014).

It incorporates key components of various holistic pedagogies, including Montessori and Waldorf. There are a variety of features, which J. P. Miller (2008, 2012, 2016) points out, that compose the fundamental learning foundations and teaching methods at Equinox Holistic Alternative School.

Holistic Connections for a Whole Curriculum

At Equinox Holistic Alternative School, the curriculum is based on a holistic learning vision that incorporates the following six curriculum connections:

1. Subject connections: there should be an inherent connection between different subjects, sometimes known as the "integrated curriculum."

2. Mind-body connections: this is the connection between the body and the mind, for instance, the practice of meditation.
3. Spirit connections: this is about nurturing the heart or the "mysterious energy that [gives] meaning to our lives" (J. P. Miller, 2012, p. 74) by using practices such as infusing art and outdoor learning into the curriculum.
4. Earth connections: there should be experiences with the earth through outdoor education. For instance, children at Equinox Holistic Alternative School start their day outside and meet in a circle gathering, regardless of the weather.
5. Community connections: creating a learning community in the school and the classroom. For example, there is an acorn ceremony at the beginning of each school year where the grade eight students welcome the kindergarten students to the school community.
6. Thinking connections: the integration of thought and feeling when analyzing, reflecting, and problem-solving. (J. P. Miller, 2016)

The most crucial element in the whole curriculum is its emphasis on the interconnectedness of things, people, places, and relationships that we have with each other, our surroundings, and the world at large. Activities and lessons are geared toward conjuring the recognition of this interconnectedness. Incorporating these six connections into the teaching and learning process will help to engage students' bodies, minds, and hearts.

THE HOLISTIC TEACHER: THE IMPORTANCE OF HEAD, HEART, AND ACTION

The holistic teacher is one who cares about and makes it a priority to nurture all aspects of their teaching, including their pedagogy, content knowledge, and the human dimension of teaching. The human dimension of teaching includes the teacher's attributes, the relational aspects of teaching, and the teacher's inner life. These are often ignored in postsecondary teacher education and professional teacher development (Gatto, 2000; Kottler, Zehm, & Kottler, 2005; Palmer, 2007; Reilly, 2015). Even in research literature, the human aspect of teaching is often ignored (Clark, 1995). Instead, research literature will often focus on teachers' knowledge of curriculum content, teachers' mental lives, and their knowledge of methods and techniques of teaching as indicators of effective teaching (Clark, 1995).

To teach holistically, and to embody characteristics of a holistic teacher, it is vital for educators to combine the elements of head, heart, and action into their daily teaching. It is the rich interplay of all three factors that makes a teacher's teaching practice and their teaching presence holistic. Simply put, what we do with what we know is dependent on who we are. As one of my professors once said to us in a graduate course, "What do you make of what you've been made of?" (K. Cooper, personal communication, May 6, 2017).

Head: The Teacher's Vision

The head refers to the teacher's mental conception of their teaching vision and purpose, stemming from their knowledge of subject matter, the curriculum, and what they have learned from their background and life experiences. Your vision in teaching includes your views on how you plan, implement, perceive, and experience the curriculum program with your students. It comprises what you do and how you do it, with one other major factor that most teacher education programs often ignore: why you do what you do in your teaching.

In line with this, Reilly (2015) and Sinek (2009) state that having a conception of why you do what you do and operating from the inside out is what makes a teacher (or leader) who inspires and motivates. Sinek (2009) mentions that most people can articulate what they do and how they do it. However, it is rare for people to have a firm grasp of the rationale behind what propels them in the first place. Reilly (2015) shares similar sentiments when he explicitly discusses the importance for teachers to make it a priority to develop self-awareness through reflecting on what they bring from themselves into their teaching and to teach from the inside out. Teaching from the inside out equates to teaching from one's heart, from one's "underlying purpose—the 'big picture'" of why they became teachers in the first place (Reilly, 2015, pp. 11–12).

Heart: We Teach Who We Are

In Clark's (1995) research on thoughtful teaching, he found that the majority of teacher research focuses on the technical aspects of teaching, such as subject matter knowledge, knowledge of methods and techniques of teaching, and objective assessments, as indications of effective teaching. However, when he compiled interviews with teachers and students on what makes an effective, thoughtful teacher, although teachers will highlight the previously

Box 5.3: Teaching with Vision: Some Examples

In her article "Pedagogy of the Distressed," Tompkins (1990) provides an honest and moving account of eye-opening insights that she gained from self-reflection on her purpose in teaching. She was initially teaching for the sake of being approved of and being seen as intelligent by her students. She shifted from that intention to one of a student-centred perspective where students' voices are heard and their narratives are honoured. Tompkins's (1990) insight and realization capture the importance of knowing one's teaching vision vividly:

> I have come to realize that the classroom is a microcosm of the world; it is the chance we have to practice whatever ideals we may cherish. The kind of classroom situation one creates is the acid test of what it is one really stands for. (p. 656)

In my teaching practice as an early childhood studies field advisor, I have often asked my students to think about what their "why" is in their philosophy of early childhood studies. Often, I notice that when I ask them this question, they are taken aback at first, not quite sure how to articulate it. However, with asking that question and planting that seed in their minds (and hopefully their hearts too), I often hear a shift in the way they perceive and approach their practice. In one of my former students' words,

> As Lovisa mentioned in the seminar, I had thought of "what" and "how" of my teaching, but not much about "why." My "why" is to foster trust and to support and extend children's possibilities, and to be a listener to them. Once I found my "why," every moment at internship became more valuable and motivated me. (Anonymous, personal communication, December 10, 2017)

Whether we are seasoned or novice educators, it is essential to continually reflect on our vision and purpose in teaching and learning and our authentic mission in why we do what we do; this will begin to bring wholeness into our teaching journey.

mentioned factors, they stress interpersonal relationships as the critical indicator instead. Students also agree with the teachers' responses to the primary importance of interpersonal relationships.

My research on inspirational teaching aligns with Clark's (1995) findings as well. Back in 2009, I conducted in-depth interviews with exemplary teachers on their views on effective teaching. What stood out, despite their differences in subject expertise and personal background experiences, was their utmost regard for the importance of being caring, thoughtful, and authentic in the way they relate to their students as the foundation of good teaching (Fung, 2010). J. P. Miller (2012, 2018) discusses the combination of a teacher's attributes and the way they relate to their students in the classroom as a "teacher's presence." He points out that holistic educators are teachers who have a presence in the classroom that profoundly touches the students:

> I believe that more than anything students want our full, authentic presence, and through this presence the teacher connects with the students.... If we recall the teachers that have had an impact on us, it is often not the material that they taught that we remember but their "presence" that somehow touched us deeply. (2012, p. 97)

Holistic educators seek to not only master subject-matter knowledge and pedagogical knowledge, but they also make it a priority to develop their inner life. They fully recognize and acknowledge that who they are and the presence they bring into the classroom matters just as much as the knowledge and methods they use in the classroom.

Action: Teaching as a Calling, Teaching as a Work of the Soul

The merging of the head and heart also requires that holistic educators can translate that connection into action in their daily teaching. The relationships and connections that teachers develop with students should be authentic and come from the heart for the child to reach their inherent potential. To grow as whole teachers, there are several essential practices that holistic educators can participate in on a regular basis. These include self-reflection, contemplative practices such as meditation, and individualized reflections of and attention to each student.

In Waldorf's teacher training, teachers are required to do "heart homework" where they reflect on each child while doing yoga, meditation, or quiet sitting. These practices not only strengthen teachers' attention, awareness, and connection to each child, but also sharpen their intuition skills about themselves and their surroundings (Sobo, 2014). According to J. P. Miller (2014), part of a holistic educator's practice in honing their presence is engaging in contemplative practices. Contemplation is about being open, fully aware, and present in the current moment. A common form of contemplation is the practice of meditation. Meditation comes in many forms, including sitting, walking, and using mantras. It can also be in the form of visualization with guided audio for imagery. Meditation is not the only way to practice contemplation. Being present in the moment can be a pure awareness to stop your worries and thoughts while completing an everyday task, such as washing the dishes. Through contemplation, "[it] allows the individual to gradually overcome [their] sense of separateness" (J. P. Miller, 2014, p. 7). Contemplation aligns with one of the leading elements that make up the framework of holistic education: the spiritual worldview of connectedness to and a reverence for life.

By having attentiveness and awareness of themselves, teachers have a better capacity to bring their full presence into the classroom; having individualized attention and connection with each student is also important. For instance, Reilly (2015) recalls a teacher he had who chose a different book for each child according to what she felt would be meaningful for that particular child and gave it to the child to keep. Years later, as adults, these students spoke of how this meaningful gesture touched them and stayed with them. A gesture like this sends out a message to each child that they are unique individuals who are worth the time to connect with and to get to know.

Essentially, a holistic educator's head, heart, and action are not separate: they work harmoniously to inform, impact, and influence one another. When all three are in harmony, a teacher is teaching holistically, coming from a place of wholeness in their being.

CONCLUSION

Holistic education is a child-centred teaching philosophy that focuses on nurturing the child's inner potential. Many influential figures contributed to the history and evolution of holistic education, including Pestalozzi, Rousseau, and Neill. These key figures have a common thread of being displeased with the mainstream education system of their time, including its purposes and goals, the teaching methods being used, and the conception of children and learning. Alternative schooling approaches such as Waldorf and Montessori continue to be prevalent today as an appealing alternative to mainstream education. With a variety of alternative holistic schooling approaches and their differences, they are held together with common features, including facilitation of the unfolding of inherent potential in children, a spiritual worldview of reverence for life, and a focus on nurturing the whole child. To complement the holistic teaching framework, it is imperative that teachers, through the use of contemplative and reflective practices, carry out their teaching using a balanced combination of head, heart, and action.

REFERENCES

Cahn, S. (1997). Summerhill: A. S. Neill. In *Classic and contemporary readings in the philosophy of education* (pp. 368–376). New York, NY: McGraw-Hill.

Clark, C. M. (1995). *Thoughtful teaching.* New York, NY: Teachers College Press.

Edwards, C. P. (2002). Three approaches from Europe: Waldorf, Montessori, and Reggio Emilia. *Early Childhood Research & Practice.* Retrieved from http://ecrp .uiuc.edu/v4n1/edwards.html

Freire, P. (2000). *Pedagogy of the oppressed* (30th anniversary ed.). New York, NY: Bloomsbury Academic.

Fung, L. (2010). *Reinventing the teacher: A look at inspirational teaching* (Unpublished masters thesis). University of Toronto, Toronto, ON.

Gatto, J. (2000). *A different kind of teacher: Solving the crisis of American schooling.* Berkeley, CA: Berkeley Hills Books.

Kottler, J. A., Zehm, S. J., & Kottler, E. (2005). *On being a teacher: The human dimension* (3rd ed.). Thousand Oaks, CA: Corwin.

McKenna, M. K. (2010). Pestalozzi revisited: Hope and caution for modern education. *Journal of Philosophy and History of Education, 60,* 121–125.

Miller, J. P. (2008). *The holistic curriculum* (2nd ed.). Toronto, ON: University of Toronto Press.

Miller, J. P. (2012). *Whole child education.* Toronto, ON: University of Toronto Press.

Miller, J. P. (2014). *The contemplative practitioner.* Toronto, ON: University of Toronto Press.

Miller, J. P. (2016). Equinox: Portrait of a holistic school. *International Journal of Children's Spirituality, 21,* 283–301.

Miller, J. P. (2018). *Love and compassion: Exploring their role in education.* Buffalo, NY: University of Toronto Press.

Miller, R. (1990). *What are schools for? Holistic education in American culture.* Brandon, VT: Holistic Education Press.

Montessori, M. (1967). *The discovery of the child*. New York, NY: Ballantine.

Montessori, M. (1995). *The absorbent mind*. New York, NY: Henry Holt.

Ontario Ministry of Education. (2014). *How does learning happen? Ontario's pedagogy for the early years*. Toronto, ON: Queen's Printer of Ontario.

Palmer, P. (2007). *The courage to teach: Exploring the inner landscape of a teacher's life* (10th ed.). San Francisco, CA: Jossey-Bass.

Petrash, J. (2002). *Understanding Waldorf education*. Lewisville, NC: Gryphon House.

Reilly, P. (2015). *A path with heart: The inner journey to teaching mastery*. Tomkins Cove, NY: Irimi Horizons.

Robinson, K., & Aronica, L. (2009). *The element: How finding your passion changes everything*. New York, NY: Penguin Group.

Shell, B. (1992). A look at Waldorf and Montessori. *Special Delivery*. Retrieved from http://link.galegroup.com/apps/doc/A125612/AONE?u=utoronto_main&sid= AONE&xid=be04a05f

Sinek, S. (2009). *Start with why: How great leaders inspire everyone to take action*. New York, NY: Portfolio.

Sobo, E. J. (2014). Play's relation to health and well-being in preschool and kindergarten: A Waldorf (Steiner) education perspective. *International Journal of Play, 3*(1), 9–23. doi: 10.1080/21594937.2014.886102

Taylor, J. B. (2008, February). *Jill Bolte Taylor: My stroke of insight* [Video file]. Retrieved from https://www.ted.com/talks/jill_bolte_taylor_s_ powerful_stroke_of_insight

Tompkins, J. (1990). Pedagogy of the distressed. *College English, 52*(6), 653–660.

CHAPTER 6

Experiencing Education in the Early Years

Susan Jagger

GUIDING QUESTIONS:

1. What are Dewey's ideas about education, school, curriculum, pedagogy, and social progress?
2. Draft your own personal philosophy of early years education and care. What would your philosophy entail?

> Education ... is a process of living and not a preparation for future living.
> (Dewey, 1897/1998, p. 230)

With these words in mind, John Dewey brought the practice of teaching and experience of learning and living to the very heart of education. His philosophies of education have been central to the reconceptualization of curriculum and pedagogy since the late 19th century, and his ideas can be traced throughout various contemporary approaches to schooling and society. Dewey was prolific, and his impact was far reaching: he published more than 38 books and 800 articles and pamphlets. Without Dewey, educational research and pedagogical practice today would be very different. This chapter first recounts the life experiences, both in the academy and out, of John Dewey, arguably the most influential educational theorist of the

20th century. Next, it outlines some of the ideas central to Dewey's works and considers the place of experience in his notions of education, school, curriculum, instruction, and social progress.

THE LIFE EXPERIENCES OF JOHN DEWEY

John Dewey was born in Burlington, Vermont, in 1859, at the beginning of a time of tensions, conflicts, and change. In that same year, *On the Origin of Species* by Charles Darwin, *A Contribution to the Critique of Political Economy* by Karl Marx, and *On Liberty* by John Stuart Mill were published. The United States was two years ahead of a civil war that followed Abraham Lincoln's presidential inauguration and was motivated by the Union and Confederate states' opposing views on slavery. Dewey's father, Archibald, fought in the war with the Vermont cavalry and was away from his wife, Lucina, and four young children for six years. Dewey's mother recognized the importance of education and encouraged her children in their studies, providing them with books and materials to support their explorations. Following her grandfather, who was a US congressman, and her father, who was a member of the Vermont General Assembly, she was active in the community and worked hard to support the poor in Burlington.

In high school, John Dewey followed a structured classical education of English, French, Greek, Latin, and mathematics; however, his childhood and youth were rich with experiences in the outdoors and informal learning opportunities. He enjoyed time spent on his grandparents' farm, hiking and canoeing in the mountains around Lake Champlain and north into Canada, and later he had jobs delivering newspapers and working in lumberyards. Dewey was not yet 16 years old when he enrolled at the University of Vermont to study social and political philosophy. Upon graduation, he taught high school in Pennsylvania, from 1879 to 1881, before beginning graduate studies at Johns Hopkins University in Baltimore, Maryland. Here he studied under G. Stanley Hall, a pioneer in child psychology and education who helped to establish child study as an area of research.

With his PhD in hand, Dewey took a position at the University of Michigan and taught philosophy and psychology. It was at Michigan that Dewey began thinking about progressivism and how democracy might inform the growing scientific, urban, and industrial realms of society. Dewey was also troubled by how he saw schools and schooling not responding to the major social changes of the late 19th century and the research findings of studies on child development. After one year at the University of Minnesota, Dewey returned to Michigan in the role of chair of the Department of Philosophy.

Dewey met Alice Chipman, a student at the University of Michigan and a suffragette who was an enthusiastic social and educational activist, and they married in 1886. They had three sons and three daughters, and two of their sons, Morris and Gordon, died in childhood. The Deweys later adopted a young son while travelling in Italy.

In 1894, the Deweys relocated to Chicago, where John took the position of head of the Department of Philosophy and Psychology at the University of Chicago. The university had been founded only four years earlier but was already establishing itself as a research-focused institution. Education and pedagogy were to fall under Dewey's charge, and he was to start a laboratory school to explore and apply his evolving ideas about learning and teaching, and study curriculum and child development. The Dewey School, later called the Laboratory School, was established in 1896.

After a 10-year tenure at the University of Chicago, Dewey and his family moved to New York City, as he had taken a position at Columbia University. It was here that he would stay for 47 years, during 25 of which he taught at the university. While he did not run a laboratory school at Columbia, Dewey remained active in social issues and activism, supporting the civil rights and women's suffragette movements. Dewey lectured and published widely on curriculum and pedagogy and was a consultant on many educational systems internationally.

In 1927, Dewey's wife passed away, and he stayed single until 1946, when he married Roberta Lowitz Grant. Soon after, they adopted two children. Dewey maintained his activity in writing, thinking, and being involved in public and social issues up until his death on June 1, 1952.

Extending from his life experiences and guided by the five articles of his philosophy of education, *My Pedagogic Creed* (1897), the following outlines some of Dewey's key ideas and assertions about education, school, curriculum, instruction, and progress, and how experience underpins each.

WHAT EDUCATION IS

The question of education, of what it is and what it could be, was a topic of much discussion at the beginning of the 20th century, and Dewey's voice resonated then as it continues to do now. Looking across provincial and territorial mission statements, we see similarities and differences in ideas about education and in its aims and goals:

> Ontario is committed to the success and well-being of every student and child. Learners in the education system will develop the knowledge, skills, and characteristics that will lead them to become personally successful, economically productive and actively engaged citizens. (Ontario Ministry of Education, 2014, p. 1)

> The purpose of the British Columbia school system is to enable [students] to develop their individual potential and acquire the knowledge, skills, and abilities needed to contribute to a healthy society and a prosperous and sustainable economy. (British Columbia Ministry of Education, n.d., p. 1)

> The mission for New Brunswick public schools is to have each student develop the attributes needed to be a lifelong learner, to achieve personal fulfillment, and to contribute to a productive, just, and democratic society. (New Brunswick Education and Early Childhood Development, 2018, p. 1)

Each of these three statements has a shared and desired end product—a successful, engaged, and healthy citizen who contributes productively to society and the economy. Knowledge, skills, abilities, and attitudes are the requirements for learners to reach this goal. Arguably, the shared purpose of education is to prepare learners for the future, for future participation in society, and to ensure that this future is bright.

Dewey asserts otherwise, that education itself is realized in the active and present engagement of the individual in the social consciousness (1897/1998). These experiences begin soon after the child is born and guide their developing habits, ideas, and emotions. To Dewey, the child's psychological instincts and behaviours are the starting point of education. However, the child's psychological structure works with and in sociological contexts and stimuli. These two sides to the process of education, the psychological and sociological, are inextricably linked and continually shape and inform each other. Education is a social process, and recognizing the unique and dynamic social conditions within which we dwell, interact, learn, and grow allows for a richer interpretation and understanding of the individual and social educative processes and products. Education is for the present and for the future and occurs through our psychological and sociological engagements and experiences (Dewey, 1897/1998).

These notions of education have been taken up, to varying degrees, in educational models that have been proposed and embraced. Two such models, traditional education and progressive education, have been in opposition at points through history since the early movement to a more progressive education in the late 19th century, elements of which can be traced to our thinking about education today.

On one hand, the purpose of traditional education was to "prepare the young for future responsibilities and for success in life, by means of acquisition of the organized bodies of information and prepared forms of skills which comprehend the material of instruction" (Dewey, 1938/1997, p. 18). It focused on predetermined and static content and skills to be transmitted to learners. Well-established standards and rules framed learning so as to best develop and train moral actions. The organization of schools and within schools was distinct and set apart from other social institutions. Patterns of daily schedules and timings, examinations, promotion to higher grades, and classification and priority of subject areas, and the roles and interactions among students and teachers helped to define and bound what we understand to be school and education more broadly. Student were to be receptive to content and take up the expected moral conduct; "the attitude of pupils, must, upon the whole, be one of docility ... and obedience" (Dewey, 1938/1997, p. 18). Books were the primary source of information for students, and teachers were the relayers of content and skills and enforcers of conduct. While taken up widely then, and in many instances now, traditional education is organized in a top-down way and from outside of the school, imposing adult ideals and methods on students that are disconnected from the understandings and experiences of children. Participation of students in guiding curriculum and their education is non-existent, as what has been taught in the past remains what is taught, regardless of the rapidly changing social and environmental contexts within which education occurs.

Traditional education is in stark contrast to a more progressive education. Following Locke and Rousseau, progressive education allows for the expression and growth of individuality. Learning is through experience and free activity rather than structured solely by teachers and textbooks. Instead of a focus on preparation for a far-off and predetermined future, learning is organically embedded in opportunities to actively engage in living in the

ever-changing and dynamic present. What is central in a progressive education is the recognition and fostering of relations and relationships. Curriculum is informed by the interests, needs, and well-being of students, with the
teacher as a facilitator or guide. The whole child is nurtured and reflected
in teaching and learning, and home and school are inherently connected in
curriculum and pedagogy. Students are encouraged to work collaboratively
and learn together with their peers and their community rather than in quiet
isolation. Reflective of research in the field of child studies, progressive education is responsive to students, society, and environments, and changes
accordingly. The Progressive Education Association (1919–1955) was committed to promoting the ideals of this "new" education and outlined its central tenets in the Seven Principles of Progressive Education:

1. Children's freedom to develop naturally
2. Children's interest as the motivation for educational work
3. Teacher as guide
4. School record-keeping to promote the study of child development
5. Focus on children's physical development
6. Cooperation between the home and school in meeting the child's
   needs and interests
7. Progressive schools as leaders in education

It is important to note that while progressive education was increasingly
widespread in the early to mid-1900s, it fell out of favour following World
War II and through the 1950s, 1960s, and 1970s with the rise of conserva-
tism, nationalism, school standardization, and disciplinary knowledge that
followed the launch of Sputnik and that accompanied the Cold War.

WHAT THE SCHOOL IS

Dewey's conception of what school is extends from his educational focus on
the child and on living relationships of the learner, society, and the environment. Given that education is a social process, it follows that the school is a
social institution and a part of the community collective. He asserts "that the
school must represent present life—life as real and vital to the child as that
which he carries on in the home, in the neighbourhood, or on the playground"
(Dewey, 1897/1998, pp. 230–231) and states that education that proceeds
otherwise, through disconnected and inauthentic activity, "is always a poor

substitute for the genuine reality and tends to cramp and to deaden" (p. 231). Thus, school and schooling must grow out of the child's existing home and social life and continue those social experiences and engagements in a focused and simplified way. As such, Dewey maintains that the child will come to make meaning of their everyday lived experience and participate in those relationships. Furthermore, this close connection of home and school allows for moral values and training from home to be built upon and deepened at school. The teacher's role is as a member of the community and as a guide in children's experiences and their responses to those experiences.

When considering traditional education and schools, the recognition of the school as a form of community life is often missing. Instead, the school is a site for the transmission of information, lessons, and habits that are predetermined from outside of the community and that work to prepare the student for the future. "The child must do these things for the sake of something else he is to do ... [and] as a result they do not become a part of the life experience of the child and so are not truly educative" (Dewey, 1897/1998, p. 231). Dewey asserts that in schools informed by traditional education, the connections between children's work and thought tend to be neglected or even dismantled, and this makes it difficult and, in some cases, impossible for children to participate in learning and practising morals and values. The teacher directs and controls, thus eliminating positive community social interaction in the class curriculum and instruction.

Dewey's progressive ideas about education and what school is were realized in 1896 when he and his wife, Alice, brought together interested parents and established the Dewey School, later renamed the Laboratory School, at the University of Chicago, with an enrolment of 15 children in its first year. The stated primary purpose of this new school was the following:

1. To exhibit, test, verify, and criticize theoretical statements and principles
2. To add to the sum of facts and principles in its special line (Mayhew & Edwards, 1965/2007, p. 3)

Here, the strong influence of science is clear in the terminologies and goals stated, but the school was more than a sterile and controlled laboratory of experimentation. It was a space within which developing ideas and approaches were brought into practice and curriculum and instruction was recentred on the children and their lived experiences. As Dewey states, "in this school the life of the child becomes the all-controlling aim. All the media necessary to further the growth of the child centre there. Learning?—certainly, but living primarily, and learning through and related to this living" (1899, p. 53).

The school and its teachers began not with a set of learning objectives and fixed rules but rather with four broad questions or concerns to actively guide curriculum and instruction:

1. What can be done, and how can it be done, to bring the school into closer relation with the home and neighbourhood life—instead of having the school a place where the child comes solely to learn certain lessons? What can be done to break down the barriers which have unfortunately come to separate the school life from the rest of the everyday life of the child?...

2. What can be done in the way of introducing subject matter in history and science and art, that shall have a positive value and real significance in the child's own life; that shall represent, even to the youngest children, something worthy of attainment in skill or knowledge; as much so to the little pupil as are the studies of the high school or college student to him?...

3. How can instruction in these formal, symbolic branches—the mastering of the ability to read, write, and use figures intelligently—be carried on with everyday experience and occupation as their background and in definite relations to other studies for more inherent content, and be carried on in such a way that the child shall feel their necessity through their connection with subjects which appeal to him on their own account?...

4. Individual attention.... This is secured by small groupings—eight or ten in a class—and a large number of teachers supervising systematically the intellectual needs and attainments and physical well-being and growth of the child.... It requires but a few words to make this statement about attention to individual powers and needs, and yet the whole of the school's aims and methods, moral, physical, intellectual, are bound up in it. (Dewey, 1899, pp. 118–119)

The Laboratory School closely followed Dewey's ideas about education, learning, and schools. The home experiences of the child were reflected in school activities, and academic skills were constructed out of those engagements. Work and thought were inextricably linked at the Laboratory School. Children's interactions were encouraged, as they were recognized as part of a learning community in which cooperation and collaboration were integral to curriculum and pedagogy. Motivations to learn were internal to the child, and the experiences and teachers' knowledge of their students' interests and needs determined the problems and activities planned for them. The school's physical structure supported this experience-centred way of teaching, as it included shops for children's hand-work: shop-work with wood and tools was done in the carpentry room; cooking work was done in the kitchen; and sewing, weaving, and textile work was done in the sewing room. All children participated in the different types of hand-work with girls working with wood and tools and boys cooking, sewing, and weaving. The organization and activities of the school were in stark contrast to the very traditional schools of the late 19th century, which reinforced children's place in society and unequal gender roles.

The Laboratory School at the University of Chicago continues to educate children and youth from nursery to high school following the principles and practices of John Dewey. The school is still responsive to societal and environmental changes, and this is reflected in its mission statement: "The Laboratory Schools are home to the youngest members of the University of Chicago's academic community. We ignite and nurture an enduring spirit of scholarship, curiosity, creativity, and confidence. We value learning experientially, exhibiting kindness, and honoring diversity" (University of Chicago Laboratory Schools, n.d., p. 3).

In Canada, Dewey's work and the Laboratory School motivated the foundation of St. George's School for Child Study (later the Dr. Eric Jackman Institute of Child Study) at the University of Toronto in 1925. The school was established by Dr. William E. Blatz, a psychologist and pediatrician, and was the first of the University of Toronto's multidisciplinary research centres. Its focus on the child and child study has persisted through the years, and today the school is home to approximately two hundred children from nursery to grade six:

> The Dr. Eric Jackman Institute of Child Study shares characteristics that are common to many great schools across North America: a focus on children and learning; involved parents; competent and reflective teachers; responsive leadership; a caring environment; and curricular, teaching, and assessment strategies that are appropriate and effective. (OISE/University of Toronto, n.d.)

THE SUBJECT MATTER OF EDUCATION

When we think of curriculum, we often think of the structured and pre-scribed learning objectives set out in subject- and grade-specific documents from our respective provincial and territorial ministries of education. These frameworks are informed by Ralph Tyler's (1949) four curricular and instructional parts (known as the Tyler Rationale)—(1) defining learning objectives; (2) introducing learning experiences; (3) organizing experiences; and (4) evaluating learning and revising less-effective components—and little has changed since they were set out 70 years ago. What is missing in this organization is the voice of children. Where does the child fit into our curriculum and what we teach?

Looking etymologically at curriculum, we can trace the term's roots to a course, a path taken, a route followed. But, rather than begin the race, as it were, with the curriculum document as we so often do, perhaps we should recentre the starting gate. Dewey asserts that it is essential to consider the child and their world when we plan for the subject matter of our teaching and children's learning:

> The child is the starting point, the centre, and the end. His [*sic*] development, his [*sic*] growth, is the ideal. It alone furnishes the standard. To the growth of the child all studies are subservient; they are instruments valued as they serve the needs of growth. Personality, character, is more than subject-matter. Not knowledge or information, but self-realization, is the goal. (1902, p. 13)

A child-centred approach recognizes that the experience of the child is fluid and ever changing, and inherently and seamlessly brings together their personal and social interests and motivations. Learning occurs through authentic and organic connection and assimilation that begins within the child. It does not reach in, but rather it reaches out. As such, it is the child, not the subject matter, that determines learning. Indeed, in schooling, the curriculum that is separate from and even subordinates the child and their experience is one that is lifeless, mechanical, and dead.

On the other hand, those in the formal-curriculum camp might assert that children's experience as it is should be widened by a breadth of understandings across disciplines. This breadth can make for a very long road to be travelled, and thus topics are reduced into studies, studies into lessons, and lessons into a series of specific concepts and ideas. The children then move step by step through these parts, making their way along the curricular path. The steps are sequenced and, when followed, bring understanding and knowledge.

What we see formed is a binary in the opposition of the child and the curriculum and a perceived juxtaposition of the child versus the curriculum. This is taken up in the motivations, underpinnings, and asserted characteristics of each camp and in their critiques of each other. Some of these are summarized in table 6.1.

Rather than perpetuate this polarity, Dewey maintains that we must instead let go of the notion that there is, in fact, a gap between the child and their experience and the curriculum and the subject matter of study. The curriculum is not fixed and outside of the experience of the child. Similarly, the child and their experience are not set but rather are dynamic and evolving. Instead, the child and the curriculum exist along a continuum.

> The child and the curriculum are simply two limits which define a single process. Just as two points define a straight line, so the present standpoint of the child and the facts and truths of studies define instruction. It is continuous reconstruction, moving from the child's present experience out into that represented by the organized bodies of truth that we call studies. (Dewey, 1902, p. 16)

It is not a matter of following the child or the curriculum located at either end of the continuum. The child must not be solely placed on a path to

Table 6.1: The Child versus the Curriculum

CHILD	CURRICULUM
Interest	Discipline
Psychological	Logical
Empathy and knowledge of child	Teacher training and scholarship
Freedom and initiative	Guidance and control
Spontaneity	Law
Change and progress	Conservation
Chaos and anarchism	Inertness and routine
Neglect of sacred authority of duty	Suppression of individuality through tyrannical despotism

follow, as rigid adherence to "old education" might encourage, and neither should they be expected to develop facts or truths out of their own mind without guidance. As Dewey purports, "development does not mean just getting something out of the mind. It is a development of experience and into experience that is really wanted" (1902, p. 24). The role of the educator, working along the continuum between the child and the curriculum, is to plan environments with both the child's interests and understandings in mind and thus guide experiences indirectly.

THE NATURE OF METHOD

Activity is central in Dewey's assertions about how education, schooling, and teaching should proceed and be realized in our pedagogical enactments. He maintains that, in the development of the child, activity comes ahead of passivity, expression before impression, muscular development before sensory, and movements before conscious sensation. When education and schooling proceed counter to this sequencing, Dewey claims, learning will not follow:

> The neglect of this principle is the cause of a large part of the waste of time and strength in school work. This child is thrown into a passive, receptive, or absorbing attitude. The conditions are such that he is not permitted to follow the law of his nature; the result is friction and waste. (1897/1998, p. 233)

Through the child's activity, intellectual and rational ideas are developed and refined as the action is repeated and similarly sharpened.

As noted above, children's interests should guide curriculum, and they should also inform pedagogical approaches. A deep understanding of the interests and needs of the child will allow the educator to see what concepts and contexts the child is ready to explore and engage with and what materials are best suited to enriching and extending those experiences. When we fail to take children's interests into consideration in pedagogy, Dewey states, our repression is a substitution of the adult for the child and, in turn, leads to limited intellectual curiosity and inquisitiveness, reduced children's initiative and self-motivation, and minimized interest.

Learning, to Dewey, proceeds from activity, and thus the method of teaching ought to focus on children's engagement in curricular experiences. Teachers, then, are to set out things for children to do, rather than objectives to learn, and these activities are to require thought, not just action. The actions will then be elevated to meaningful experiences:

> On the active hand, experience is trying—a meaning which is made explicit in the connected term experiment. On the passive, it is undergoing. When we experience something we act upon it, we do something with it; then we suffer or undergo the consequences. We do something to the thing and then it does something to us in return; such is the peculiar combination. The connection of these two phases of experience measures the fruitfulness or value of the experience. Mere activity does not constitute experience. (Dewey, 1916/2009, p. 109)

Experiences change the learner in some way, requiring them to adjust and adapt, and in these alterations, understandings and knowledge of the experience, of the thing under study, are developed and deepened.

Play is central in children's meaning-making and in pedagogical methods. Not only does a focus on play make school more enjoyable for children to attend, through play, home and school environments are easily connected and deeper understandings realized. Children learn about the world that they live with and in through their creative play, how the processes of life work, and how to keep those processes going. However, as with activities, "it is not enough just to introduce plays and games, hand work and manual exercises. Everything depends upon the way in which they are employed" (Dewey, 1916/2009, p. 152). Mindful inclusion and infusion of activity, experience, and play are key.

Along with meaningful experience and play, and following that education is a social process, collaboration and collective experiences are of importance in pedagogy. Classrooms and learning centres informed by principles of progressive education are noisy and busy places. There is active discussion between children, and between children and educators. Members of the learning community support and help each other to solve problems and co-construct knowledge.

> A spirit of free communication, of interchange of ideas, suggestions, results, both successes and failures of previous experiences, becomes the dominating note of the recitation. So far as emulation enters in, it is the comparison of individuals, not with regard to the quantity of information personally absorbed, but with reference to the quality of work done—the genuine community standard of value. (Dewey, 1899, p. 30)

An important part of pedagogy, according to Dewey and still foundational in many educational models, is problem-based or project-based learning.
Dewey's criteria for projects (or occupations, as they were identified) are that
they are of interest to children, stimulate and motivate thinking, and pique
curiosity and take children into new areas of thinking, and that investigations
of them last for an extended period of time. Within project-based learning,
children might participate in role play, field trips, experiments, and research.
Some projects proceed loosely following the scientific method, though not
necessarily in sequential steps and in the order outlined in Dewey's five steps
for solving problems:

1. Defining the problem
2. Observing the problem and its context
3. Forming hypotheses
4. Outlining consequences of each hypothesis
5. Testing the hypotheses to determine which best solves the problem

THE SCHOOL AND SOCIAL PROGRESS

To Dewey, the school played a critical and essential role in society and in social progress. Schools needed to embrace a community life and reflect present
societal ideals and goals. Really, schools served as a microcosm of society. As
such, the school allowed for children's participation and for their voices to be
heard in education, school, curriculum, and pedagogy. By doing so, children
learned about democracy and equality among citizens, both contested issues
during Dewey's time that continue to be hard fought for in many communities and societies. Education, teaching, and learning can have the power to be
transformative and empower learners to make positive changes in society and
the environments that they live with and in. In Dewey's words, "education is
the fundamental method of social progress and reform" (1897/1998, p. 234).
    Societal norms are reflected in the goals of schools and schooling and
in the purpose of education. In the late 19th and early 20th centuries, children were to be prepared for later life, to be fitted into predetermined roles
and institutions, and to perpetuate desired societal norms. Change, reform,
equality, and democracy did not feature in the mission of schools and education. Today, we see many of the same goals persisting, as can be interpreted in mission statements of educational systems and schools. Learners
can be, and should be, change agents, and schools are the place for positive

societal and environmental change and progress to begin. As Dewey noted over 100 years ago,

> It is the business of every one interested in education to insist upon the school as the primary and most effective instrument of social progress and reform in order that society may be awakened to realize what school stands for, and aroused to the necessity of endowing the educator with sufficient equipment properly to perform his task. (1897/1998, p. 235)

Now, perhaps more than ever, the role of education in the life of the child and the place of school in society renders Dewey's work essential for our (re)thinking about how to create relevant and transformative teaching and learning experiences for the betterment of ourselves and our communities. Together, education, schools, curriculum, and pedagogy can empower young citizens to be active change agents and participate in creating a more democratic, just, and equitable society and environment for all. The legacy of John Dewey can be seen in the history of curriculum change as it becomes refocused on the child and their experience as both learner and citizen in a dynamic world.

REFERENCES

British Columbia Ministry of Education. (n.d.). Ministry of Education. Retrieved from https://www2.gov.bc.ca/gov/content/governments/organizational-structure/ministries-organizations/ministries/education

Dewey, J. (1897/1998). My pedagogic creed. In L. A. Hickman & T. M. Alexander (Eds.), *The essential Dewey: Pragmatism, education, democracy* (Vol. 1, pp. 229–235). Bloomington, IN: Indiana University Press.

Dewey, J. (1899). *The school and society.* London, UK: Forgotten Books.

Dewey, J. (1902). *The child and the curriculum.* Chicago, IL: University of Chicago Press.

Dewey, J. (1916/2009). *Democracy and education.* London, UK: Merchant Books.

Dewey, J. (1938/1997). *Experience and education.* New York, NY. Touchstone.

Mayhew, K. C., & Edwards, A. C. (1965/2007). *The Dewey School: The Laboratory School of the University of Chicago, 1896–1903.* New York, NY: Atherton Press.

New Brunswick Education and Early Childhood Development. (2018). Education and early childhood mandates. Retrieved from http://www2.gnb.ca/content/gnb/en/departments/education/contacts/dept_renderer.151.html#mandates

OISE/University of Toronto. (n.d.). The Laboratory School at the Dr. Eric Jackman Institute for Child Study. Retrieved from https://www.oise.utoronto.ca/jics/j-ics-lab-school/

Ontario Ministry of Education. (2014). *Achieving excellence: A renewed vision for education in Ontario*. Toronto, ON: Queen's Printer. Retrieved from http://www.edu.gov.on.ca/eng/about/renewedVision.pdf

Tyler, R. W. (1949). *Basic principles of curriculum and instruction*. Chicago, IL: University of Chicago Press.

University of Chicago Laboratory Schools. (n.d.). Lab. Retrieved from http://www.ucls.uchicago.edu/uploaded/admissions/Lab_viewbook_spreads.pdf?1468942014016

CHAPTER 7

The Great Debate Applied to Developmentally Appropriate Practice (DAP): Moving beyond Dichotomies in the Early Years

Kristy Timmons

GUIDING QUESTIONS:

1. What are DAP, its core components, and related common misconceptions?
2. Critically reflect on DAP and the presence of dichotomies in early years education and care. How might we move forward as a field?

INTRODUCTION

This chapter provides an overview of the historical perspectives of developmentally appropriate practice (DAP) and the organization that published the position statement, the National Association for the Education of Young Children (NAEYC). The core components of DAP and the principles of child development and learning that inform practice in the early years are presented. A critical exploration is undertaken, which includes an examination of potential misunderstandings and misconceptions of DAP, and a call to move beyond dichotomies in the early years is suggested. Despite a common desire from parents, teachers, researchers, and policy-makers to increase the quality of learning environments for all children, tensions exist concerning the "best" or most "appropriate" way to support development and learning. In order to move forward as a community of early learning professionals, we must come together to recognize the ways in which different practices support the development of children's social, emotional, cognitive, and physical skills, while moving away from extremes of "this" versus "that" thinking. The chapter concludes with suggestions for continual refinement in understanding evidence-based practices in the early years.

WHERE DID DAP COME FROM?

Conceptually, the idea that an activity, instruction, or a lesson may be developmentally appropriate for children, or not, had been discussed by educators and psychologists alike long before NAEYC addressed it. Despite the use of the terminology prior to the 1980s, it was not until the mid-1980s that a more specific description for DAP became necessary. The need for a clearly operationalized conception of DAP arose when NAEYC created a system to accredit early childhood programs. This accreditation involved guidelines that required early childhood programs to provide "developmentally appropriate experiences and materials for children" (Copple & Bredekamp, 2006), making it necessary for NAEYC to be specific about what was meant by DAP.

In 1986, a position statement on developmentally appropriate practice for preschool children was published. In 1987, these guidelines were expanded to include the entire span of development from birth to age eight, and these publications included an outline of appropriate and inappropriate practices (Bredekamp, 1987). The understanding from the initial publication was that the position statement on DAP would be revisited periodically to reflect the emerging knowledge in the field of early childhood.

In 1988, the Association for Childhood Education International (ACEI) published an article that confirmed the importance of play (Isenberg & Quisenberry, 1988). Two years later, in 1990, the National Association of Elementary School Principals (NAESP) expanded its own standards for quality early childhood programs, which were then revised again in 2005 (NAESP, 2005). This was followed by the National Association of State Boards of Education (NASBE), which included statements as part of the National Task Force on School Readiness (NASBE, 1991). Additional position statements that may be of interest are included in box 7.1.

Box 7.1: Additional Position Statements

Anti-Discrimination	Linguistic and Cultural Diversity
Code of Ethical Conduct and	Literacy
Statement of Commitment	Mathematics
Standards for Professional	Media Violence
Preparations	Professional Development
Accreditation	Public Policy
Child Abuse Prevention	Quality Standards
Curriculum, Assessment, and	School Readiness
Program Evaluation	Science
Early Learning Standards	Teacher Certification
Inclusion	Technology
Kindergarten	Violence
Licensing and Public Regulation	

The first major revision of NAEYC's position statement and guides for DAP were published in 1997, entitled *Developmentally Appropriate Practice in Early Childhood Programs*, Revised Edition (Bredekamp & Copple, 1997). The preface of the 1997 publication included an acknowledgement that the changing knowledge base in the field of early childhood education would require a review process and revised document approximately every 10 years (Gestwicki, 2017). The second revision and most recent position statement was published in 2009 (Copple & Bredekamp, 2009).

WHAT IS DAP?

DAP involves meeting children where they are while supporting each child in accomplishing challenging yet achievable goals. This involves knowledge of how young children learn, from a developmental perspective, and knowledge of the individual, including the social and cultural contexts in which children live. Therefore, educators should consider the children's interest, age, social and cultural contexts, and developmental level when determining whether practices are developmentally appropriate. DAP also requires that goals and experiences are challenging in order to encourage continued interest for the children, individually and as a group. One way of achieving this is through having high yet realistic expectations for all students.

Several decades of research in the area of teacher expectations have provided convincing evidence that educator expectations influence student performance and achievement (Babad, 1993; Timmons, 2018; Weinstein, 2002; Zhang, 2014). Teachers use information related to a variety of individual characteristics in forming expectations of their students (de Boer, Bosker, & van der Werf, 2010; Keogh, 2000; Timmons, 2018). Many researchers over the past three decades have explored how individual characteristics such as ethnicity, gender, social class, social skills, stereotypes, exceptionalities, prior achievement, parent background, and teacher-student relationships influence teacher expectations (Baron, Tom, & Cooper, 1985; McKown & Weinstein, 2002; Obiakor, 1999; Tenenbaum & Ruck, 2007; Timmons, 2018; Woodcock & Vialle, 2011; Zhang, 2014). There has been a particular focus on the characteristics of ethnicity and social class given the noted gap in academic achievement for minority groups and families in low socio-economic classes (Hattie, 2003; Muller, Katz, & Dance, 1999; Pellegrini & Blatchford, 2000; Rubie-Davies, Hattie, & Hamilton, 2006; Tenenbaum & Ruck, 2007; Weinstein, 2002).

Teacher expectations may be enacted through differentiated instruction, which can result in inequitable learning opportunities for some students. There are often justified pedagogical reasons for differentiated instruction; however, the ultimate goal should always be to enhance the learning opportunities and experiences of all children, and oftentimes this requires differentiated practices. It is essential, however, that educators pay attention to the ways their expectations and beliefs influence their instruction, ultimately influencing the learning experiences of children. Fang (1996) documented the many ways in which teacher beliefs impact practices. This literature review focused on the ways teachers' implicit beliefs impact reading and writing approaches and revealed that teachers' beliefs do, in fact, influence teaching pedagogy. Similarly, Zohar, Degani, & Vaaknin (2001) interviewed teachers about the suitability of higher-order thinking methods for students of differing abilities. Forty-five percent of the teachers believed that higher-order thinking approaches were not appropriate for low-ability students. In fact, 30 percent reported never using higher-order questioning with students they characterized as low ability (Zohar et al., 2001). Findings suggest that teacher beliefs and expectations lead to differing instructional interactions, which ultimately affects what children learn and demonstrates a need to critically reflect on what is truly meant by DAP. Comprehensive, effective curriculum is essential; however, an educator's daily interactions with children are the most influential determinant of children's learning outcomes (Copple & Bredekamp, 2009).

The goal should be to reduce the gap between high- and low-achieving students, and this can be accomplished at the teacher level. In fact, one of the key messages of the position statement on DAP is a call to reduce the achievement gap. Research has continually noted substantial achievement gaps related to demographic variables including, but not limited to, family income and education, ethnicity, and language background (de Boer et al., 2010; Keogh, 2000; Van den Bergh, Denessen, Hornstra, Voeten, & Holland, 2010). These disparities can have significant impacts on children's opportunities to learn; thus, it must be a priority for early childhood educators, researchers, and policy-makers to continue to narrow this gap. Given the known disparities and the goal of reducing the achievement gaps in early learning, early childhood programs must invest in extended and enriched learning opportunities for children who do not have these experiences outside of school. Developmentally appropriate practice extends beyond the opportunities provided directly to children and requires engagement with parents and families, health services, and mental health supports (Copple & Bredekamp, 2009).

In considering the importance of engaging parents and families, a strength-based funds of knowledge perspective is crucial (Di Santo, Timmons, & Pelletier, 2015; Moll, Amanti, Neff, & Gonzalez, 1992; Riojas-Cortex, Flores, & Clark, 2003; Timmons & Pelletier, 2014). It is important that educators "recognize the children within the context of their unique system and natural home environment" (Carter, Chard, & Pool, 2009, p. 520). I am advocating for a family-strengths approach that acknowledges, validates, and builds on the funds of knowledge of families and embeds "learning opportunities within meaningful and contextually relevant everyday experiences" (Carter et al., 2009, p. 520). In highlighting the knowledge that families and children bring to their learning, educators can ensure that DAP includes the unique social and cultural contexts in which children live.

WHAT IS THE POSITION STATEMENT?

The purpose of the NAEYC position statement on DAP is to "promote excellence in early childhood education by providing a framework for best practice. Grounded both in the research on child development and learning and in the knowledge base regarding educational effectiveness, the framework outlines practices that promote young children's optimal learning and development" (Copple & Bredekamp, 2009, p. 1). In addition to providing a rationale for the position statement, NAEYC provides a discussion on the current context and critical issues in early education and development. The revisions intend to reflect the continuity and change within the field. Despite revisions to the publication, NAEYC's commitment to "excellence and equity" and the "core understanding of how children learn" has remained a fundamental commitment.

Core Components of DAP

Teachers are tasked with making a multitude of decisions each and every day. In making these decisions, teachers should be intentional about the goals they make for children's learning and the ways in which they support children in accomplishing these goals (Copple & Bredekamp, 2009). Being intentional requires that these goals are challenging yet achievable.

The NAEYC position statement identifies three areas of knowledge that early childhood practitioners must consider in their work (Copple & Bredekamp, 2009, pp. 9–10).

1. *Knowledge of child development and learning:* "What is known about child development and learning—referring to knowledge of age-related characteristics that permits general predictions about what experiences are likely to best promote children's learning and development."

   Knowledge of child development and learning should not be based on assumptions, but rather informed by empirical research and early childhood theory (box 7.2). Early childhood training should include a focus on child development theory, diverse practice experiences in the field, and instruction in how to critically review and reflect on empirical research. Educators should continue to review and be critical of empirical research as part of their ongoing professional practice. Knowledge of child development and age-related characteristics allows educators to make general predictions on what type of experiences are likely to promote learning and development and to make initial decisions about setting up the environment (Gestwicki, 2017).

2. *Knowledge of what is individually appropriate:* "What is known about each child as an individual—referring to what practitioners learn

about each child that has implications for how best to adapt and be responsive to that individual variation."

It is crucial to be aware of the principles of child development that influence learning; however, knowledge of child development theory is only a small part of ensuring practices are developmentally appropriate. Beyond knowledge of child development, practitioners need to know children on an individual level. Educators should strive to build strong relationships with all children. Building strong relationships with children involves spending informal time getting to know their interests, dislikes, strengths, and challenges. Formal and informal assessments should take place on a regular basis. Educators can learn about the uniqueness of children in their classroom through regular observations, clinical interviews, conversations with families, collection of work samples, and engagement in documentation with the child. Responding and interacting with children as unique individuals is the key to DAP. Kaurez (2013) suggests that sometimes the use of the phrase *developmentally appropriate practice* can raise red flags for some and recommends the phrase *differentiated instruction*. Despite the language used in discussing what is individually appropriate, it is crucial that learning experiences are challenging and achievable. As mentioned, the goal of differentiated instruction and DAP must always be to enhance learning opportunities and experiences of children.

3. *Knowledge of what is culturally important:* "What is known about the social and cultural contexts in which children live—referring to the values, expectations, and behavioral and linguistic conventions that shape children's lives at home and in their communities that practitioners must strive to understand in order to ensure that learning experiences in the program or school are meaningful, relevant, and respectful for each child and family."

Getting to know the values and expectations that influence children's lives at home and in their larger communities involves recognizing the important role that families have as their children's first teacher. Children grow up within a family system and bring with them their lived experiences. Educators should be careful not to make any assumptions about children or families but instead work with families to understand what is important to them for their child's learning and development. Learning from families about important cultural contexts and practices ensures that our interactions with children are meaningful and respectful (Copple & Bredekamp, 2009). Just as knowledge of the individual child and general child development is critical to DAP, the important role of culture needs to be recognized and supported in respectful ways.

PRINCIPLES OF CHILD DEVELOPMENT AND LEARNING THAT INFORM PRACTICE

The NAEYC makes it clear that DAP, as defined in the position statement, is not based on assumptions of what we "think" or "want to believe" about children. Instead, DAP is informed by and based in empirical research on learning and development (Copple & Bredekamp, 2009). The NAEYC acknowledges that, despite integrating a comprehensive list of principles on child development and learning, it is not an all-encompassing list. In discussing the 12 principles, the NAEYC references 54 research papers that shed light on the importance of these interrelated principles. In considering the importance of remaining current, I recommend that the principles and their supporting research be updated more frequently than every 10 years to reflect emerging research and understanding of the field.

"IT DEPENDS": CAN WE REALLY BE CERTAIN WHEN PRACTICES ARE DEVELOPMENTALLY APPROPRIATE?

This section is inspired by many conversations with teacher candidates in the early primary concentration at Queen's University. I have had numerous discussions with teacher candidates about the importance of considering the contextual factors that influence the decisions we make as early years educators. When reviewing the results of empirical research studies, teacher candidates often begin to unpack the contextual factors that play a role in understanding and interpreting the findings. Teacher candidates often respond to discussion questions by initially acknowledging that we must consider a multitude of contextual variables, including teacher education and training, program quality, and demographic variables, among many other factors, in unpacking and understanding the results. It is not uncommon for pre-service teachers to respond by saying "it depends," as part of critically

Box 7.2: Principles of Child Development and Learning

1. All the domains of development and learning—physical, social and emotional, and cognitive—are important, and they are closely interrelated. Children's development and learning in one domain influence and are influenced by what takes place in other domains.

2. Many aspects of children's learning and development follow well documented sequences, with later abilities, skills, and knowledge building on those already acquired.

3. Development and learning proceed at varying rates from child to child, as well as at uneven rates across different areas of a child's individual functioning.

4. Development and learning result from a dynamic and continuous interaction of biological maturation and experience.

5. Early experiences have profound effects, both cumulative and delayed, on a child's development and learning, and optimal periods exist for certain types of development and learning to occur.

6. Development proceeds toward greater complexity, self-regulation, and symbolic or representational capacities.

7. Children develop best when they have secure, consistent relationships with responsive adults and opportunities for positive relationships with peers.

8. Development and learning occur in and are influenced by multiple social and cultural contexts.

9. Always mentally active in seeking to understand the world around them, children learn in a variety of ways; a wide range of teaching strategies and interactions are effective in supporting all these kinds of learning.

10. Play is an important vehicle for developing self-regulation as well as for promoting language, cognition, and social competence.

11. Development and learning advance when children are challenged to achieve at a level just beyond their current mastery, and also when they have many opportunities to practice newly acquired skills.

12. Children's experiences shape their motivation and approaches to learning, such as persistence, initiative, and flexibility; in turn, these dispositions and behaviors affect their learning and development.

Source: Copple & Bredekamp, 2009, pp. 10–25

reflecting on topics and/or research findings. Likewise, it is imperative that we consider the multiple contextual factors that play a role in making choices and deciding when practices are developmentally appropriate—or not.

Pre- and in-service educators have struggled with understanding how the philosophy of DAP translates to decisions and interactions in the daily practices of the classroom. In doing so, educators may ask themselves, "Can we really be certain when practices are developmentally appropriate?" In reflecting on this question, it is important that educators realize that whether or not what happens in early years classrooms is developmentally appropriate goes beyond the decisions of teachers; it is the result of decisions that are made on multiple levels by government, administrators, policy-makers, families, and educators (Copple & Bredekamp, 2009). However, the position statement includes guidelines that address the decisions that teachers can make in five interrelated areas of practice: (1) creating a caring community of learners; (2) teaching to enhance development and learning; (3) planning curriculum to achieve important goals; (4) assessing children's development and learning; and (5) establishing reciprocal relationships with families. Additional descriptions of the guidelines are beyond the scope of this chapter and can be found as part of NAEYC's position statement (pp. 16–23). These guidelines are designed to support educators in translating the DAP framework into quality interactions and experiences with children (Copple & Bredekamp, 2009).

Despite the inclusion of the guidelines for effective teaching in the position statement, uncertainty regarding whether practices are developmentally appropriate persists. Determining whether or not a practice is appropriate or not requires consideration for the context surrounding the practice. In considering how difficult it is to determine whether or not a situation, interaction, or practice is developmentally appropriate or not, I present five situations:

1. An early years professional reads an environmental print picture book to a group of preschoolers.
2. A teacher stands at the smartboard and conducts a teacher-directed whole group literacy lesson for children in grade one.
3. A full-day kindergarten classroom has a one-hour block of free-choice time.
4. An activity for three-year-olds lasts for thirty minutes, during which the children mostly watch and listen to the teacher.
5. Children in a grade two classroom sit at table groups.

At first look, you may quickly identify situations 1, 3, and 5 as developmentally appropriate and situations 2 and 4 as inappropriate. However, if provided with additional contextual information about each situation, you quickly realize that determining whether or not practices are developmentally appropriate is quite complex. For example, in situation 3, you may think that a one-hour block of free choice is aligned with the guidelines for effective teaching; however, when informed that children in this full-day kindergarten classroom are only provided with this one-hour block of choice every three days, you may quickly change your vote. Furthermore, if you found out that this one-hour open block took place in an undersized classroom with limited resources, you again would likely change your opinion. Likewise, you may change your mind in regard to situation 2, where the grade one teacher delivers a teacher-directed whole group literacy lesson, if you knew that this was a five-minute teacher-directed reading of the poem of the week, where the teacher was modelling concepts of print, word recognition, and rhyming. This teacher-directed component was key to the balanced literacy program followed in this classroom. These examples highlight how important it is to consider the context of the lessons and the social and cultural context in which children live in reflecting on the developmental appropriateness of a practice. Context affects whether a practice should be used or adapted. This complexity in reflecting on developmental appropriateness of practices has me questioning whether *appropriate* is the best terminology to use, as the word *appropriate* denotes a dichotomy of practice—something that is appropriate or not. For this reason, I propose the use of developmentally *aligned* practices to acknowledge the multitude of ways in which practices can be beneficial for promoting well-being, learning, and development of young children.

Despite the complexity in determining the developmental appropriateness of practices, the NAEYC statement provides information that is helpful to early years professionals in supporting the learning and development of children from birth through age eight. In the 2009 publication, the NAEYC provides examples to consider in clarifying understanding. The document outlines practices in chart form in two categories: (1) developmentally appropriate and (2) in contrast. The practices are organized developmentally for infant and toddler years (zero to three years), preschool years (three to five years), kindergarten (five to six years), and primary (six to eight years). In providing examples to consider for infants and toddlers, the chart is divided into six areas important to infant/toddler care: (1) relationships between caregiver and child, (2) environment, (3) exploration and play, (4) routines, (5) reciprocal relationships with families, and (6) policies. The preschool, kindergarten, and primary years all cover practices in five areas important to the teacher's role: (1) creating a caring community of learners, (2) teaching to enhance development and learning, (3) planning curriculum to achieve important goals, (4) assessing children's development and learning, and (5) establishing reciprocal relationships with families. In addition to the charts, a comment section expands on the practice examples and speaks to the cultural factors that should be considered in determining when practices should be used.

To unpack the complexities further, Copple and Bredekamp (2009) created a list of practices with general agreement in the field as to whether or not they were developmentally appropriate (box 7.3) and a second list of practices with less agreement and clarity from the field (box 7.4).

Box 7.3: Agreed-Upon Practices for Children Three to Eight Years of Age

Developmentally appropriate:

- Curriculum and experiences that actively engage children
- Rich, teacher-supported play
- Integrated curriculum
- Scope for children's initiative and choice
- Intentional decisions in the organization and timing of learning experiences
- Adapting curriculum and teaching strategies to help individual children make optimal progress

Developmentally inappropriate:

- Highly linear instruction, especially when it follows an inflexible timeline
- Heavy reliance on whole group instruction
- Fragmented lesson without connections that are meaningful to children
- Rigid adherence to a packaged, "one size fits all" curriculum

---

Box 7.4: Less Agreed-Upon Practices for Children Three to Eight Years of Age

These practices are often quickly rejected, yet require further consideration:

- Structured learning experience, such as small groups with planned focus and sequence
- Use of packaged curricula
- Use of teacher "scripts," such as questions teachers find useful to have at their fingertips
- Child testing/assessment
- Scope and sequence
- "Academics"

In contrast, practices below may require additional scrutiny, as they are more likely to be quickly accepted:

- Curriculum lacking in sequence and sustained focus
- Curriculum developed by a teacher or program without grounding in up-to-date knowledge about outcomes/standards, curriculum, and pedagogy
- Purportedly child-centred classrooms in which many opportunities for learning are missed
- Curriculum focused on social-emotional development without attention to cognitive development
- Observations without the follow-up needed to help children move forward
- Maturationist approach in which teachers simply wait for children to acquire the skill or concept

Gestwicki (2017) argues that the crux of the "appropriate" versus "inappropriate" discussions lies in the differing responses to the following questions:

1. How do children effectively learn at this age?
2. What is most important for children to learn at this age, whether they are in a program of one sort or another or at home?

3. What are the repercussions later in the child's school years, adolescence, and adult life of the academic preschool experience versus experience in a developmentally appropriate program?

I would add two questions to this list: How do we ensure that the social and cultural contexts in which children live are respected, and how do we embed these contexts into our practice? Given the complexity of DAP, it is not surprising that it is still subject to misinterpretations and misconceptions. Copple and Bredekamp (2009) identified three of the most persistent myths (p. 47):

1. Direct instruction is always inappropriate.
2. DAP is maturationist (i.e., teachers are encouraged to simply wait for children's development to unfold rather than actively promoting it).
3. Developmentally appropriate practice is soft (i.e., teachers are urged to put off introduction of robust subject content until later grades).

Copple and Bredekamp (2009) suggest that in order to challenge these myths, as a field we must communicate more clearly, and we need to widen our lens on how we view practice, while becoming more precise in how we describe effective practices. Similarly, Gestwicki (2017) identified resistance in establishing DAP stemming from "less than thorough" grounding in development, oversimplifying or closing conversation that should continue to be debated and discussed, and standards being identified as fixed. Gestwicki identified ten misunderstanding of DAP:

1. There is only one right way to carry out DAP.
2. DAP classrooms are unstructured.
3. Teachers teach minimally or not at all in DAP classrooms.
4. Developmentally appropriate programs do not include academics, generally interpreted to be the formal skills of learning reading, writing, and arithmetic.
5. Developmentally appropriate programs are effective only for particular populations.
6. In developmentally appropriate classrooms, there is no way to tell if children are learning.
7. DAP can be achieved simply by acquiring certain kinds of toys and materials.

8. DAP uses no goals or objectives.
9. In DAP, the curriculum is child development.
10. Developmental appropriateness is just one in a sequence of changing trends in education.

Continual discussion in reflecting on what truly is developmentally appropriate demonstrates the forward thinking of the early years profession. In continuing to move forward, I suggest that educators remember to not only reflect on "what" type of practices are developmentally appropriate but also strive to unpack the "why." Why do certain practices promote learning and development in certain contexts? Just as we would avoid simply providing teachers with a list of lesson plans to integrate into their practice, we too should not simply provide pre- and in-service educators with a list of appropriate practices. We need to recognize that we must move beyond a focus on "which" activities are developmentally appropriate and move toward continual refinement in understanding "why and how" we can work together with children to create environments and opportunities that are optimal for learning and development.

MOVING AWAY FROM DICHOTOMIES IN EARLY LEARNING: PLAY AS DEVELOPMENTALLY APPROPRIATE PRACTICE

Much like the debates and dichotomies that are present in the literature and discussion around DAP, debates and dichotomies exist in empirical research and conversations on the appropriateness, value, and role of play and play-based learning in early years contexts. These debates extend beyond the value of play and include conflicting perspectives around which activities can actually be counted as play (Danniels & Pyle, 2018). A prominent debate in the play literature is a focus on the benefits of play for social and emotional development versus the benefits of play for academic learning outcomes. Growing evidence reveals that free play and teacher-guided play contribute to development and academic learning in varying ways (Danniels & Pyle, 2018; Pyle, 2018; Pyle & Danniels, 2017). Convincing evidence points to the benefits of free play for the development of social, emotional, and self-regulation skills (Pascal, 2018; Pyle, 2018; Timmons, Pelletier, & Corter, 2015). Furthermore, empirical research demonstrates that teacher-guided play impacts the development of cognitive abilities and academic skills (Pyle, 2018; Timmons, 2018). The work of the Play Learning Lab, headed by Angela Pyle at the Dr. Eric Jackman Institute of Child Study at OISE/University of Toronto, highlights the need to for an integrated, balanced approach that combines the social and emotional benefits of free play with the academic benefits of teacher-involved play. Pyle recognizes that both developmental and academic outcomes can and should be achieved through play-based learning and advocates for an integrated and effective balance between the extremes of a "totally child-driven approach" and a "totally educator-driven approach" (2018). Pascal (2018), building on the work of Pyle, suggests that early learning design and policy can be difficult due to the lack of "evidentiary consensus" in the field. We must begin to understand how we can move forward together as a field to figure out how to combine the practices we know are crucial for social and emotional development with the more teacher-guided practices that have shown to be so beneficial for children's academic development. To do this, we need to recognize the benefits that come from a variety of practices in the early years and avoid a narrow dichotomy in thinking. With that, I again suggest a movement from the language of developmentally "appropriate" practice toward developmentally "aligned" practice so as to shift away from the dichotomy that we so easily can get caught in. This is not to say that all practices are appropriate. Of course, there are practices that are inappropriate and would not be suitable for children. For example, it would not be appropriate to demand a child struggle through an activity without providing them with support. Nor would it be appropriate to restrict the sensory exploration of infants or have overstimulating environments. However, with the goal of moving forward as a field, it is important to recognize that there are practices that are not suitable for the development and learning of young children, while also recognizing that there are a variety of practices that support the development of various skills. Advocating for a balanced approach is essential to ensure optimal learning and development of our earliest learners.

Pyle and Danniels (2017) facilitate the integration of play-based learning practices into early years contexts through developing a broader definition of play-based learning that moves away from the dualistic division between pretend play and learning and conceptualizing play-based learning as a continuum. This continuum aims to enhance the benefits of play-based pedagogies in the early years for teachers and students (Pyle & Danniels, 2017). This continuum can support educators in implementing play-based pedagogies in their practice. The continuum of teacher involvement acknowledges the variation in the types of play that children engage in as well as the varying roles teachers take in play. On one end of the continuum is play that would be described as child-directed and on the other end of the spectrum is teacher-directed play. The middle of the continuum includes play that can be classified as collaborative. More specifically, the continuum of play includes free play, inquiry play, collaboratively designed play, playful learning, and learning through games (beginning with more child-directed play, moving toward collaborative types of play, and ending with teacher-directed play). Child-directed play, collaboratively created play, and teacher-directed play all provide opportunities for social, personal, and academic learning (Pyle & Danniels, 2017). Detailed descriptions of the five types of play are beyond the scope of this chapter but can be found in Pyle and Danniels (2017). More information and examples of activities can also be found on the Play Learning Lab website (www.playlearninglab.ca).

CONCLUSION: SUGGESTIONS FOR CONTINUAL REFINEMENT IN UNDERSTANDING EVIDENCE-BASED, DEVELOPMENTALLY "ALIGNED" PRACTICES IN THE EARLY YEARS

A growing commitment toward accountability in early years education has resulted in changes to early years curriculum and pedagogy. Despite a common desire from parents, teachers, researchers, and policy-makers to increase the quality of learning environments for all children and reduce achievement gaps, a tension exists regarding the "best" or most "appropriate" way to support development and learning. In order to move forward as a community of early learning professionals, we must come together to recognize the ways in which different practices support the development of children's social, emotional, cognitive, and physical skills, while moving away from extremes of "this" versus "that" thinking. Pascal (2018) notes that "research and policy that can demonstrate the ever-evolving role of the educator in a learning environment that provides opportunities for play opportunities that balance child-centered and adult-directed play, and where the provision of these opportunities is guided by the learning goals, can provide a promising framework for play-based programming that addresses children's learning in a comprehensive manner" (p. 45). In striving for this balance, I provide the following suggestions for continual refinement and reflection in understanding evidenced-based, developmentally aligned practices:

- Recognize that different aspects of children's development can be promoted through a variety of pedagogical strategies.
- Acknowledge the benefits of play and play-based learning for learning and development.
- Continue to invest in extended and enriched learning opportunities for children who do not have these experiences outside of school.
- Recognize the importance of engaging with children, families, parents, health services, and policy-makers.
- Continue to ask how we can ensure that the social and cultural contexts in which children live are respected and how we embed these contexts into our practice.
- Move beyond "what" type of practices are developmentally appropriate toward unpacking the "why." Why do certain practices promote learning and development in certain contexts?
- Update the principles and their supporting research more frequently to reflect emerging research and understanding of the field.
- Move beyond false dichotomies (Pascal, 2018) from "best" and "appropriate" practices toward "evidence-based practices."

REFERENCES

Babad, E. (1993). Teachers' differential behavior. *Educational Psychology Review, 5*(4), 347–376.

Baron, R. M., Tom, D., & Cooper, H. M. (1985). Social class, race, and teacher expectancies. In J. B. Dusek, V. C. Hall, & W. J. Meyer (Eds.), *Teacher Expectations* (pp. 251–269). Hillsdale, NJ: Lawrence Erlbaum Associates.

Bredekamp, S. (1987). *Developmentally appropriate practice in early childhood programs serving children from birth through age eight.* Washington, DC: NAEYC.

Bredekamp, S., & Copple, C. (1997). *Developmentally appropriate practice in early childhood programs* (Rev. ed.). Washington, DC: NAEYC.

Carter, D. R., Chard, D. J., & Pool, J. L. (2009). A family strengths approach to early language and literacy development. *Early Childhood Education Journal, 36*(6), 519–526.

Copple, C., & Bredekamp, S. (2006). *Basics of developmentally appropriate practice: An introduction for teachers of children 3 to 6.* Washington, DC: NAEYC.

Copple, C., & Bredekamp, S. (Eds.). (2009). *Developmentally appropriate practice in early childhood programs serving children from birth through age 8* (3rd ed.). Washington, DC: NAEYC.

Danniels, E., & Pyle, A. (2018). Defining play-based learning. In R. E. Tremblay, M. Boivin, R. and Peters (Eds.), *Encyclopedia on early childhood development* [online]. Retrieved from http://www.child-encyclopedia.com/play-based-learning/according-experts/defining-play-based-learning.pdf

de Boer, H., Bosker, R. J., & van der Werf, M. P. (2010). Sustainability of teacher expectation bias effects on long-term student performance. *Journal of Educational Psychology, 102*(1), 168–179.

Di Santo, A., Timmons, K., & Pelletier, J. (2015). "Mommy that's the exit.": Empowering homeless mothers to support their children's daily literacy experiences. *Journal of Early Childhood Literacy, 16*(2), 1–26. doi: 10.1177/1468798415577872

Fang, Z. (1996). A review of research on teacher beliefs and practices. *Educational Research, 38*(1), 47–65.

Gestwicki, C. (2017). *Developmentally appropriate practice: Curriculum and development in early education.* Boston, MA: Cengage Learning.

Hattie, J. (2003). *New Zealand education snapshot: With specific reference to the yrs 1–13 years.* Paper presented at Knowledge Wave 2003: The Leadership Forum. Auckland, New Zealand.

Isenberg, J., & Quisenberry, N. (1988). Play: A necessity for all children. *Childhood Education, 64*(3), 138–145.

Kaurez, K. (2013). *Developmentally appropriate practice in preK–third grade: It can be done.* Speech recorded at NAEYC Institute of Professional Development, 2013.

Keogh, B. K. (2000). Risk, families and schools. *Focus on Exceptional Children, 33*(4), 1–12.

McKown, C., & Weinstein, R. S. (2002). Modeling the role of child ethnicity and gender in children's differential response to teacher expectations. *Journal of Applied Social Psychology, 32*(1), 159–184.

Moll, L. C., Amanti C., Neff, D., & Gonzalez, N. (1992). Funds of knowledge for teaching: Using a qualitative approach to connect homes and classrooms. *Theory into Practice, 31*(2), 132–141.

Muller, C., Katz, S. R., & Dance, J. (1999). Investing in teaching and learning. *Urban Education, 34*(3), 292–337.

National Association for the Education of Young Children. (1986). Position statement on developmentally appropriate practice in programs for 4- and 5-year-olds. *Young Children, 41*(6), 20–29.

National Association of Elementary School Principals. (2005). *Leading early childhood learning communities: What principals should know and be able to do.* Alexandria, VA: Author.

National Association of State Boards of Education. (1991). *Caring communities: Supporting young children and families: The report of the national task force on school readiness.* Alexandria, VA: Author.

Obiakor, F. E. (1999). Teacher expectations of minority exceptional learners: Impact on accuracy of self-concepts. *Exceptional Children, 66*(1), 39–53.

Pascal, C. E. (2018). Moving beyond false dichotomies in the play-based learning domain: Overall commentary. In R. E. Tremblay, M. Boivin, & R. Peters (Eds.), *Encyclopedia on early childhood development* [online]. Retrieved from http://www.child-encyclopedia.com/play-based-learning/according-experts/moving-beyond-false-dichotomies-play-based-learning-domain

Pellegrini, A. D., & Blatchford, P. (2000). *The child at school: Interactions with peers and teachers.* London, UK: Arnold.

Pyle, A. (2018). Play-based learning. In R. E. Tremblay, M. Boivin, & R. Peters (Eds.), *Encyclopedia on early childhood development* [online]. Retrieved from http://www.child-encyclopedia.com/sites/default/files/dossiers-complets/en/play-based-learning.pdf

Pyle, A., & Danniels, E. (2017). A continuum of play-based learning: The role of the teacher in a play-based pedagogy and the fear of hijacking play. *Early Education & Development, 28*(3), 274–289. doi: 10.1080/10409289.2016.1220771

Riojas-Cortex, M., Flores, B. B., & Clark, E. R. (2003). Los niños aprenden en casa: Valuing and connecting home cultural knowledge with an early childhood program. *Young Children, 58*(6), 78–83.

Rubie-Davies, C. M., Hattie, J., & Hamilton, R. (2006). Expecting the best for students: Teacher expectations and academic outcomes. *British Journal of Educational Psychology, 76*(3), 429–444.

Tenenbaum, H. R., & Ruck, M. D. (2007). Are teachers' expectations different for racial minority than for European American students? A meta-analysis. *Journal of Educational Psychology, 99*(2), 253–273.

Timmons, K. (2018). Educator expectations in full-day kindergarten: Comparing the factors that contribute to the formation of early childhood educator and teacher expectations. *Early Childhood Education Journal, 46*(6), 613–628. http://rdcu.be/HcwF

Timmons, K., & Pelletier, J. (2014). Understanding the importance of parent learning in a school-based family literacy programme. *Journal of Early Childhood Literacy, 15*(4), 510–532. doi: 10.1177/1468798414552511

Timmons, K., Pelletier, J., & Corter, C. (2015). Understanding children's self-regulation within different classroom contexts. *Early Child Development and Care, 186*(2), 249–267. doi: 10.1080/03004430.2015.1027699

Van den Bergh, L., Denessen, E., Hornstra, L., Voeten, M., & Holland, R. W. (2010). The implicit prejudiced attitudes of teachers: Relations to teacher expectations and the ethnic achievement gap. *American Educational Research Journal, 47*(2), 497–527.

Weinstein, R. S. (2002). *Reaching higher: The power of expectations in schooling.* Cambridge, MA: Harvard University Press.

Woodcock, S., & Vialle, W. (2011). Are we exacerbating students' learning disabilities? An investigation of preservice teachers' attributions of the educational outcomes of students with learning disabilities. *Annals of Dyslexia, 61*(2), 223–241.

Zhang, Y. (2014). *Educational expectations, school experiences and academic achievements: A longitudinal examination.* Retrieved from http://repository.upenn.edu/cgi/viewcontent.cgi?article=1021&context=gansu_papers

Zohar, A., Degani, A., & Vaaknin, E. (2001). Teachers' beliefs about low-achieving students and higher order thinking. *Teaching and Teacher Education, 17*(4), 469–485.

CHAPTER 8

Children's Rights: Raising Awareness amongst Professionals Working with and for Children

Aurelia Di Santo and Bethany Robichaud

GUIDING QUESTIONS:

1. Which historical events and treaties led to the creation of the United Nations Convention on the Rights of the Child, and how do the articles relate to and depend on each other?

2. How might the United Nations Convention on the Rights of the Child and its four general principles inform early years education and care?

INTRODUCTION

The United Nations Convention on the Rights of the Child (UNCRC) is an international human rights treaty that declares that all children 18 years of age and younger have a set of rights specific to their survival, development, protection, and participation in matters affecting their lives. The UNCRC has been ratified by all but one United Nations (UN) member nation, thus affording a common ethical and legal framework from which to promote and protect children's rights and to ensure their participation in matters that affect them (UNICEF, 2005). Canada ratified the UNCRC on December 13, 1991. Ratifying the treaty signifies Canada's commitment to ensuring that children's rights are reflected in the country's laws and policies. The federal, provincial, and territorial governments all have responsibility for implementing the UNCRC (Standing Senate Committee on Human Rights, 2007). Furthermore, governments have an obligation to "make the principles and provisions of the Convention widely known, by appropriate and active means, to adults and children alike" (UN General Assembly, 1989, Article 42).

In spite of 195 UN member nations ratifying the treaty, children remain one of the most marginalized populations globally (Bentley, 2005), a fact that can be attributed in part to their lack of understanding of their rights and those of others. Therefore, the question that arises is why Canadians continue to lack awareness of the UNCRC. This is an important question to address if we are to increase both an awareness and understanding of children's rights. One way to combat this issue is through education at all levels. To this end, this chapter responds directly to the Committee on the Rights of the Child (CRC) (2012) statement that Canada should

> take more active measures to systematically disseminate and promote the Convention, raising awareness among the public at large, among professionals working with or for children, and among children. In particular, the Committee urges the State party to expand the development and use of curriculum resources on children's rights, especially through the State party's extensive availability of free Internet and web access providers, as well as education initiatives that integrate knowledge and exercise of children's rights into curricula, policies, and practices in schools. (p. 5)

HISTORY

To understand the UNCRC, it is important to recognize the early beginnings of children's rights. Prior to 1989, a number of legally and non-legally binding treaties were established. In 1919, the International Labour Organization (ILO), a United Nations agency dealing with labour standards and relations, stated that one of its aims would be the "protection of children, young persons and women, including the abolition of child labour, limitations on the labour of young persons and the provision for child welfare and maternity protection" (Rodgers, Lee, Swepston, & van Daele, 2009, p. 8). Child labour conventions related to the minimum age for working in industry at sea (14 years old) and for night work and working on steam engines (18 years old) were adopted in 1919 (Rodgers et al., 2009).

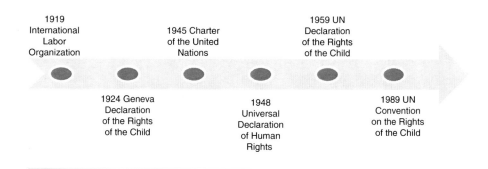

Figure 8.1: Historical Timeline for the United Nations Convention on the Rights of the Child

Eglantyne Jebb, the founder of Save the Children, is credited for shifting the view that children need protection (objects of concern) to children as subjects of rights. In 1923, Jebb drafted the first version of the Declaration of Child Rights, which guided the work at Save the Children. Jebb read her Declaration of Child Rights at the 1924 League of Nations convention in Geneva, and it was adopted by the League of Nations on September 26, 1924, as the Geneva Declaration of the Rights of the Child (GDRC) (League of Nations, 1924; Save the Children, 2018). The declaration comprises five articles:

> By the present Declaration of the Rights of the Child, commonly known as "Declaration of Geneva," men and women of all nations, recognizing that mankind owes to the Child the best that it has to give, declare and accept it as their duty that, beyond and above all considerations of race, nationality or creed:
>
> 1. The child must be given the means requisite for its normal development, both materially and spiritually;
> 2. The child that is hungry must be fed; the child that is sick must be nursed; the child that is backward must be helped; the delinquent child must be reclaimed; and the orphan and the waif must be sheltered and succored;
> 3. The child must be the first to receive relief in times of distress;
> 4. The child must be put in a position to earn a livelihood, and must be protected against every form of exploitation;
> 5. The child must be brought up in the consciousness that its talents must be devoted to the service of fellow men. (League of Nations, 1924)

These five rights were not focused on what children should "'do' or [how] to 'act' independently as individuals. Instead they were rights to 'receive' in the form of things that should be done for the child" (Kosher, Ben-Arieh, & Hendelsman, 2016, p. 15).

Following this milestone and the end of World War II, the United Nations General Assembly adopted the Universal Declaration of Human Rights (UDHR) in 1948. Specific to children's rights, Article 1 states that "all human beings are born free and equal in dignity and rights" (UN General Assembly, 1948, p. 2) and Article 25 states that "motherhood and childhood are entitled to special care and assistance" and "all children, whether born in or out of wedlock, shall enjoy the same social protection" (UN General Assembly, 1948, p. 5). Although not legally binding, the General Assembly requested that member countries disseminate the UDHR in educational settings. Indeed, it is disconcerting that 70 years later, we are still lagging behind in the dissemination of children's rights and still advocating for raising children's rights awareness in all sectors of society.

Both the 1924 GDRC and 1948 UDHR provided the foundation for the Declaration of the Rights of the Child (DRC), which was adopted by the United Nations in 1959 (Fass, 2011). Similar to the UDHR, the General Assembly requested "Governments of Member States ... to publicize as widely as possible the text of the Declaration of the Rights of the Child" and "to use every means at his disposal to publish and distribute texts in all languages possible" (UN General Assembly, 1959, 1387 XIV). Thirty years later, on November 20, 1989, the UNCRC was adopted, and it entered into force as international law on September 2, 1990.

The UNCRC sets out 54 articles that convey the rights that all children possess, "irrespective of the child's or his or her parent's or legal guardian's race, colour, sex, language, religion, political or other opinion, national, ethnic or social origin, property, disability, birth or other status" (Article 2) and include their civil, political, economic, social, and cultural rights. Articles 1 through 41 are substantive rights that focus on provisions for children. These articles outline the human rights afforded to children and contain rights not addressed in the 1948 UDHR and the 1959 DRC, namely the right to participation and the use of *he* and *she* pronouns, as opposed to the general *he*, to refer to males and females (Flowers, Brederode-Santos, Claeys, Schneider, & Szelényi, 2007). Articles 42 through 54 set out the governments' responsibilities for the implementation and monitoring of children's rights. However, despite the UNCRC's near-universal ratification, which indicates state signatories' ostensible commitment to all children and their inherent rights, the systematic realization of children's rights remains largely unimplemented (Canadian Coalition for the Rights of Children, 2018; UNICEF Canada, 2010; UNICEF Innocenti Research Centre & UNICEF Canada, 2009).

IMPLEMENTING THE UNCRC

It is vital that we understand that all of the articles in the UNCRC are of equal importance and that they are all "indivisible, interrelated, and interdependent" (UNICEF, 2014, para. 4). Take, for example, Article 28, a child's right to free primary education. This right would be difficult to achieve if a child is not registered at birth (Article 7) or if the child's right to survival and to a healthy development is compromised (Article 6). Similarly, consider the connection between children engaged in labour and their right to play and leisure (Article 31). The latest statistics from the ILO indicate that in 2016 there were 218 million children working on a daily basis. These children ranged in age from 5 to 17 years of age. Of these children, 152 million were in child labour, of which 73 million were engaged in hazardous child labour (International Labour Organization, 2017). Given these statistics, how can children realize their right to play and leisure activities (Article 31)? For Article 31 to be realized, then, children cannot be engaged in child labour, as this will affect their right to play and leisure and their other rights, such as the ones listed above—the rights to survival, a healthy development, and education.

Most importantly, we must hold governments accountable to their commitment to Article 42, that is, to "undertake to make the principles and provisions of the Convention widely known, by appropriate and active means, to adults and children alike" (UN General Assembly, 1989). It is difficult for children and youth to know they have rights if they and society in general are not aware of or do not understand the UNCRC.

There are several ways that the UNCRC may be reviewed and understood. The CRC (2003, 2005) has established the following four general principles for implementing children's rights during the early childhood period: Article 2—the right to non-discrimination; Article 3—the best interests of the child shall be a primary consideration in all actions concerning children; Article 6—the right to life, survival, and development; and Article 12—respect for the views and feelings of the child in matters that affect the child.

The right to non-discrimination means that no matter the circumstances, we must not discriminate against children and youth. The best interests of children should always be considered when making decisions that will directly or indirectly impact them. Children have an inherent right to life, and governments "are urged to … create conditions that promote the well-being of all young children during this critical phase of their lives … [and] from an early age, children should themselves be included in activities promoting good nutrition and a healthy and disease-preventing lifestyle" (CRC, 2005, p. 4). As capable human beings with agency, children have the right to express their views in all matters that affect them. More importantly, adults must take children's views into consideration when making decisions. When making decisions with (e.g., child choice activities, planning for the day) and for (e.g., planning a program, developing policies and procedures, classroom organization) children, these four general principles should be the focus and centre of our intentions. Refer to table 8.1 for connections between the four general principles and the implementation of the UNCRC.

CHILDREN'S RIGHTS MONITORING AND EVALUATION FOR RAISING AWARENESS

Prominent theorists such as Lev Vygotsky, Jean Piaget, Maria Montessori, Margaret Mahler, Erik Erikson, B. F. Skinner, John Bowlby, Urie Bronfenbrenner, and Howard Gardner have chiefly informed much of what we have historically held true concerning children's growth and development and their experiences of childhood. However, since the establishment of the UNCRC in 1989, conceptualizations of children and childhood have begun to shift, as prior perceptions of children's development, learning, and status are giving way to a school of thought that recognizes all children as active, rights-bearing social agents (e.g., Harcourt, 2011; Mayall, 2013; Quennerstedt & Quennerstedt, 2014; Wells, 2015). From this perspective, children are no longer viewed as incapable and disengaged but rather as competent agents with the capacity and right to participate in matters related to and affecting their lives and learning. While this shift in thinking has not yet received universal acknowledgement and widespread application, international human rights treaties, such as the UNCRC, have been slowly and steadily informing and guiding a myriad of work with and for children in various disciplines, such as education, health, law, Indigenous studies, and environment and climate change. In fact, there are several significant programs and initiatives that

Table 8.1: Connecting the Four General Principles to UNCRC Articles for Implementation

GENERAL PRINCIPLE	IMPLEMENTATION OF UNCRC ARTICLES
Article 2: the right to non-discrimination	Protection from violence and exploitation (Articles 19, 32, 34, 36) Access to nutrition (Article 24) Access to care (Articles 3, 7, 18, 20, 23, 24, 38, 40) Opportunities for play (Article 31) Access to education (Articles 28, 29) Freedom of expression (Article 13) Discrimination against children with disabilities (Article 23) Indigenous and minority rights (Articles 17, 29, 30)
Article 3: the best interests of the child shall be a primary consideration in all actions concerning children	"The principle of best interests appears repeatedly within the Convention (including in articles 9, 18, 20 and 21, which are most relevant to early childhood)" (CRC, 2005, p. 6)
Article 6: the right to life, survival, and development	"Other provisions of the Convention, including rights to health, adequate nutrition, social security, an adequate standard of living, a healthy and safe environment, education and play (arts. 24, 27, 28, 29 and 31), as well as through respect for the responsibilities of parents and the provision of assistance and quality services (arts. 5 and 18)" (CRC, 2005, p. 4)
Article 12: respect for the views and feelings of the child in matters that affect the child	"The child shall have the right to freedom of expression; this right shall include freedom to seek, receive and impart information and ideas of all kinds, regardless of frontiers, either orally, in writing or in print, in the form of art, or through any other media of the child's choice" (UN General Assembly, 1989, Article 13). "The right to express views and feelings should be anchored in the child's daily life at home (including, when applicable, the extended family) and in his or her community; within the full range of early childhood health, care and education facilities, as well as in legal proceedings; and in the development of policies and services, including through research and consultations" (CRC, 2005, p. 7). "States parties should take all appropriate measures to promote the active involvement of parents, professionals and responsible authorities in the creation of opportunities for young children to progressively exercise their rights within their everyday activities in all relevant settings, including by providing training in the necessary skills. To achieve the right of participation requires adults to adopt a child-centred attitude, listening to young children and respecting their dignity and their individual points of view. It also requires adults to show patience and creativity by adapting their expectations to a young child's interests, levels of understanding and preferred ways of communicating" (CRC, 2005, p. 7).

have chosen to place children's rights at the heart of their work. In 2007, the Landon Pearson Resource Centre for the Study of Childhood and Children's Rights, located at Carleton University, began Shaking the Movers—Canada-wide workshops that are driven and led by youth. These workshops focus on empowering children and youth to exercise their right to engage in matters affecting their lives, to have their voices listened to and heard, and to examine aspects of the UNCRC in relation to their lived experiences (Landon Pearson Resource Centre, 2018). In Hampshire County, England, schools have made a pedagogical shift by developing rights with respect to education that aims to realize, teach, and embody children's rights within the school environment (Hampshire County Council, 2016). With the understanding that children can play an essential role in contributing to building child-friendly communities, towns, or cities, UNICEF's Child Friendly City Initiative upholds the view that "the voices, needs, priorities and rights of children are an integral part of public policies, programmes and decisions" (UNICEF, 2018, para. 2).

Although rights-oriented programs, policies, and services undoubtedly exist, there remains a paucity of information regarding the impact of these initiatives and, more specifically, how they are monitored and evaluated. Thus, a need for more comprehensive monitoring and evaluation of children's rights at the local, national, and international levels prevails, for if we do not have a thorough understanding of what does or does not work and why, with respect to children's rights, then children's rights cannot and will not be fully realized. Garnering insight into effective practice in the implementation of the UNCRC includes gathering information from a range of stakeholders (e.g., educators, health practitioners, lawmakers, policy developers) who work with and for children and must include young people's views, as "children are not only entitled to have their views given due weight ... but ... adults working with them [must] ensure that their participation is compliant with the [UNCRC]" (Lundy & McEvoy, 2012, p. 140). Children, experts in their own right, must be meaningfully engaged, consulted, and involved in the monitoring and evaluation of initiatives that seek to ameliorate their individual and collective rights. For students and professionals[1] concerned with children and their rights, monitoring and evaluation is of vital importance, as "evaluation helps achieve better results for children" (UNICEF, 2017, para. 1). Lansdown and O'Kane (2014) provide definitions for distinguishing between monitoring and evaluation programs (refer to table 8.2). It is important to understand the differences; monitoring is a continuous assessment of a program, whereas evaluation is assessing a program at a specific point in time.

Table 8.2: Lansdown and O'Kane's Descriptors for Monitoring and Evaluation of Programs

MONITORING	EVALUATION
Is: "the systematic and continuous assessment of the progress of a piece of work over time" (p. 10)	**Is:** "an assessment of the programme at a specific point in time, based on the information gathered in the monitoring process" (p. 11)
Includes: ongoing monitoring to ensure that a service or program is on course to achieve its goals	**Includes:** a review of "what you set out to do, what you have achieved, and how you achieved it" (p. 11)
Results: yields information that guides the implementation of *ongoing* improvements to the program/initiative	**Results:** helps to assess a program's or an initiative's "relevance, effectiveness, efficiency, impact, and sustainability" and "can explore both the positive and negative outcomes ... and should result in recommendations" for improvements (p. 11)
Source: Lansdown & O'Kane (2014)	

In accordance with Article 4 of the UNCRC, states parties are legally obliged to realize and monitor the articles enshrined in the treaty and must "undertake all appropriate legislative, administrative, and other measures for the implementation of the rights recognized in the present Convention" (UN General Assembly, 1989, Article 4). Monitoring of the implementation of the UNCRC is undertaken by the CRC, which is "composed of 18 independent experts who are persons of high moral character and recognized competence in the field of human rights" (United Nations Human Rights Office of the High Commissioner, 2018). In accordance with UNCRC Article 44,

> States Parties [will] undertake to submit to the Committee, through the Secretary-General of the United Nations, reports on the measures they have adopted which give effect to the rights recognized herein and on the progress made on the enjoyment of those rights (a) Within two years of the entry into force of the Convention for the State Party concerned; [and] (b) Thereafter every five years. (UN General Assembly, 1989)

The CRC reviews the state's report and develops a response highlighting the committee's concerns with and recommendations for the state's obligations for implementing children's rights. In addition to receiving, reviewing, and issuing concluding observations to UNCRC state signatories, in accordance with Article 45 of the UNCRC, the committee also receives and reviews reports from "other competent bodies" (UN General Assembly, 1989, Article 45), for instance, NGOs and "specialized agencies" (UN General Assembly, 1989, Article 45) such as the ILO—a UN agency that "brings together governments, employers and workers representatives of 187 member states to set labour standards, develop policies and devise programmes promoting decent work for all" (ILO, 2018, para. 2); the World Health Organization (WHO)—"the directing and coordinating authority on international health within the United Nations' system" (WHO, 2018, para. 1); the United Nations Educational, Scientific and Cultural Organization (UNESCO)—a UN organization created to "build peace through international cooperation in Education, the Sciences and Culture" (UNESCO, n.d., para. 2); and the United Nations Children's Fund (UNICEF)—which works "to overcome the obstacles that poverty, violence, disease and discrimination place in a child's path" (UNICEF, 2016, para. 4). These organizations work to monitor the implementation of the UNCRC "in areas falling within the scope of their respective mandates ... and activities" (UN General Assembly, 1989, Article 45).

In Canada, the federal, provincial, and territorial governments share responsibility for the implementation, monitoring, and evaluation of the UNCRC. Canada's fifth and sixth reports on the UNCRC were officially filed in February 2019. According to the Canadian Coalition for the Rights of Children (CCRC), Canadian children are not doing as well as children in countries where the UNCRC has been implemented on a consistent basis (CCRC, 2018). Furthermore, the CRC's concluding observations on Canada's combined third and fourth periodic report state that the committee is "especially concerned that there has been little effort to systematically disseminate information on the Convention and integrate child rights education into the school system" (p. 5). However, the CCRC's current analysis of raising awareness through curricula and government websites indicates that "no province integrates children's rights into its curriculum and children cannot easily find useful information on government websites" (CCRC, 2018). Children's rights should be included in both the content of the curriculum and educational processes in "the home, school, or elsewhere" because "children do not lose their human rights by virtue of passing through the school gates" (CRC, 2001, p. 3).

THE IMPORTANCE OF RAISING CHILDREN'S RIGHTS AWARENESS

Educating children about their rights and the rights of others from a young age is essential not only to ensure their well-being but also to foster civic engagement. Canadian children frequently lack the capacity to realize their rights or stand up for the rights of others. Although research about child rights education among young children is limited, there are many advantages to integrating child rights into the curriculum. Several important studies clearly demonstrate the many benefits of integrating child rights into early years curriculum. For example, Covell and Howe undertook a multi-year evaluation (in 2005, 2007, 2008, 2009, 2011) of one application of the Hampshire Rights, Respect, and Responsibility (RRR) human rights education program, which has the UNCRC at its core, in schools in Hampshire County, England. The researchers found that when children understand their rights, they tend to be more socially responsible and to participate in more facets of their education (2011).

Increasing children's participation in matters that affect them is a key focus of the UNCRC. Howe and Covell (2013) found that children who are taught their rights tend to be more open to learning about social justice and to engage in "critical thinking, persuasive argument, decision-making, and collaborative learning" (p. 179). Education about rights combined with child participation was shown to foster self-regulation and lead to increased understanding about responsibilities and respect for others (Covell, Howe, & McNeil, 2008). Howe and Covell (2013) also found that students in schools where children's rights are integrated into the curriculum exhibited "steady increases in ... achievement scores on the standardized assessment tests" (p. 179). In an era where grades appear to supersede learning for the sake of learning, one would expect that this finding alone would motivate provincial and territorial ministries of education to integrate children's rights into the curricula at all educational levels.

Scholars have also found that schools integrating children's rights into the curriculum have more of a sense of community and foster respect and participation among students (Xiaofeng & Meyer, 2005). Other research has shown that the use of democratic teaching and positive classroom management can foster prosocial behaviours such as cooperation and communication (Campbell & Rose-Krasnor, 2007). Additionally, schools that integrate human rights education tend to have less bullying and exclusion (Hampshire Services, 2014). It is clear that rights-based education can lay the foundation for civic participation in which children are understood "as holders of human rights and capable of agency and participation in the present, as well as, the future" (Kinlen, Hansson, Keenaghan, Canavan, & O'Conner, 2013, p. 2).

Even though the research shows positive outcomes of integrating children's rights into practice, it is disconcerting that, in general, rights are being relegated to the area of theory and not practice. This is especially true among young children because early childhood and primary grades curricula are often deficient in providing education specifically intended to foster children's understanding of their rights (Jerome, Emerson, Lundy, & Orr, 2015). Sadly, Ontario's *Kindergarten Program* mentions rights only once, and it is in relation to the right to play (Ontario Ministry of Education, 2016). In their discussion paper to prepare for Canada's 5th/6th periodic review to the CRC, the Canadian Coalition for the Rights of Children states that although the provinces refer to the teaching of human rights, "there are only sporadic references to children rights and fewer explicit references to learning about the Convention on the Rights of the Child" (CCRC, 2017, p. 3). Moreover, the CCRC highlights the fact that the CRC's recommendation in their last report to Canada to "integrate the knowledge and exercise of children's rights into curricula, policies, and practices in schools" has not been met. This supports Jerome and colleagues' (2015) finding that Canadian curricula for children lack consistency with regard to child rights. We should not be surprised, therefore, that there is a lack of awareness of rights amongst children, youth, and society as a whole. Furthermore, a United Nations survey of 26 countries, including Canada, found that teachers are not adequately trained in children's rights or the UNCRC and they are not required to be educated about children's rights (Jerome et al., 2015). How can we expect professionals to raise children's rights awareness if they are most likely not exposed to the UNCRC during their pre-service education? Given the lack of integration of the UNCRC into school curricula at all educational levels, it is imperative that we begin to shift toward a "rights-integrative approach" (Di Santo & Kenneally, 2014) to teaching and learning.

In contrast to provincial education curricula, children's rights and their best interests are at the core of many Canadian early learning frameworks (e.g., in British Columbia, New Brunswick, Ontario, Prince Edward Island, Saskatchewan). However, there appears to be a gap in the application of theory (references to children's rights) to practice (application to classroom practice).

Because Canadian curricula and classroom practices for younger children do not explicitly include rights-based approaches (Di Santo & Kenneally, 2014), critical opportunities to educate young children on their rights are overlooked. Therefore, the lack of awareness about child rights among Canadian children (Pearson & Li, 2015; UNICEF Innocenti Research Centre & UNICEF Canada, 2009) needs to be addressed because children "who know their rights are better able to claim them" (UNICEF, 2009, para. 4). They will also have the knowledge and power to combat injustice and are likely to be more civically engaged in the future (Melton, 1999).

It is evident from the literature and from the many organizations working in the area of children's rights that there is a lack of attention on raising awareness of rights amongst children and youth. These gaps may be a result of several factors, including educators' fear that teaching children their rights will lead children to challenge their authority/control in the classroom; lack of cooperation and collaboration among and between policy-makers, professionals, curriculum developers; lack of knowledge of the UNCRC among professionals and the general public; and the notion that rights-based approaches to teaching may not be suitable for young children. However, research shows that children as young as three are capable of understanding the UNCRC articles, contributing their own ideas, and sharing their knowledge about children's rights with others (Dunn, 1988; Rowe, 2006). Hall and Rudkin (2011) asked a group of four-year-old children to create a list of their rights. Titled Boulder Journey School Charter on Children's Rights, the children compiled a list of 61 rights over several weeks. Several examples of their rights include the right to "plant flowers and plants with other people; clean air; clean, fresh food to eat and if the food is dirty, they can say, 'NO!'; never, never go to jail; not be called names; have their words heard by other people; paint their fingernails, boys and girls, with their moms; and to have fun" (pp. 8–9). The full charter can be found in Hall and Rudkin's (2011) *Seen & Heard: Children's Rights in Early Childhood Education*. This comprehensive list of rights is evidence of young children's capability to think about their rights and, in addition, the rights of others. Thus, the aim should be to broaden all children's awareness so that they know their rights, recognize when their rights or those of others are being violated, and feel empowered to act. To achieve this goal, we must shift society's beliefs that children already have enough rights and the misconception that by understanding their rights it will take away the rights of the significant adults in their lives, such as their early childhood educators, teachers, and parents.

IMPLICATIONS FOR PRACTICE

Children are rights-holders! The 2012 CRC's report about Canada stated that "awareness and knowledge of the Convention remains limited amongst children, professionals working with children, parents, and the general public" (p. 5, #24). This is still largely ignored by member countries, as is evidenced in the statistics regarding children's rights awareness. During the week of National Child Day 2017, approximately two hundred children and youth participated in 17 children's rights workshops across Canada. Information gathered during the workshops was presented at the #CanadaWe-Want 2018 conference. In total, more than five hundred children and youth participated and contributed to a report that informed the Public Health Agency of Canada's 2018 report to the United Nations. One of the most noteworthy findings that bears highlighting is that children and youth realize there continues to be a lack of awareness amongst young people of their rights (Student's Commission, 2018). Similarly, a 2009 joint report of the UNICEF Innocenti Research Centre and UNICEF, *Not There Yet: Canada's Implementation of CRC General Measures of the Convention on the Rights of the Child*, outlines the lack of education with respect to children's rights at the provincial, territorial, and federal level.

As professionals studying to work with and for children, we must learn to distinguish between children's rights and their needs and interests. Rights are not rewards given to children as adults see fit. Children are "relatively powerless and depend on others for the realization of their rights" (CRC, 2005, p. 5); however, this does not mean that adults should subscribe to the belief that they hold the power to control children's rights. Children's rights are inherent, and they must be respected. It is key that we keep in mind that in contrast to rights, children's needs and interests "may be arbitrary, [whereas] rights are principles and formally agreed entitlements and standards, as in the UNCRC" (Montgomery, 2010, p. 156). As future and current professionals working with and for young children and youth, you have an important role to play, that is, of a duty bearer. In other words, professionals have "duties and obligations under the UNCRC, legally binding them to respect, protect and fulfil children's rights" (European Commission, 2018, para. 1). Refer to table 8.3 for a description of the four general principles, suggestions for applying the principles to practice, and how to monitor the implementation of the general principles.

Table 8.3: Applying and Monitoring the UNCRC in Practice

UNCRC GENERAL PRINCIPLE	HOW CAN I APPLY THIS PRINCIPLE TO PRACTICE?	HOW CAN I MONITOR THIS PRINCIPLE IN PRACTICE?
Article 2: The right to non-discrimination	Under no circumstances should a child be discriminated against; this includes overt and covert discriminations. Children's particular risk for multiple discriminations is recognized, understood, and kept at the forefront of practice. All children are welcomed, respected, and supported equally and equitably. A sense of safety, security, and belonging is created and maintained for all children. Policies, procedures, and programming are inclusive, reflective, and supportive of children's diversities, including cultures, (dis)abilities, gender, languages, traditions, sex, and socio-economic status. Environments, both built and natural, are supportive of children's diverse and evolving capacities.	Refer to government policies and regulations (e.g., regulation checklists, quality assurance checklists) to ensure criteria are met. How can you / do you exceed the criteria in your practice to ensure criteria go beyond structural requirements (e.g., number of books reflective of persons with disabilities)? Refer to your organization's anti-discrimination policies and procedures to assess your practice. How are you meaningfully applying the policy recommendations in your practice? How are children welcomed into and respected in the program? How do you create a sense of belonging for all children, individually and collectively, and as members of a larger community? Based on an environmental scan, how does the environment support *all* children?
Article 3: The best interests of the child shall be a primary consideration in all actions concerning children	Children's reliance on adults and responsible authorities to assess and fulfill their rights and best interests is acknowledged; however, it is further recognized that children are not passive recipients of this care and attention. Children's individual and collective best interests are meaningfully considered. Policies, procedures, and programming are child-centred. Children's parents/guardians, families, and those who work with and for children are supported and assisted in adequately realizing children's rights. Children's views and evolving capacities are supported and acknowledged as essential to the fulfillment in all actions concerning them.	Do policies clearly and explicitly state that decisions will be made in the best interest of the child, in all matters affecting them? How is the child's best interest acknowledged and upheld in my program planning? This includes children's best interest, both individually and collectively. How are children involved in program planning? Are parents/guardians also provided opportunities for involvement? How are children's best interests supported and reflected in the environment?

(continued)

Table 8.3: (Continued)

UNCRC GENERAL PRINCIPLE	HOW CAN I APPLY THIS PRINCIPLE TO PRACTICE?	HOW CAN I MONITOR THIS PRINCIPLE IN PRACTICE?
Article 6: The right to life, survival, and development	Children's survival and development are supported holistically and continually.	Are all aspects of children's growth, development, health, wellness, safety, and security acknowledged holistically? Is it further acknowledged that these aspects are different for each individual child?
	Education is recognized as integral to children's holistic development; children are provided opportunities to learn and grow progressively.	Are children of all ages able to access child-centred, equitable education that encourages them to flourish, thrive, and develop to their full potential?
	The natural environment is recognized as integral to children's holistic development.	*Where does children's learning primarily occur? Are children provided opportunities to learn and grow holistically both indoors and outdoors?*
	Parents/guardians are supported in their responsibility to fulfill children's right to a full and healthy life.	Are children encouraged to develop a respect for and to learn from nature?
	Children's right to play is supported and acknowledged as essential to children's survival, development, health, and well-being; it is further acknowledged that, in line with children's diversities and evolving capacities, play looks different for each child.	Are children involved in activities or programs focused on their health? How are parents/guardians included and supported in realizing their child's right to survival and development?
	Children, experts in their own right, are included in any and all activities that promote their health, wellness, and development.	What opportunities do children have to promote their own growth, development, health, and wellness?
Article 12: Respect for the views and feelings of the child in all matters affecting the child	Children's ideas, views, and feelings are heard and respected—not in a tokenistic manner, but heard and respected meaningfully.	*How are children provided opportunities to express their ideas, views, and feelings? Are children's diversities acknowledged, recognizing that children do not all communicate in the same manner?*
	A child-centred attitude and approach is adopted.	How are children's opinions and suggestions heard, acknowledged, validated, and realized?
	Children are recognized and respected as active social agents.	Do children have opportunities to incorporate their ideas into policies, procedures, and programming?
	Children are provided space and opportunities to communicate their ideas, views, and feelings in ways that are meaningful to them; children's preferred modes of communication may not always be spoken or written language.	Can children develop a charter of rights for the specific environment(s) that they inhabit? Is it reflective of the children within the program and made accessible to all?
	Children are consulted and actively participate in and contribute to matters that affect them.	How are parents/guardians, those working with and for children, and the community at large included in validating and realizing children's individual and collective right to have their views and feelings heard and acknowledged?
	Parents/guardians, those working with and for children, and the community at large are supported in their responsibility to uphold children's right to express their views and feelings.	

Source: Adapted from UN Committee on the Rights of the Child, 2005.

As duty bearers, all members of society have a responsibility to raise awareness amongst adults and children. This is especially true of those individuals who are in pre-service education wishing to work with and for children and current professionals already working in their field. The overarching goal that should be at the centre of practice is to enhance rights awareness so that all children know their rights, recognize when their rights or those of others are being violated, and are empowered to act.

NOTE

1. Throughout this chapter, the term *professional* is inclusive of ECEs, teachers, and all other practitioners working with and for children.

REFERENCES

Bentley, K. A. (2005). Can there be any universal children's rights? *International Journal of Human Rights, 9(1)*, 107–123.

Campbell, K., & Rose-Krasnor, L. (2007). The participation rights of the child: Canada's track record. In R. B. Howe & K. Covell (Eds.), *Children's rights in Canada: A question of commitment* (pp. 209–239). Waterloo, ON: Wilfred Laurier University Press.

Canadian Coalition for the Rights of Children. (2017). Children's rights and education: More than a right to go to school. Discussion paper to prepare for Canada's 5th/6th review. Retrieved from http://rightsofchildren.ca/wp-content/uploads/2017/10/Discussion-Paper-on-Childrens-Rights-and-Education-2017.pdf

Canadian Coalition for the Rights of Children. (2018). *Raising the bar for children's rights.* Retrieved from http://rightsofchildren.ca/services_item/raising-the-bar-for-childrens-rights/

Committee on the Rights of the Child. (2001). General comment no. 1, Article 29 (1): The aims of education. United Nations. Retrieved from http://www.right-to-education.org /resource /crc-general-comment-1-article-29-1-aims-education

Committee on the Rights of the Child. (2003). General comment no. 5: General measures of implementation of the Convention on the Rights of the Child, CRC/GC/2003/5. Retrieved from http://www.refworld.org/docid/4538834f11.html

Committee on the Rights of the Child. (2005). General comment no. 7: Implementing child rights in early childhood. United Nations. Retrieved from http://www2 .ohchr.org/english/bodies/crc/docs/AdvanceVersions/GeneralComment7Rev1.pdf

Committee on the Rights of the Child. (2012). *Concluding observations on the combined third and fourth periodic report of Canada.* Retrieved from https://www.ohchr.org/en/countries/lacregion/pages/caindex.aspx

Covell, K., & Howe, R. B. (2011). *Rights, respect and responsibilities in Hampshire County: RRR and resilience report.* Children's Rights Centre: Cape Breton University. Retrieved from http://www3.hants.gov.uk/rrr-in-hampshire-rrr-and-resilience-report.pdf

Covell, K., Howe, R. B., & McNeil, J. K. (2008). "If there's a dead rat, don't leave it": Young children's understanding of their citizenship rights and responsibilities. *Journal of Education, 38* (3), 321–339.

Di Santo, A., & Kenneally, N. (2014). A call for a shift in thinking: Viewing children as rights-holders in early childhood curriculum frameworks. *Childhood Education, 90*(6), 395–406. doi: 10.1080/00094056.2014.982969

Dunn, J. (1988). *The beginnings of social understanding.* Cambridge, MA: Harvard University Press.

European Commission. (2018). *Rights holders and duty bearers.* Retrieved from https://europa.eu/capacity4dev/sites/default/files/learning/Child-rights/2.8.html

Fass, P. S. (2011). Historical context for the United Nations Convention on the Rights of the Child. *The Annals of the American Academy, 633,* 17–29.

Flowers, N., Brederode-Santos, M. E., Claeys, J., Schneider, A., & Szelényi, Z. (2007). *Compasito: Manual on human rights education for children.* Council of Europe, Budapest.

Hall, E. L., & Rudkin, J. K. (2011). *Seen & heard: Children's rights in early childhood education.* New York, NY: Teachers College Press.

Hampshire County Council. (2016, October 14). *Getting started.* Retrieved from http://www3.hants.gov.uk/education/hias/rights-respecting-education/gettingstarted.htm

Hampshire Services. (2014). *RRR evidence of impact.* Hampshire County Council. Retrieved from http://www3.hants.gov.uk/rrr-evidence-of-impact.pdf

Harcourt, D. (2011). An encounter with children: Seeking meaning and understanding about childhood. *European Early Childhood Education Research Journal, 19(3),* 331–343.

Howe, R. B., & Covell, K. (2013). *Education in the best interests of the child: A children's rights perspective on closing the achievement gap.* Toronto, ON: University of Toronto Press.

International Labour Organization. (2017). *Global estimates of child labour: Results and trends, 2012–2016.* Geneva, Switzerland: ILO Publications.

International Labour Organization. (2018). *Mission and impact of the ILO: Promoting jobs, protecting people.* Retrieved from http://www.ilo.org/global/about-the-ilo/mission-and-objectives/lang--en/index.htm

Jerome, L., Emerson, L., Lundy, L., & Orr, K. (2015). *Teaching and learning about child rights: A study of implementation in 26 countries.* Queen's University Belfast & UNICEF. Retrieved from: http://www.unicef.org/crc/files/CHILD_RIGHTS_EDUCATION_STUDY_final.pdf

Kinlen, L., Hansson, U., Keenaghan, C., Canavan, J., & O'Connor, U. (2013). *Education for civic engagement in post-primary schools in Ireland and Northern Ireland: A rights perspective.* NUI Galway OÉ Gaillimh & University of Ulster. Retrieved from http://www.childandfamilyresearch.ie/sites/www.childand-familyresearch.ie/files/cyp_book_5_full_report.pdf

Kosher, H., Ben-Arieh, A., & Hendelsman, Y. (2016). *Children's rights and social work.* Cham, Switzerland: Springer Nature.

Landon Pearson Resource Centre. (2018). *Shaking the movers.* Retrieved from https://carleton.ca/landonpearsoncentre/shaking-the-movers/

Lansdown, G., & O'Kane, C. (2014). *A toolkit for monitoring and evaluating children's participation: Introduction* (Booklet 1). Retrieved from https://resourcecentre.savethechildren.net/node/8102/pdf/me_toolkit_booklet_1.pdf

League of Nations. (1924, September 26). *Geneva declaration of the rights of the child.* Retrieved from http://www.un-documents.net/gdrc1924.htm

Lundy, L., & McEvoy, L. (2012). Children's rights and research processes: Assisting children to (in)formed views. *Childhood, 19*(1), 129–144. doi:10.1177/0907568211409078

Mayall, B. (2013). *A history of the sociology of childhood.* London, UK: Institute of Education Press.

Melton, G. B. (1999). Parents and children: Legal reform to facilitate children's participation. *American Psychologist, 54*(11), 935–944.

Montgomery, H. (2010). The rights of the child: Rightfully mine! In D. Kassem, L. Murphy, & E. Taylor (Eds.), *Key issues in childhood and youth studies* (pp. 149–160). New York, NY: Routledge.

Office of the High Commissioner for Human Rights. (2001). Convention on the Rights of the Child: General comment No. 1: The aims of education: Article 29 (1). Geneva, Switzerland: United Nations.

Ontario Ministry of Education. (2016). *The kindergarten program.* Toronto, ON. Retrieved from https://files.ontario.ca/books/kindergarten-program-en.pdf?_ga=2.164252285.390369392.1531616556-77923470.1531616556

Pearson, L., & Li, L. (2015). *A Canada fit for children 2015: Identity, rights and belonging.* Landon Pearson Resource Centre for the Study of Childhood and Children's Rights. Retrieved from http://www.landonpearson.ca/uploads/6/0/1/4/6014680/a_canada_fit_for _children_ 2015.pdf

Quennerstedt, A., & Quennerstedt, M. (2014). Researching children's rights in education: Sociology of childhood encountering educational theory. *British Journal of Sociology of Education, 35*(1), 115–132. doi:10.1080/01425692.2013.783962

Rodgers, G., Lee, E., Swepston, L., & van Daele, J. (2009). *The International Labour Organization and the quest for social justice, 1919–2009*. Geneva, Switzerland: International Labour Organization.

Rowe, D. (2006). Taking responsibility: School behavior policies in England, moral development and implications for citizenship education. *Journal of Moral Education, 35(4)*, 519–531.

Save the Children. (2018). *Our founder: The woman who started Save the Children*. Retrieved from https://www.savethechildren.org/us/about-us/why-save-the-children/eglantyne-jebb

Standing Senate Committee on Human Rights. (2007). *Children: The silenced citizens: Effective implementation of Canada's international obligations with respect to the rights of children*. Retrieved from: https://sencanada.ca/en/committees/

Student's Commission: Centre of Excellence for Youth Experience. (2018). *Children's rights in Canada*. The Canada We Want Conference Series. Retrieved from http://www.studentscommission.ca/cww_conf/resources/Children's-Rights-Report-June13.pdf

UNESCO. (n.d.). *UNESCO in brief*. Retrieved from https://en.unesco.org/about-us/introducing-unesco

UN General Assembly. (1948). Universal declaration of human rights, 10 December 1948. (217 [III] A). Retrieved from http://www.refworld.org/docid/3ae6b3712c.html

UN General Assembly. (1959). Declaration of the rights of the child, 20 November 1959, A/RES/1386(XIV). Retrieved from http://www.refworld.org/docid/3ae6b38e3.html

UN General Assembly. (1989). Convention on the rights of the child, 20 November 1989. United Nations, Treaty Series (Vol. 1577, p. 3). Retrieved from www.refworld.org/docid/3ae6b38f0.html

UNICEF. (2005). *The state of the world's children 2005: Childhood under threat*. New York, NY: United Nations Children's Fund. Retrieved from http://www.unicef.org/publications/files/SOWC_2005_(English).pdf

UNICEF. (2009). *20 years: The Convention on the Rights of the Child*. Retrieved from https://www.unicef.org/rightsite/whatyoucando_356.htm

UNICEF Canada. (2010). *Children's rights education: Applying a rights-based approach to education*. Retrieved from http://www.unicef.ca/sites/default/files/imce_uploads/UTILITY

UNICEF. (2014, May 19). *Background on human rights*. Retrieved from http://www.unicef.org/crc /index_30196.html

UNICEF. (2016, March 3). *About UNICEF*. Retrieved from http://www.unicef.org/about/who/index _introduction.html

UNICEF. (2017). *Evaluation and good practice*. Retrieved from http://www.unicef.org/evaluation/

UNICEF. (2018). *What is a child-friendly city?* Retrieved from https://childfriendlycities.org/what-is-a-child-friendly-city/

UNICEF Innocenti Research Centre & UNICEF Canada. (2009). *Not there yet: Canada's implementation of the general measures of the Convention on the Rights of the Child*. Florence, Italy: United Nations Children's Fund (UNICEF).

United Nations Human Rights Office of the High Commissioner. (1996–2018). *Human rights committee: Membership*. Retrieved from https://www.ohchr.org/en/hrbodies/ccpr/pages/membership.aspx

Wells, K. (2015). *Childhood in a global perspective*. Cambridge, UK: Polity Press.

World Health Organization. (2018). *About WHO: What we do*. Retrieved from http://www.who.int/about/what-we-do/en/

Xiaofeng, S. L., & Meyer, J. P. (2005). Teachers' perceptions of their jobs: A multilevel analysis of the teacher follow-up survey for 1994–1995. *Teachers College Record, 107*, 985–1003.

CHAPTER 9

Children *in* Society—Thinking Sociologically about Children and Childhood in a Canadian Context

Noah Kenneally

GUIDING QUESTIONS:

1. What is the sociology of childhood, and how do the conceptual tools of sociological thinking apply to children and childhood?
2. How might engaging with sociological and historical ideas reframe your interactions with children?

INTRODUCTION

When we think about childhood or children, we do not often think about large, overarching dynamics such as history, politics, economics, or cultural systems of value and belief. More often than not, when early childhood professionals think about children or childhood, we think about particular children or specific circumstances—what is happening with *this* child, in *this* place, at *this* moment. However, the places and moments we find ourselves in are profoundly shaped by those larger overarching dynamics. The time in history, the place, the predominant philosophies or cultural systems of value, and the politics of the day exert enormous influence on how things happen and are understood. When we take these larger overarching dynamics and consider how they are shaping the lived experiences of particular people in a particular place at a particular moment in time, we are thinking sociologically. Sociology is the scientific study of how humans negotiate the daily work of living together—how they organize themselves and live in their societies. It looks at the ways that larger overarching dynamics shape the lives of people and how the lives of people shape those larger dynamics. Sociology is the study of social life at the broadest, most macro-social levels and at the most personal micro-social levels.

The approach to sociological thinking taken in this chapter is relational and constructive, and framed around a perspective that puts children's lived experiences at the centre. This approach is at the heart of a particular branch of sociology—the sociology of childhood, which looks at how both large social dynamics and daily living shape and influence children and childhood. This chapter is inspired by C. Wright Mills, who described sociology as the intersection of history and biography (1959/2000). It will explore the ways in which the history of Canada influences contemporary social contexts and children's lives and how understanding the influence of history can help us think sociologically about children and childhood. Through a process of historicization—the act of situating events within a historical context—it is possible to trace some of the roots and routes that shape societies in the present.

This chapter will first briefly describe what sociology is and does and then trace the development of the sociology of childhood as a field of research and a framework for understanding children's lives. Then, three conceptual tools of thinking sociologically—social context, social action, and social construction—are outlined. Following this, the social context of Canada is explored—with a focus on elements in Canadian history that shape contemporary social dynamics. Concluding the chapter are some thoughts on the ways that these large dynamics influence how childhoods have taken shape in Canada and some examples of thinking sociologically about children and childhood in Canadian contexts.

SOCIOLOGY

Sociology investigates the ways the large dynamics of history and politics direct the social organization of our societies, how this affects our personal lives, and vice versa, the ways our personal lives affect the social organization of society (Bauman & May, 2001; Bourdieu & Waquant, 1992; Mills,

1959/2000; Weber, 1956/1978). It tries to answer questions about social life and social organization, such as how do our societies work, why might they work in those particular ways, and how do we learn how to be a part of our society?

Sociologists have explored these questions in several ways. Sociology is a complex discipline, and sociologists use different perspectives and frameworks to conduct their investigations of social life. For example,

- Positivist sociologists feel that there are fundamental truths around which societies organize themselves and generally work on large, macro-level scales using quantitative methods to determine general patterns.
- Interpretive sociologists focus more on the interpersonal ways that small groups and individuals make meaning of their social worlds.
- Constructivist sociologists understand society and social life to be co-created by the individuals, groups, and structures involved.

Sociological studies can be conducted on a large scale, with quantitative studies exploring social dynamics at population levels using statistics to track broad patterns, movements, and trends. They can also be carried out at a more personal scale, in qualitative studies interpreting the meanings that smaller groups and even individuals attribute to the negotiations necessary for humans to live with other humans. Looking at the interplay between these large tides in society and personal trajectories can show us the ways that history, politics, and social structures influence personal interactions and can also highlight that those histories, politics, and social structures are made up of many personal interactions combined together.

Early sociology worked to apply the same scientific positivist perspectives common in other branches of science at the time (Macionis, Jansson, & Benoit, 2009; Wallace & Wolf, 2006). It struggled to discover universal laws about how humans organized the ways that they lived together. It was also preoccupied with the structures that maintained the social order and how people learned the rules of how to behave and function within their society. At the time of the development of sociology as a field of study, much attention was paid to the new social structures that industrialization and increased urbanization—for example, the shift into mechanical mass manufacturing and the movement of the majority of people from rural farm life into urban settings—were having on society. Economics, systems of value, and work became central focuses of sociology after Marx made his profound contributions to the field (Marx, Moore, Aveling, & Engels, 1904; Marx, 1913). Parsons's functionalist theory was a dominant approach for a period of time, following philosophical perspectives that there was a fundamental social order and that societies operated much like machinery—social components working together to form a well-ordered whole (Parsons, 1975). However, this normative approach to understanding social life was soon to be challenged.

After the First and Second World Wars, the understanding that language and culture mattered and shaped social life and lived experience in different ways started to become more commonly accepted. This philosophical change is known as the linguistic or cultural turn—meaning a shift from a search for universals to an exploration of differences, expressed primarily in language and culture (Macionis et al., 2009; Wallace & Wolf, 2006). At the same time, social movements fighting against discrimination and oppression were taking shape (e.g., the labour rights, civil rights, and feminist movements). These important social movements called attention to the classist, racist, and sexist dynamics that shaped our societies in discriminatory and violent ways. They focused on the lived experiences and perspectives of marginalized people—workers, people experiencing poverty, racialized populations, and women—and saw value in their ideas and perspectives, reconceiving them as important members of society. A growing number of sociological studies, intent on investigating the perspectives of these marginalized groups, opened up a new realm of interpretive inquiry. People began to think sociologically about these different groups—about the ways that history, politics, and social structures interacted with the lived experiences of these groups and how that shaped society. Riding this wave, the sociology of childhood was established—investigating the lived experience of people whose life experiences were different because of their age.

THE SOCIOLOGY OF CHILDHOOD

In the field of early childhood, theoretical frameworks from developmental psychology, medicine, and biology have dominated the ways that we understand children and childhood. These disciplines generally view childhood as a cumulative and progressive process in which young humans achieve standardized milestones and develop increasingly complex cognitive faculties necessary for a properly functioning adulthood. This ages-and-stages perspective guides practice in early childhood as well as dominant ideas in popular thinking about children and childhood. In this chapter, this way of thinking is referred to as the developmental perspective. It emphasizes universal and normative patterns of development and tends to view differences as deviant. Sociology perceives difference in other ways, and the sociology of childhood emerged as a response to the universalizing point of view of the developmental perspective.

Traditionally, sociology theorized that children learned expectations and behaviour from either observing the adults around them over time and/or being explicitly taught codes of conduct. By growing up around adults and then going through formalized learning, either through apprenticeships or by going to school, children were thought to be socialized through a one-way flow of information, as if they were empty vessels waiting for grown-ups to pour knowledge, culture, social dynamics, and values and beliefs into them. As time passed and the linguistic/cultural turn demonstrated how important difference, language, and culture were, the interactive dynamic of socialization began to become better understood, and sociologists began to see the ways that children participated in their own socialization. It became clear that not only were children participating in their own socialization but that they were also active in the socialization of other children through peer and friend relationships. It also became gradually understood that children were involved in socializing adults as much as children were being socialized by adults and that this multidirectional socialization also influenced societies in large-scale ways (James & James, 2004; James, Jenks, & Prout, 1998; Qvortrup, 1993). This shift in thinking about children followed in the footsteps of the civil rights and other social movements. Attention began to turn toward the ways that differences led to marginalization based on class, race, and gender. Similarly, children's place as part of society began to be rethought, and children's particular lived experiences and their vulnerabilities, needs, and contributions began to be reconsidered. Discrimination based on age began to be understood as a marginalizing social force as well (Pierce & Allen, 1975).

This shift in understanding happened over several decades and solidified in the late 1980s and early 1990s as the academic, political, and popular thinking about children and childhood focused on their place in society. Children's rights thinking flourished alongside this shift as the United Nations, after decades of labour, drafted and ratified the United Nations Convention on the Rights of the Child (UNCRC) (UN General Assembly,

1989). A record number of member nations signed on to the UNCRC very quickly, an indication that children and childhood were taking a new priority on the international stage.

Social researchers began to think about children and childhood from these perspectives and build a body of knowledge, literature, and theory regarding childhood and children's lived experiences (Corsaro, 2011; Gabriel, 2017; James & James, 2004; James et al., 1998; James & Prout, 2015; Mayall, 2002; Qvortrup, 1993). This body of knowledge and a growing movement in the social studies of childhood were referred to as the "new" sociology of childhood and became consolidated around several core principles:

- Childhood should be considered an important topic of study. Studying childhood can help us understand aspects of social life that we cannot learn about in other ways and can yield important insight into a diversity of seemingly unrelated topics.
- Childhood is an enduring social category that shapes and is shaped by environment and context. Childhood is a part of every society and has significant influence on social life in a diversity of ways. Although the members of this social category age out of it as they grow into adulthood, the category of childhood itself persists.
- Children are social agents. Children are not passive objects but active subjects whose presence and actions have real consequence on the social lives of those around them.
- Children have rights and perspectives that should be acknowledged and included. Children are subject to particular circumstances due to their physical and social vulnerabilities in a world organized for and by adults. However, these circumstances do not diminish their capacities as active subjects, and they still need to be taken seriously as members of their communities and societies with their own developing perspectives and ideas. This does not mean that children should run the show but that spaces should be made where their perspectives can be considered and they can participate in decision-making processes.

While these ideas are no longer "new," they have yet to seep into our popular notions regarding children and childhood. Although Canada participated in the groundbreaking international study Childhood as a Social Phenomenon (Pence, 1991; Qvortrup, 1993), and some scholars have begun to use the principles and frameworks (see Chen, Raby, & Albanese, 2017), thinking sociologically about children and childhood has yet to make its way into the mainstream studies of childhood in Canada. The next section will discuss three conceptual tools used in thinking sociologically: social context, social action, and social construction. These three tools are interrelated, but for the sake of clarity we will look at them individually. Understanding these conceptual tools can help to think about Canadian society and the ways that children and childhood are a part of it.

Social Context

The previous sections have made mention of the larger social dynamics and structures that shape and maintain society. Put all together, we can call these dynamics and structures social context. Social context is the setting in which social life is happening. It consists of a number of elements:

- The physical environment—where in the world are these relationships happening?
- The historical moment—when in time are these relationships happening, and what has led to this moment in time?
- The cultural sphere—who is having these relationships, what do they value and believe, and what languages, customs, and meanings do they use to make sense of the world?
- The political landscape—how is power being negotiated in these relationships, how are decisions made, and how is the allocation of resources negotiated?
- The social structures—what institutions are responsible for maintaining the ways that these relationships take shape?

Social context is complex and has very real material consequences. The ideas at work in a social context are often taken for granted as the "way things are" everywhere. Social context can be understood on a large scale (e.g., the social context of nations, cultures, or communities) and at a smaller scale (e.g., the context of a school, a neighbourhood, a classroom, or a family). Social context is maintained by a variety of elements, including populations (i.e., who is part of the society), histories (i.e., what has happened that has led to this society being in the particular configuration it is in), and social structures (i.e., the organizing institutions that make the ideals, politics, and values of a society concrete and material). While social context can be personal in that it is a part of the lives of individual people, it goes beyond the personal to connect people together. It is the larger frame we live inside of, the stage with all the set-dressing, props, and costumes that we use to act out our life-stories.

Social Action

Social action, on the other hand, consists of the daily interactions that we have in relation to others. If social context is the stage and setting of the play of society, then social action is the doing and the acting that makes the story. Weber (1956/1978) explained sociology as being the study of the subjective meanings of social action. For him, action was any human behaviour that people attached meaning to, and social action was, therefore, any meaningful behaviour that was done in relation to/with/for/about others. Humans are social creatures, and throughout history we have organized the way we live together with other humans. For Bauman and May (2001), it is impossible for us to not be in relationship with people, and this approach to sociology explores what this profound interdependence means to different groups and people. Bauman asks,

> [why] does it matter that in whatever they do or may do people are dependent on other people; in what sense does it matter that they live always (and cannot but live) in the company of, in communication with, in an exchange with, in competition with, in cooperation with other human beings? (p. 8)

In this personal way, humans are constantly in contact with each other, and their actions, ideas, beliefs, and practices influence the lives of everyone else. We call these fields of constant relationship the social aspects of society.

What we do is always in relation to others, seen and unseen, acknowledged and unacknowledged. Social actions are the small building blocks that we use to make up the dynamics and larger relationships that in turn make up our societies. The small, individual actions that we take with each other reflect and reinforce the values and ideas that make up the social context. The overarching values of our societies filter into our everyday exchanges; so, for example, if women and giving birth are valued in a society, then women and mothers will take a central place in that society and be accorded a high status, and people will treat mothers with respect in their everyday interactions. It is in this way that history and biography, and social structure and individual agency, interact and shape each other.

Social Construction

The third conceptual tool is social construction. Social construction refers to the ways in which an aspect of social life is given meaning in a particular context and brought to life through social interaction (Berger & Luckmann, 1967). Actions, phenomena, or events mean different things in different communities, places, and times and can also mean different things to the different people who are involved in them. For instance, in one context it may make perfect sense to eat a particular animal, whereas in another context that animal may be invested with particular meaning and, therefore, never be consumed as food. The ways we interact with other people, with other groups of people, and with social structures largely depend on these particular meanings.

Additionally, because the meanings of our social constructions are so contextual, it can be difficult for us to see that our meaning is socially constructed. Most aspects of our context tell us that this is the way to do things, or that a particular thing has a particular meaning, so we take it for granted as common sense. This can lead to difficulties when interacting with others. Each party can take their own socially constructed meaning for granted as the true meaning and not understand the other's position. Understanding the notion of social construction can help to reveal the influence of context on social interaction, and, in this way, it is a powerful tool to understand how people negotiate social life.

These three conceptual tools are incredibly useful when thinking sociologically about children and childhood. Childhoods take different shapes according to the history, politics, and cultural values of a particular place and time, so they are profoundly influenced by social context. Children are also constantly involved in social action (e.g., no infant would survive without the attention of others), and we are all embedded in a continuous web of social interaction with others (Bauman & May, 2001). Finally, childhood and children have different meanings attached to them, depending on their context. In different places and at various times in history, children have been valued as good workers, innocent angels, sin-riddled demons in need of redemption, and unformed animals who need to be actively civilized. Childhood itself is a social construction, and understanding that can provide useful information and strategies for professionals working with children in Canadian contexts. However, what exactly is the Canadian context? This next section will examine what constitutes our understanding of Canadian society, paying particular attention to Canadian history.

THE CANADIAN CONTEXT

In the late 1930s, Gibbon proposed a mosaic as a useful metaphor for describing Canadian society (Gibbon, 1938). A mosaic is made up of small pieces of coloured tile that create a larger uniform and coherent picture. When applied to Canadian society, this image describes one way to think about individual people and different groups coming together to make a big picture of Canada. The image of the mosaic, which at first glance values diversity and difference, is considered very different from a traditional image used to describe society in the United States—the melting pot. The melting pot combines people and groups into a unified American whole, adopting the dominant traits of American culture. Since the 1960s, both of these metaphors have been critiqued for not matching the actual lived experiences of people living in Canada (Fieras, 2014; Kelley and Trebilcock, 2010; Kunz and Sykes, 2007; Porter, 1965).

To understand Canadian society, it is important to think about the social context of Canada. As discussed above, the social context is a multifaceted concept made up of many elements—the physical environment, the cultural values, the politics, social structures, and histories of a particular place at a particular time. It is beyond the scope of this chapter to look at all the elements of the Canadian social context in depth. Therefore, after a brief overview of these different elements, and following C. Mills Wright, this chapter focuses on how history influences the social context of Canada and thus the lives of Canadian children.

Canada's physical environment is vast and various, covering almost 10 million square kilometres and eight different climatic regions. Much of the population resides within one hundred kilometres of the southern border, although there are pockets of inhabited areas scattered sparsely throughout the rest of the country. The expansive geographic variation means an equally high level of variation in how childhood is experienced. For example, children living in southern regions might have access to the outdoors unencumbered by winter gear over longer periods during the year; children living in coastal regions might have easier access to beaches and ocean life; and children living in cities are more likely to have access to a wider-ranging assortment of resources, programming, and supports than children in rural areas.

Canada is described as a multicultural country, although this description is often critiqued. Canada's cultural identity has evolved, and for much of the nation's history, Canadian cultural identity was derived from French and British colonial heritages, often described as the "Charter" nations. Over the 20th and 21st centuries, waves of immigration from all parts of the world, alongside an increasing awareness of the necessity for the acknowledgement of Indigenous cultures and presence, have made clear that Canada's cultural makeup has become far more complex (Fieras, 2014; Kelley and Trebilcock, 2010). While multicultural policies work toward equality for all in theory, in practice, racism and systemic oppression mean that some groups of people are more equal than others. These conflicting cultural dynamics have important implications for children, who are particularly vulnerable to negative stereotyping and the vagaries of popular opinion. This is especially true for Indigenous people and Indigenous children, who have experienced grave injustice in struggling with Canadian cultural identity. The Truth and Reconciliation Commission of Canada (TRC), which was in official session between 2008 and 2015 and documented the history of Indigenous people's experiences in the residential school system and the impacts of those experiences, provides a framework for Canadian society to acknowledge and reconcile with Indigenous people and societies through its 94 calls to action (TRC, 2015). It is now far more realistic to think of the cultural sphere of Canada as being composed of many threads and streams weaving together to create a complex tapestry of practices, traditions, and systems of belief and value.

Politics can be defined in many ways. In this chapter, politics are defined as the ways that societies negotiate decision-making, access to power, and access to resources and support. Generally speaking, Canadian politics have been based on ideas of individual rights, constitutional methods of governance, and equal rights to education, health care, employment, and social security (Whitehorn, 2015). Historically, Canada's politics are based in its colonial past. Both France and Britain governed their colonies from overseas through representatives of their respective governments. When an independent government did develop, it was based on the British parliamentary system, which evolved into the federal parliamentary democracy in place now. Canada has a multi-party system, with the different parties working to secure representation in their regions so as to contribute to decision-making processes at both the federal and provincial levels. Politics have a profound influence on childhood in the Canadian context, as more socially responsive governments provide more supports and resources for children, while governments oriented toward individual responsibility are less likely to invest in social structures that shape the social landscapes of childhood.

Initially, Canada relied on its vast spaces and material resources to establish what is known as a staples economy. The economy was primarily based on basic commodities (fur, fish, lumber, agricultural material, and minerals) used domestically and exported as trade. In the post-war economic boom, an attitude of social responsibility prevailed in Canada, and socialized medicine and unemployment insurance, markers of a socially interventionist state taking responsibility for the welfare of its citizens, became available to Canadians. In recent years, economic downturns have led to more austere economic practices, and capitalist dynamics in the global economy have concentrated wealth and access to resources into the hands of a shrinking percentage of the population (Wells, 2015). Canadian politics and economics have been influenced by these global trends and moved toward more neoliberal approaches. Neoliberal models of governance and economics focus on economic growth as the primary measure of value. Neoliberalism looks to the free market to achieve social progress and access to resources, shifting systems of value toward trade and capital and emphasizing individual responsibility. The economy, and the socio-economic status of the population, has a significant bearing on children's lived experiences. When families have greater access to resources, they can provide their children with a wider range of experiences, thus having a direct effect on the material and social aspects of childhood.

Due to the country's socialist democratic political approach, the primary social structures in Canada are built on the idea of equal access. In practice, however, politics and discrimination furnish some citizens with more access and others with less. The social structures that have a significant influence on the shape of Canadian society are the following: the representational government system, which engages people in decision-making processes; the socialized medical system, which is meant to provide everyone with the health care they need; the education system, which provides publicly funded elementary and secondary schooling for children and youth; and the social welfare system, which works to secure basic resources, supports, and benefits for those in need in cases of unemployment, disability, poverty, and other special circumstances.

In the following section, key elements of Canada's complex history receive a brief summary. These elements have significant bearing on the shape of contemporary Canadian society and, therefore, on Canadian childhoods as well.

Indigenous Societies

Indigenous people have lived in the territories that became Canada for thousands of years. Throughout Canadian history, they have experienced terrible wrongdoing. When European settlers began to colonize North America, they considered Indigenous people primitive and in need of civilization and religious salvation. Settlers claimed Indigenous territories for their own or signed treaties with Indigenous societies to gain access to resources and territories (Indigenous and Northern Affairs Canada, 2017). The Canadian government has consistently neglected to honour treaty agreements with Indigenous societies and has instead worked to eliminate what was considered "the Indian problem" by actively developing assimilationist and discriminatory policies. Under-resourced reserve territories, residential schools, and the sixties scoop and the subsequent over-representation of Indigenous children in state-organized foster care are all examples of how colonial historical dynamics have played out in Canadian society. The colonial legacy of Canada continues to shape Canadian society and Canadian childhoods and has extremely negative effects on Indigenous children.

Early Colonial Settlement

Settlements were founded as a way to establish new territories for European empires and to draw on the resources found in North America in the forms of furs, lumber, and fish. Many settlements were overseen by large commercial ventures, such as the British Hudson's Bay Company and the French Compagnie des Cent-Associés. The colonial economy was based on extracting resources and sending them back to European markets. According to Parr (1982), although many in the first waves of settlers were trappers and military men, family became one of the primary organizing elements of early settlement life. Given that areas were sparsely populated and that settlers were from diverse areas in their countries of origin, regional customs were rarely carried over into the new settlements, and social patterns tended to be organized along family lines rather than any other system common in France or England at the time. Children tended to stay close to the family farm or take up the family trade. This established family-centric social patterns that would hold fast for many years.

France and Britain

While several European countries made expeditions to North America, France and Britain were the primary colonial powers. France established colonies and settlements along the St. Lawrence Valley and called the territory Nouvelle France, working to consolidate a strong hold over the fisheries and the fur trade to Europe. Britain had settlements to the south and east in the northeast areas of what is now the United States, known as New England. Tensions between Britain and France spilled over into their colonial territories, and at the end of the Seven Years' War (1756–1763), the first war fought on a global scale over colonial territories in India and America, Britain emerged victorious and claimed most of the territories in North America. This lasted until the Revolutionary War (1775–1783), when many of the colonies declared independence from the British government and became the United States of America. Quebec and Nova Scotia did not participate in the Revolutionary War and remained British colonies. Hostility between the French-speaking and English-speaking colonists led to New Brunswick being established and Quebec being separated into two provinces: Upper Canada for the English and Lower Canada for the French. Later, in a political bid to pacify their hostility, these two separate provinces were fused together again to create the province of Canada. This conflicted French and British colonial history set the stage for Canada's troubled relationship with identity, language, and heritage.

Canadian Confederation and Expansion

Britain retained colonial authority over its North American territories for several decades in the face of rising unrest and a gradual shift in public sentiment that the colonies should govern themselves. Eventually, a government was put in place, patterned after the British parliament, although the British government still retained overall control. Canada was established as its own nation in 1867 when the provinces of British North America— Canada (which split into Ontario and Quebec upon Confederation), Nova Scotia, and New Brunswick—came together to form a federation, a union of states that self-govern under the umbrella of a centralized government.

Western and eastern territories joined as Canada expanded, and as settlement continued it often pushed against Indigenous societies and territories. The Indian Act was established in 1876, conferring all control of Indigenous issues to the federal government, which developed several approaches to assimilate Indigenous people into the dominant culture. Canada, as a nation, covered an enormous range of territories, and power was most often consolidated in white, English-speaking urban areas along the southern border.

Cities and the Rise of Industry

New technologies and mechanized production transformed ways of life all over the developed world. In Canada, railways opened up new vistas, and settlements continued to spread west. In 1885, railroads in central Canada were connected to the west coast, in large part by the efforts of an estimated 17,000 Chinese migrant labourers (Li, 2000; Library and Archives Canada, 2007). This coast-to-coast railroad solidified the new nation. Urban areas benefitted greatly from being crossroads for the railways, both commercially and as hubs of transportation. Slowly, the Canadian population began to move away from rural subsistence farming and toward more industrial forms of work in factories in urban areas. This shift from rural to urban life began to change Canadian society as wealth, cultural life, and access to resources concentrated in urban areas. It also had profound consequences for children. While urban children had to contend with close quarters and particularities of urban life, they also had more access to supportive social structures such as centralized health care and more easily accessible education.

World War I, World War II, and Canadian Independence

The First and Second World Wars had profound influence on Canadian society. The continued close ties to Britain cultivated a deep sense of responsibility in the Canadian population, and although the Canadian government was hesitant to deploy troops, many Canadians enlisted to fight, and high numbers were killed. After the First World War, the popular feeling was that Canada had proved itself as an independent nation on the international stage. In 1931, the Statute of Westminster proclaimed Canada an independent nation, although amendments to the constitution required approval by the British government. It was not until the Canada Act in 1982 that Canada was declared entirely separate from Britain.

Multicultural Canadian Society

As populations all over the world rose, Canada, with its space and access to resources, became a place to immigrate to in order to establish a new and better life. Canada's vast territories were sparsely populated, and the only way to maintain its population growth was through encouraging immigration. A diversity of people from different parts of the world have come to make Canada their home, although not all people were welcomed equally. Some groups were considered more desirable than others. While many white immigrants from Northern Europe were offered free land to settle on and farm in Canada's early years, other groups, such as the Chinese labourers who built the railway, were charged a high fee per person to bring their families to settle with them. Immigration from South Asia was banned from 1907 until the 1940s. During World War I and World War II, immigration to Canada was restricted, and during World War II, anti-Japanese discrimination led to the government forcibly moving Japanese Canadians to internment camps. It was not until the 1960s that Canadian immigration policies went through radical reform and the racial discrimination that had governed immigration to Canada began to shift. For many years, Canada had been described as "bicultural," an acknowledgement of its British and French cultural heritages. However, Canadian society had become much more culturally diverse. In 1971, Prime Minister Pierre Trudeau officially declared a policy of multiculturalism, and Canada became a model nation for using a multicultural framework as overt social policy to address the changing demography and cultural makeup of its society (Winter, 2015). The Multicultural Act, legislation that protects cultural, racial, religious, and linguistic diversity in Canada, was passed in 1988. Multiculturalism has been a double-edged sword in Canada; making everyone equal can sometimes obscure important differences that need to be taken into consideration.

All of these elements interact in complex ways to create social context. Considering the general social context of Canada as a nation; the specific social contexts of different places, spaces, and groups within Canada; and how these contexts shape our understanding of Canadian society provides an important backdrop when thinking sociologically about children and childhood.

CHILDREN *IN* SOCIETY

Children are an important part of Canadian society. Many aspects of our society involve children and childhood, and yet childhood issues are rarely prioritized. According to the latest census from 2016, 19.3 percent of Canadians are under the age of 17; nearly a fifth of the population of Canada are children (Statistics Canada, 2017). Our federal budget devotes significant funding to social structures and services that directly affect children's lives: our education systems, health care, and social support programs such as the Canada Child Benefit (Government of Canada, 2018). However, because of their youth and common-sense ideas about their intellectual capacities, most of the time, children are excluded from political discourse and civic engagement in Canada. We rarely hear about issues that pertain to childhood or children's perspectives regarding social life. This is where thinking sociologically about children and childhood can really be of assistance, particularly to early childhood professionals. Let's consider how each of the main aspects of this chapter—the framework of the sociology of childhood, the three conceptual tools of sociology, and an awareness of how history influences contemporary lived experience—can help us think sociologically about children and childhood in Canada. I do not claim to come to any conclusions in this next section, but instead propose ways that thinking sociologically about children and childhood can help us deepen our understanding.

Let's first recall the four principles of the sociology of childhood: childhood is an important topic of study; childhood is an enduring social category that affects environment and context; children are members of their societies whose presence and actions have consequence; and children's particular circumstances need to be accounted for and their perspectives given space to be heard and included in social life. Assessing Canadian society according to these principles shows that mainstream thinking in Canada follows along very different lines. Canadian society does not consider childhood an important topic of inquiry, as evidenced by ongoing political disinterest and a severe gap in knowledge about children and issues of childhood across the country (Albanese, 2009). Childhood is not considered an enduring social category that shapes and is shaped by society in Canada. If it was, there would be a more concerted effort to provide the supports that children and their families need, such as a universal and accessible federal system of child care. Children are not thought of as social actors—prevalent discourses in Canada primarily describe children from the developmental perspective—not yet having the capacities required to be functioning members of society. Finally, children's perspectives are not taken seriously, nor are they involved in decision-making processes at the society level; there are very few mechanisms in place to allow for children to engage in decision-making or to make their views known.

The tide is shifting, however, as there are a growing number of scholars across the country who are working with these principles, and their research is slowly moving into mainstream attitudes toward children and childhood. Using these principles can give early childhood professionals some concrete areas to question, explore, and strategize new ways of framing children and childhood in their practice and interactions. Early childhood professionals already feel that children and childhood are important, and they are in a position to pass on this perspective to the wider population. They are also aware that children are social actors; their classrooms and professional settings are full of material evidence and interactions that prove that children's actions have consequence on their environment and context. It is also possible for people working in childhood settings to help children live in ways that make their rights concrete, encourage them to form and share their own views, and help to create platforms where those views can be shared.

The three conceptual tools of thinking sociologically outlined earlier in this chapter—social context, social action, and social construction—can support new and different thinking about children and childhood in Canada. First, the complex interweaving of social and structural elements that make up the varying social contexts in Canada needs to be taken into consideration when thinking about childhood and children's lived experiences. Where they are, what kinds of resources they and their family have access to, how much difference they experience day-to-day, their and their family's socio-economic status, the cultural beliefs present in their context—all of these factors influence the ways in which childhood will take shape. Considering the interplay of these factors and how they impact on children's lives can widen our lens of understanding. Understanding social context is a crucial tool for early childhood professionals, and doing so can help them foster interactions, design interventions, and nurture relationships that acknowledge who each child is, so that these things may be tailored to each child and therefore be most effective.

Second, children's social actions and the meaningful interactions children have can reveal important information about their lived experiences and also about Canadian society. How children behave at school, the ways they make friends, debates about screen time and media consumption, where they go and what they do when they play, and the surveillance they are subject to—looking at these social dynamics can tell us a lot. Early childhood professionals are in an excellent position to observe children's social actions and to reflect on how those actions reflect dynamics in their social environment.

What can these actions tell us about children's lives? Additionally, early childhood professionals are well placed to nurture more inclusive, supportive, and thoughtful social action, both directed toward children and childhood and among children themselves.

Third, what social constructions are at work in Canada? What significance do we invest in childhood and in our children? These are deeply complex questions, as social constructions are based on cultural beliefs and values. In Canada's pluralist and multicultural society, many value systems and ideologies exist, some harmoniously, while others are contradictory in profound ways. Beliefs about children and childhood are as varied. We can, however, see some of the most popular underlying ideas by looking at the general organization of Canadian society. Children across the country spend a large part of their childhood going to school and learning material prescribed for them by adults. They are legally prohibited from certain behaviours. For example, children in Canada are not allowed to work, vote, drive, or drink alcohol until young adulthood. If children do engage in anti-social or criminal behaviours, they are subject to a different criminal code than adults are. Children are also rarely involved in decision-making processes, whether at a community or governmental level. These and many other social dynamics reveal that in Canada, children are thought of as being less capable than adults and not really participating members of their society. While it is clear that children are dependent on the adults in their lives, it is equally clear that they are capable of many things and that many of the traits we associate with adulthood and functioning members of society are not necessarily age-related (Lee, 2001). Early childhood professionals can be powerful agents for change regarding the meanings we invest in childhood in Canada. Already well-versed in the dominant developmental perspective, by adding sociological thinking to their conceptual toolkit early childhood professionals could make a significant contribution to shifting the mainstream ways that we understand children toward perspectives that acknowledge them as contributing members of society and investing children and childhood with new and more nuanced meaning.

A famous saying goes, "those who ignore history are doomed to repeat it." Being conscious of Canadian history can help trace the sources of enduring structures in our society and can also help us understand why they take the shapes that they do (Seixas, 2004). Knowledge of colonial history and the Canadian government's ongoing conflicted relationship with Indigenous people helps reveal why some parts of those communities are struggling.

An awareness of the historical tensions between France and Britain, how they played out in colonial North America, and how they are made more complex by recent immigration to Canada sheds new light on the ambiguous and complicated state of Canadian identity. Our social lives do not exist in a vacuum; they grow out of the social lives and contexts that came before them. Structures, institutions, policies, laws, and social dynamics are built upon those that came before. History is alive in the present and all around us: in the built environments of our schools and homes, in the ways that our laws determine correct and deviant behaviour, in the ways that we make decisions as communities and as a country. Early childhood professionals equipped with historical knowledge can understand the dynamics leading to the social circumstances of the present and are better able to respond to how those historical dynamics interact with the lives of the children they work with. Thinking sociologically can help us better understand children marginalized by the social structures built upon the decisions of the past, and early childhood professionals capable of historicizing childhood are better equipped to support children in the present.

REFERENCES

Albanese, P. (2009). The missing child in Canadian sociology: Is it time for change? *Jeunesse: Young People, Texts, Cultures, 1*(2), 136–146.

Bauman, Z., & May, T. (2001). *Thinking sociologically* (2nd ed.). Malden, MA: Blackwell.

Berger, P. L., & Luckmann, T. (1967). *The social construction of reality.* New York, NY: Anchor.

Bourdieu, P., & Wacquant, L. J. (1992). *An invitation to reflexive sociology.* Chicago, IL: University of Chicago Press.

Chen, X., Raby, R., & Albanese, P. (Eds). (2017). *The sociology of childhood and youth in Canada.* Toronto, ON: Canadian Scholars.

Corsaro, W. A. (2011). *The sociology of childhood* (3rd ed.). Thousand Oaks, CA: Pine Forge Press.

Fieras, A. (2014). *Racisms in a multicultural Canada: Paradoxes, politics, and resistance.* Waterloo, ON: Wilfrid Laurier University Press.

Gabriel, N. (2017). *The sociology of early childhood: Critical perspectives.* Thousand Oaks, CA: SAGE.

Gibbon, J. M. (1938). *Canadian mosaic: The making of a northern nation.* Toronto, ON: McClelland and Stewart.

Government of Canada. (2018). *Equality + growth.* Retrieved from https://www
.budget.gc.ca/2018/docs/themes/growth-croissance-en.html

Indigenous and Northern Affairs Canada. (2017). *First Nations in Canada.* Retrieved
from https://www.aadnc-aandc.gc.ca/eng/1307460755710/1307460872523#chp2

James, A., & James, A. L. (2004). *Constructing childhood: Theory, policy and practice.*
Hampshire, UK: Palgrave Macmillan.

James, A., & Prout. A. (2015). *Constructing and reconstructing childhood: Contemporary
issues in the sociological study of childhood* (3rd ed.). Oxford, UK: Routledge, Taylor &
Francis.

James, A., Jenks, C., & Prout, A. (1998). *Theorizing childhood.* Cambridge, UK: Polity
Press.

Kelley, N., & Trebilcock, M. (2010). *The making of the mosaic: A history of Canadian immigration policy* (2nd ed.). Toronto, ON: University of Toronto Press.

Kunz, J. L., & Sykes, S. (2007). *From mosaic to harmony: Multicultural Canada in the
21st century.* Ottawa, ON: Policy Research Initiative.

Lee, N. (2001). *Childhood and society: Growing up in an age of uncertainty.* Berkshire,
UK: Open University Press.

Li, J. N. (2000). *Canadian steel, Chinese grit: A tribute to the Chinese who worked on
Canada's railroads more than a century ago.* Toronto: Paxlink Communications.

Library and Archives Canada. (2007). *Chinese.* Retrieved from https://www
.collectionscanada.gc.ca/settlement/kids/021013-2031-e.html

Macionis, J. J., Jansson, S. M., & Benoit, C. M. (2009). *Society: The basics* (4th
Canadian ed.). Toronto, ON: Pearson Prentice Hall.

Marx, K. (1913). *A contribution to the critique of political economy.* Chicago, IL: Charles
H. Kerr.

Marx, K., Moore, S., Aveling, E. B., & Engels, F. (1904). *Capital: A critical analysis of
capitalist production.* London, UK: S. Sonnenschein.

Mayall, B. (2002). *Towards a sociology for childhood.* Berkshire, UK: Open
University Press.

Mills, C. W. (1959/2000). *The sociological imagination.* Oxford, UK: Oxford University
Press. (Original work published in 1959).

Parr, J. (1982). *Childhood and family in Canadian history.* Toronto, ON: McClelland &
Stewart.

Parsons, T. (1975). *Social systems and the evolution of action theory.* New York, NY: The
Free Press.

Pence, A. R. (Ed.). (1991). *Childhood as a social phenomenon: National report, Canada
(No. 36).* European Centre for Social Welfare Policy and Research.

Pierce, C. M., & Allen, G. B. (1975). Childism. *Psychiatric Annals, 5*(7), 15–24.

Porter, J. (1965). *The vertical mosaic: An analysis of social class and power in Canada.* Toronto, ON: University of Toronto Press.

Qvortrup, J. (1993). Societal position of childhood: The international project childhood as a social phenomenon. *Childhood, 1*(2), 119–124.

Seixas, P. C. (2004). Introduction. In P. C. Seixas (Ed.), *Theorizing historical consciousness* (pp. 3–20). Toronto, ON: Toronto University Press.

Statistics Canada. (2017). *2016 Census: Population trends by age and sex.* Retrieved from https://www.statcan.gc.ca/eng/sc/video/2016census_agesex

Truth and Reconciliation Commission of Canada. (2015). *Honouring the truth, reconciling for the future. Summary of the final report of the Truth and Reconciliation Commission of Canada.* Winnipeg, MN: National Centre for Truth and Reconciliation.

United Nations General Assembly. (1989). Convention on the rights of the child, 20 November, 1989, United Nations Treaty Series, Vol. 1577. Retrieved from http://www.refworld.org/docid/3ae6b38f0.html

Wallace, R. A., & Wolf, A. (Eds). (2006). *Contemporary sociological theory: Expanding the classical tradition* (6th ed.). Upper Saddle River, NJ: Pearson.

Weber, M. (1956/1978). *Economy and society: An outline of interpretive sociology* (Vol. 1). Berkeley, CA: University of California Press. (Original work published in 1956).

Wells, K. (2015). *Childhood in a global perspective* (2nd ed.). Cambridge, UK: Polity Press.

Whitehorn, A. (2015). *Social democracy.* Retrieved from http://www.thecanadianencyclopedia.ca/en/article/social-democracy/

Winter, E. (2015). Rethinking multiculturalism after its "retreat": Lessons from Canada. *American Behavioural Scientist, 59*(6), 637–657.

CHAPTER 10

Thinking and Doing Otherwise: Reconceptualist Contributions to Early Childhood Education and Care

Rachel Berman and Zuhra Abawi

GUIDING QUESTIONS:

1. What are some of the reconceptualist approaches to rethinking early childhood education and care (ECEC) in terms of theory and practice?

2. How might dominant developmentalist discourses of childhood be challenged by reconceptualist contributions and lead us to re-imagine children and childhood?

INTRODUCTION

The reconceptualist movement in early childhood education and care (ECEC) began in the late 1980s, spurred on by scholars and practitioners who sought to shift away from dominant discourses of developmentalist-based theories of early childhood by implementing a multidisciplinary and multi-theoretical approach to how we think about and practise ECEC (Bloch, 2014; Curry & Cannella, 2013). Simply put, reconceptualists look to disciplines beyond developmental psychology, such as anthropology, sociology, and gender studies, and to theoretical frameworks outside constructivism and bio-ecological systems theory, such as the frameworks discussed in this chapter, in order to challenge dominant assumptions and offer other ways of conceptualizing and practising ECEC.

Reconceptualists argue that dominant narratives about early childhood and educating young children have been conceptualized through Western norms of childhood development that are standardized, colourblind, ahistorical, apolitical, and, supposedly, neutral (Iannacci & Whitty, 2009; Lubeck, 1994; MacNaughton & Davis, 2009; Pacini-Ketchabaw & Nxumalo, 2013; Silin, 1995; Taylor, 2007). These norms of development, based mostly on research with white, middle-class, able-bodied, English-speaking children, have vastly informed ECEC curriculum and pedagogy, and promote narrow ideas of children and childhood. These prescriptive norms continue to serve the status quo, despite immense growth in the diversity in social, political, economic, and technological arenas that mark globalized childhoods (Cannella, 2006; Grieshaber & Ryan, 2005; Lenz Taguchi, 2011; Pacini-Ketchabaw, 2010; Pacini-Ketchabaw & Pence, 2005). Through the reconceptualization of ECEC, new possibilities open up and new actions can be taken.

Reconceptualists take into account the multifaceted experiences, perspectives, and multiple ways of thinking about and understanding children, childhood, learning, teaching, and care in order to critique dominant practices. One such practice reconceptualists have critiqued is developmentally appropriate practice (DAP), conceptualized and promoted by the American organization of the National Association for the Education of Young Children (NAEYC). They critique DAP by arguing that it marginalizes and "others" those bodies who do not conform to its rigid categorizations, that it ignores power relations and context, such as gender, race, home language(s), home culture(s), and so forth (Bernhard et al., 1998; Brown, Souto-Manning, & Tropp Laman, 2010; Lubeck, 1994, 1998; MacNaughton & Davis, 2009; Pacini-Ketchabaw, Nxumalo, & Rowan, 2011).

Reconceputalists resist assumptions of children as helpless and passive and, rather, seek to learn from and with children (Diaz Soto & Swadener, 2005; Scheffel, 2009). They also reject the "at risk" label as deficit-based thinking and argue instead for understanding and connecting with children and families in the social, cultural, and economic context in which they live (Heydon & Iannacci, 2008; Swadener & Lubeck, 1995). They transgress traditionally constructed hierarchies that inform and implicate relationships between adults and children (Langford, 2010); children and children; and children, places, materials, and animals (Nelson, 2018; Nxumalo, 2016). They invite us to consider who gets left out when we only look to the dominant developmental theoretical frameworks. In other words, who is made invisible? Who is positioned as "abnormal" or "atypical"? Is there only one correct way to learn, and grow, and be? Where are the voices of children, of families, of teachers? What happens when we consider learning encounters with the non-human? What is the role of social justice in ECEC?

Reconceptualist work takes place in many countries throughout the world. In 2005, Pacini-Ketchabaw and Pence noted that reconceptualist perspectives in Canadian ECEC were rare. This state of affairs has changed to some degree since then, and it is worth noting that the 25th International Reconceptualizing Early Childhood Education (RECE) Conference was held in Toronto, Ontario, in 2017, and the Common Worlds Research Collective mentioned at the end of the chapter makes its home in Canada (also see Iannacci & Whitty, 2009; Pacini-Ketchabaw & Prochner, 2013). Some of the RECE scholarship discussed in this chapter takes place outside of Canada.

Reconceptualist scholars and practitioners explore and utilize theoretical approaches not traditionally taken up in ECEC in order to shed new light on our understandings of ECEC that highlight inclusivity and equity. The purpose of this chapter is to explore some of the key theoretical approaches taken up by reconceptualist scholars and practitioners, including critical race theory, feminist theory, poststructural theory, queer theory, postcolonial theory, and posthumanism, including multi-species ethnographies and the new materialism (see table 10.1). Although most of these theories are presented one at a time, they can and do overlap.

CRITICAL RACE THEORY

Critical Race Theory (CRT) (Crenshaw, 2011; Delgado & Stefancic, 2017; Ladson-Billings, 1998; Matias, Vieska, Garrison-Wade, Madhavi, & Galindo, 2014; Santamaria & Santamaria, 2012; Sleeter, 2017) is concerned with decentring power relations masked within discursive neoliberal inclusivity politics, such as colourblindness (Bonilla-Silva, 2006), the idea that racism no longer exists, and meritocracy, the notion that society is an equal playing field and if you simply work hard enough you will be rewarded. CRT emerged from the field of critical legal studies (CLS) in the United States as a response to deteriorating race relations in the 1970s following police brutality and disproportionate incarceration rates of African American men in particular (Delgado & Stefancic,

2017; Santamaria & Santamaria, 2012). Central to this theory is the idea that racism is deeply embedded in society to the extent that it appears normal and natural and is thus largely unacknowledged and unchallenged. In more recent years, blatant acts of racism seem to have once again become more normalized; however, this does not mean that the subtle or less obvious acts of racism do not require attention and dismantling.

Educator Gloria Ladson-Billings (1999) specified the four objectives of CRT as follows: (1) attention to the normalization of racism in society; (2) storytelling as a counter-narrative to white dominance; (3) the critique of liberalism, where systems of racism and racialization are silenced; and (4) the emphasis on race realism. CRT challenges racism and processes of racialization within the field of education in order to identify the racialized processes that disenfranchise and marginalize racialized and Indigenous students. Such processes include streaming, disciplinary policies and practices, and achievement gaps, which CRT challenges by asserting that the organization of society is based on racialized hierarchies that must be dismantled (Delgado & Stefancic, 2017). The deconstruction of the categories of "otherness," in which othered identities are constructed and measured in relation to the normativity of whiteness, is a central tenet of CRT. Although not widely taken up by reconceptualist thinkers in early childhood education, this theory has been adopted by some as a way to rethink race in early childhood and early childhood settings (Berman, Daniel, Butler, MacNevin, & Royer, 2017; MacNevin & Berman, 2017; Nash, 2013) and to reconceputalize refugee experiences in ECEC via RefugeeCrit (Strekalova-Hughes, Nash, & Erdemir, 2017).

Within the dominant psychological developmental norms of ECEC, it is commonly assumed that children do not notice race as they are too young to engage with concepts of race and racial identity (di Tomasso, 2012). It is not surprising, then, that in their research with early childhood educators, Han (2013), MacNaughton and Hughes (2007), and Berman and colleagues (2017) report that many pre-service teachers and practising ECEs believe that racism is not an issue in their classrooms and that treating all children the same is an adequate response to cultural and racial diversity. However, reconceptualists (along with scholars outside this movement) contend that children are constantly engaged in several meaning-making processes regarding race and are able to actively negotiate the complex power relations and fluidity of identities to develop positive ideas about race and difference (Berman et al., 2017; Boutte, 2008; Boutte, Lopez-Roberston, &

Powers-Costello, 2011; Copenhaver-Johnson, 2006; MacNaughton & Davis, 2009; Pacini-Ketchabaw & Berikoff, 2008; Skattebol, 2003). While resisting the acknowledgement of systemic racism and seeing schools as neutral spaces in early childhood education, many ECE graduates continue to enter the workforce feeling unprepared to work in classrooms with children who are different from themselves (Berman et al., 2017).

Reconceptualist concepts of race differ substantially from developmentalist ideas surrounding race; namely, the developmentalist approach views race as a biological phenomenon informed by phenotype differences (di Tomasso, 2012). Developmentalist approaches to race as a biological and static identity marker thus position whiteness as the invisible norm of identity through which all children are measured (Berman et al., 2017; Escayg, Berman, & Royer, 2017; Pacini-Ketchabaw, Nxumalo, & Rowan, 2011). Children's racial identities and identity formation in settler-colonial societies such as Canada (Tuck & Yang, 2012) are mediated and perpetuated by socializing institutions such as education (MacNaughton & Davis, 2009). Reconceptualist and CRT theorists see race as something fluid, that is, socially, politically, and historically constructed. As Escayg, Berman, and Royer (2017) suggest, Euro-dominated societies such as Canada engage in racialized discourse by normalizing and socializing whiteness whilst simultaneously touting commitments to equity, inclusion, multiculturalism, and quality child care. The narratives of multiculturalism and the celebration of diverse cultures and communities that Ontario, for example, so greatly prides itself upon fail to take into account the very racialized power relations that privilege whiteness at the expense of racialized and Indigenous peoples (Abu El-Haj, 2006; Berman et al., 2017). This colourblindness (Bonilla-Silva, 2006) effectively fails to acknowledge that Canada does indeed have a race problem (Berman et al., 2017).

A classic American study carried out in the 1940s by Kenneth and Mamie Clark (1947) found that both black and white children preferred white dolls when given a choice between two dolls (a study that has been repeated many times). A more recent study undertaken by MacNevin and Berman (2017) entailed parallel findings. The study examined performances of race in play in a child care centre located in the City of Toronto. The authors draw on the interactions between two racialized girls at play with dolls in the house centre. The girls demonstrated a clear preference for white baby dolls and discarded the black baby doll they had initially picked up. Furthermore, the children associated darker featured dolls with undesirable characteristics, such as "mean," "scary," and resembling a "witch" (MacNevin & Berman, 2017, p. 832).

In addition to CRT, it is worth noting that an anti-racist approach (Dei, 2006) has also been adopted by reconceptualist thinkers in the field of ECEC in Canada (Escayg, Berman, & Royer, 2017; Janmohamed, 2005; Pacini-Ketchabaw, 2014). Anti-racism, as CRT, challenges multicultural understandings of race and identity that tout equality without regard for the unique identities and experiences of various collective identities. Anti-racism thus problematizes how whiteness operates as a norm in institutional structures such as early childhood education to privilege white bodies and experiences while marginalizing other perspective and identities.

FEMINIST THEORY

Feminism entails multiple definitions and forms; hooks (2000) defines feminism as "a movement to end sexism, sexist exploitation and oppression" (p. 1). Based on this definition, we seek to explore feminist contributions to reconceptualizing ECEC. Gender, like race, is often considered to be obsolete and irrelevant to early childhood learning, as early childhood learning spaces are poised as gender-free, race-free neutral sites (Hogan, 2012). Adriany and Warin (2014) articulate that gendered practices by ECEs are informed by the ECEs' own preconceived beliefs and ideas about gender, which are largely grounded in larger social and political underpinnings. However, while gendered praxis in early childhood settings may not be overtly evident, gender segregation manifests itself in the learning space in subtle ways, such as classroom organization and materials (Robinson & Diaz, 2006). Gender-stereotypical practices occur through myriad processes, including gender-designated toys and centres, such as dolls and the house centre for girls and trucks and blocks for boys. As noted in the previous section regarding play and race, play is also often where gender is performed (Butler, 1990).

In revisiting the dominant norms of psychology-based developmental theories taken up in ECEC, like Erikson, Piaget, and Bowlby, we see that they are heavily grounded in dualisms, or binaries, of identity categorizations. For example, a child is either "developing" at the normal or natural pace or they are not, and thus they are othered. The developmentalist views hold the same rigidity concerning gender identity; there is the female identity on one end of the spectrum and the male on the other end, in which there is not and cannot be an in between (Grieshaber, 2007; Hogan, 2012;

MacNaughton, 2005). Feminist theory thus examines notions of male/female binaries by focusing attention on the ways power relations are enforced and maintained. Here, it is important to consider the work of influential French theorist Michel Foucault (1972) when thinking about discourse and subjectivity (and see following section on poststructuralism), namely that language is embedded in power relations and therefore is never neutral. In terms of gender discourses, these discourses create subjects enveloped in so-called universal or known truths about the nature of girls and boys (Blaise, 2005; MacNaughton, 2000; Pardhan, 2011). The polarizing identities that accompany dualisms ignore intersectionalities between gender and race, gender and sexuality, gender and dis/ability, and so forth. As Blaise (2005) contends, "child development theories not only legitimize gender as a natural category, but also reinforce gender differences, which shape the social expectations of girls and boys" (p. 29). These expectations in turn influence how children view gendered expectations and professions, including the ECEC profession, which is overwhelmingly female. The gendered nature of the profession emanates from traditional gendered processes and norms that depict males wishing to work in the field as deviants from social norms (Robinson & Diaz, 2006).

Feminist theory aims to destabilize child development's hegemonic discourses of gender in ECEC by making classrooms a safe space for children to navigate social constructs of gender informed by family, the media, and education in order to arrive at their own perspectives and identity (hooks, 1994). Adriany and Warin (2014) propose gender flexibility in ECEC spaces. The authors note that this offers a flexible approach to gender performance and simultaneously unsettles dualities of masculinity and femininity. As with race, child developmental theories depict children as too young to talk about gender and gender biases in the media, in society, and within the teaching staff (MacNaughton, 2000). However, Adriany and Warin's (2014) study suggests that it is possible to deconstruct gender binaries and stereotypes by engaging with children, as it is possible to make children aware of gender identity and performance in order to challenge these stereotypes.

POSTSTRUCTURALISM

Reconceptualists who utilize poststructuralist thinking emphasize diversity, equity, and inclusion as a means to provide a more holistic conceptualization of childhood and framing around binaries of adult and child relationality (Cannella, 2006; Dahlberg, Moss, & Pence, 2013; Grieshaber, 2007; MacNaughton, 2005; Popkewitz, 2003, 2007). This approach values multiple ways of knowing, understanding, and learning. As noted in the section on feminism, a key tool of poststructuralism is discourse (Foucault, 1972). Discourse in Foucauldian terms does not describe a world that already exists; instead, discourses make up and shape the world. In other words, for poststructuralists, the world is created through language (Taylor, 2018).

Poststructuralism allows for the dismantling, or deconstructing, of the centrality of Piaget's child-centred approaches to understanding childhood and "best" practices for educating young children by arguing that these developmentalist views gloss over the importance of social location (a person's position in society as defined by gender, age, social class, dis/ability, religion, sexual orientation, etc.) by neglecting epistemological contributions from non-Western ways of knowing (Graue, 2005; Tzuo, Yang, & Wright, 2011) and pay little attention to possibilities for childhood agency (the idea that children are able to make choices and decisions and have an impact on their world) (Silin, 1995). Poststructuralists call instead for a child-centredness that is embedded in social location, as identities and education are inherently politicized (Cannella, 2006; Slattery, 2006). Rethinking child-centred pedagogy and practice is thus a process that involves multiple and contested discourses across time and space, namely the social location and positionality of the ECE via funds of knowledge, or the understanding of where a child's learning occurs (González, Moll, & Amanti, 2005; MacNaughton, 2005; Popkewitz, 2003; Slattery, 2006).

Poststructuralism recentres ECEC to provide a voice and space for marginalized perspectives that are vehemently overlooked and excluded from dominant Eurocentric paradigms of childhood and learning (Campbell & Smith, 2001; Genishi & Goodwin, 2008; Grieshaber & Ryan, 2005). The focus therefore falls on both the educator and the child. The ECE must engage in autobiography, which entails self-examination of how the educator's positionality cannot be neutral and presumed as unbiased, as identities are political. Educators are encouraged to engage in self-reflection to consider how their social location informs their pedagogical praxis (Tzuo et al., 2011). When reconceptualizing children's learning through knowledge funds rather than adult-directed pedagogy, poststructuralism utilizes children's artistic creations, for example, to provide agency to multiple discourses and epistemologies, as Tzuo and colleagues (2011) infer "such poststructural educational projects foster learning through the sharing of discourses that represent different histories, cultures, policies, and other contexts involved in the construction of knowledge" (p. 556).

This approach can also help us rethink other aspects of ECEC, including observational practices. Campbell and Smith (2001) utilize a feminist poststructuralist framework to help dismantle assumptions regarding developmentalist-based observations of play. They demonstrate how a developmental approach to observation works to "privilege and silence particular understandings of what it is to be a child in an early childhood setting" (p. 90). They discuss a play episode that took place amongst three children and then interpret the episode according to a developmentalist perspective, where the children's choices were seen to be driven by their own individual cognitive and social abilities. The same play episode is then re-interpreted by the authors through a feminist poststructural perspective. The authors demonstrate to the reader how a feminist poststructural reading of the play episode allows for a consideration of issues of power and gender in the play, issues not considered in the developmentalist reading. By viewing the play episodes from different theoretical lenses, they effectively demonstrate the ways particular discourses constrain and open up possibilities for who children can be. In sum, reconceptualists who take up poststructuralism challenge the assumption that knowledge is impartial, neutral, and equal and open up spaces for us to think and practise otherwise.

QUEER THEORY

Reconceptualist thinkers Blaise and Taylor (2012) explain that queer theory is not a theory about gay and lesbian identity. Rather, what is queer about queer theory is that it questions the strongly held belief that there is any "normal" or correct expression of gender or sexuality. Thus, queer theory as a reconceptualist contribution seeks to challenge the pervasiveness of institutionalized heteronormativity in early learning settings, which legitimizes heteronormative and nuclear families as the norm (Gunn, 2011). As Gunn (2011) posits, "heteronormativity is the concept that heterosexual sexuality is an institutional norm and superior and privileged standard" (p. 280). The pathologization of deviations from heteronormativity stems from religious and moral underpinnings rooted in Western medicine and science (Blaise & Taylor, 2012). Within institutions such as education, heteronormativity is assumed to be everyone's norm and lived reality as well as the only norm of sexual orientation and family structure (Atkinson & DePalma, 2008; Blaise,

2005; Robinson, 2013; Taylor & Blaise, 2007). These norms govern power relations and notions of "normal" sexual- and gender-development trajectories; discourses of healthy childhood development are intricately connected to heteronormative development (Blaise & Taylor, 2012). Through the psychological, behaviourist narrative, children are rewarded for conforming to gendered norms and punished for skewing them. For example, Robinson (2013) explains the following, with regard to the former:

> Paradoxically, despite the prevalent perception that children are innocent, asexual and too young to understand sexuality, the construction of heterosexual identities and desire in early childhood is a socially-sanctioned and integral part of children's everyday educational experiences. For example, children's engagement in mock weddings is encouraged and even celebrated in many early childhood educational contexts, with games such as "Catch and Kiss" and "Mummies and Daddies" generally considered a natural and normal aspect of children's everyday play. (p. 76)

Butler (1990) refers to gender performativity as something that we are constantly performing in accordance to prescribed social and institutionalized norms of what she calls the heterosexual matrix.

The early learning setting is an ideal space to dismantle ideologies that frame gender and sexuality (Gunn, 2011; Robinson, 2013; Taylor & Blaise, 2007). Early childhood learning sites are fraught with heteronormative assumptions. For example, through play, children often perform heteronormative and gendered roles, and books and materials that depict heteronormative families and heterosexual sexuality as the normal and natural developmental ideal abound (Alloway, 1995; MacNaughton, 2000). Thus, the construction of heteronormativity is enmeshed into children's everyday lives; it is what is present in the classroom via materials and play, and it is policed by ECEs and children but never openly discussed by ECEs. Queer theory challenges what is taken for granted as the natural and normal progression of sexuality and gender identity and the marginalization of non-nuclear heterosexual family structures (Robinson, 2013).

Taylor and Blaise (2007) suggest several ways that queer theory can be enacted in early childhood learning. The first suggestion is queering the ECE curriculum and the classroom by providing same-sex resources and materials in the classroom and embedding same-sex families and queer identities into pedagogical praxis and programming. Another suggestion is queering childhood, where children can play and interact in a gender-fluid way. Thirdly, queering the family and early childhood services can encourage families to share their own epistemologies and be actively involved in their child's learning experiences without fear and pressure to "pass" as heterosexual. Fourth, early childhood research relationships might be queered by transgressing the belief that gender and sexuality are apolitical and irrelevant in early learning, and raising awareness in ECEs of how their social locations and their own performances of gender within the heterosexual matrix are politicized. Another mechanism they posit is queering childhood innocence. In the predominant Western reductionist paradigm of childhood, children are often rendered as helpless, innocent, and incapable. However, the queering of childhood innocence challenges those assumptions and argues that these conceptions in fact increase dangers by painting children as powerless, vulnerable, and lacking agency when children are not. Finally, we can queer friendships and playground interactions. Taylor and Blaise (2007) note how children's games and rhymes are highly gendered and that these friendships, interactions, and games highlight how children are actively engaged in performing gender and heteronormativity. In keeping with reconceptualist aims of decentring dualisms and binaries enforced by psychological developmentalist traditions, queer theory advocates that childhood is an ideal time and place whereby play can be gender-fluid and an opportunity for children to freely explore gender identities, roles, and resources available to themselves and their families.

POSTCOLONIAL THEORY

Postcolonial theory, or postcolonialism, as a reconceptualist contribution to early childhood education, parallels the colonization and control of non-European peoples and lands with contemporary control mechanisms and surveillance of children in the West (Cannella & Viruru, 2003; Nieuwenhuys, 2013; Viruru, 2005). European imperialism enforced total control over the "othered" non-European lands, resources, and people on justifications of moral, intellectual, and racial superiority (Said, 1978). The central tenet of colonialism was the creation of the "other," through which, as outlined in Edward Said's (1978) *Orientalism*, the "other" as an "oriental" and non-European was innately inferior to the European and the "occident" or the West. The construction of the "other" as an identity conjured a knowledge base about the characteristics of the other through demeaning representations, labels, and ultimately, imperial control (Bhabha, 1996; Cannella & Viruru, 2003). Postcolonialism involves the periods, movements, and processes following European imperialism where former colonized peoples reclaim their identities and their lands. Cannella and Viruru (2003) define postcolonialism as follows:

> Post-colonialism embodies the recognition of the Western imperialist project, followed by historical attempts to physically decolonize, while at the same time leaving nations and peoples living under one form of imperialist political and economic domination that is spreading to include power over identities and intellect. (p. 15)

The most influential discourses and narratives of childhood and children were developed during the height of Western colonization. Following World War II, colonization largely morphed from the physical appropriation and genocide of non-European peoples to a phenomenon that embodies and sustains itself through multifaceted structures such as economies, knowledge, discourse, and institutions (Cannella & Viruru, 2003). The postcolonial critique of early childhood education infers that, as with European colonization, children and childhood are othered as well through violent processes including labelling, constant surveillance, universal and simplistic representations, and being in need of controlling due to immaturity and incompetence (Cannella & Viruru, 2003; Todd, 2009). Therefore, these impositions on children and childhood as in need of adult protection and discipline stem from the same rationale whereby colonized peoples were categorized as "child-like" (Said, 1978) and children in the West are conceptualized as subject to adults. Childhood, as Cannella and Viruru (2003) note, is a "colonizing construct" (p. 64) because European representations of colonized peoples, like the West's representations of children and childhood, have constructed an oppressive ideology of such identities that has been perpetuated and sustained as dominant truths.

In addition to postcolonial theories, settler-colonialism is pertinent to the ongoing genocide and displacement of Indigenous peoples and communities on Turtle Island and elsewhere. Tuck and Yang (2012) define settler-colonialism as "different from other forms of colonialism in that settlers come with the intention of making a new home on the land, a homemaking that insists on settler sovereignty over all things in their new domain" (p. 5). Ashton (2015) calls attention to how ECEC curricula in

Canada, which claims to be inclusive and celebrate diversity, may implicitly include white settler norms and position some "diverse" children as "Other." Scholars Ritchie and Rau (2010) consider how colonial perspectives and Western developmental influences in New Zealand early childhood education privilege play as the best way in which children learn and ask us to think what other ways of knowing and being could be understood if Indigenous knowledge(s) was not rendered invisible.

POSTHUMANISM

The 21st century has witnessed substantial shifts in society, politics, demographics, and technology. While our society has rapidly changed into a globalized one with a myriad of complexities, education has been slow to keep pace with such changes and has remained relatively static (Barad, 2007; Lenz Taguchi, 2011). Presently, pedagogical practices continue to reproduce a one-size-fits-all, blanketed view of education, one that emphasizes concrete standardization at the expense of fluidity and complexity (Hultman & Lenz Taguchi, 2010; Osberg & Biesta, 2010). Contemporary educational norms consider teaching and learning as separate entities of the learner; the learner's role in this predicament is to master the materials and concepts to be studied (Lenz Taguchi, 2011). This purpose of education is grounded in the liberal humanist tradition, whereby knowledge is believed to be neutral, and thus social location is minimized. Thus, human development and learning are conceived of as being separate and distinct from race, gender, dis/ability, sexuality, and other facets of one's social location, along with the non-human (Pacini-Ketchabaw, 2010; Todd, 2009). Pedagogical assessment takes its form in the constant and compulsive documentation and surveillance of children's actions, drawings, depictions, and work to ensure childhood development adheres to the "normal," "neutral" trajectory of human development (Lenz Taguchi, 2011; Knight, 2013).

Posthumanism is an approach taken up in a number of fields that incorporates ideas from science, philosophy, technology studies, animal studies, geography, environmental studies, and more and is particularly influenced by American feminist scholars Donna Haraway, and Karen Barad (2007), along with the work of French thinkers Gilles Deleuze (1990/2004, 1994) and Félix Guattari. Reconceptualists who utilize posthumanist theory explore children's encounters/learning/relations with the non-human or more-than-human (for example, animals, plants, places, ecologies, objects, artificial intelligence, physical forces) and decentre the human, so as to seek a better world (Rautio, 2014; Rautio & Jokinen, 2015). This approach moves us away from a focus only on discourse, as in the poststructuralist approach. Citing Taylor, Moss (2019) explains that "instead of a hierarchical world, topped by humans, there are now *common worlds* that human beings 'share with all manner of others—living and inert, human and more-than-human'" (p. 144). For ECECs in Canada who take up this approach, "posthumanism is a response to the human-centred education approaches that dominate *because* they stem from and perpetuate Euro-Western anthropocentric worldviews/human exceptionalism ... this might be one method for starting to unsettle how firmly Euro-Western ontologies inform education practices in this place of ongoing settler colonialism" (Land, personal communication, December 7, 2018).

Hackett and Somerville (2017) offer that "posthuman approaches have been developed within two main traditions of scholarship in early years learning: multispecies ethnographies and new materialism, both of which aim to decentre the human in their concern for planetary well-being" (p. 376). While some may not agree with this categorization, we believe it is helpful and adopt it here for the purposes of this chapter.

MULTI-SPECIES ETHNOGRAPHY

Adopting this approach shifts us away from particular dualisms, such as the belief that humans are superior to nature and that humans are not part of nature. In this approach, early childhood researchers pay particular attention to child/animal and child/plant relations, and as stated previously, in Canada this approach is connected to ethical issues regarding unsettling settler colonialisms in our common world. For example, a group of early childhood educators connected to a forest inquiry that took place in Songhees, Esquimalt, and W̱SÁNEĆ territories, otherwise known as Victoria, British Columbia, carry out this work as they pay attention to Indigenous knowledges, Haraway, the forest, and more. The authors share their rethinking, or "stumbling," in connection with encounters in forest walks with children, as the question "what constitutes good care in troubling times?" is considered. They are clear that they are committed to thinking with more-than-human others as co-participants in caring and share what this looks like in a number of vignettes (Woods et al., 2018).

In another example of this approach, Nxumalo and Pacini-Ketchabaw (2017) examine a pet program in early childhood classrooms. They note such programs are usually considered as unproblematically beneficial for child developmental outcomes. They explain that, in their work with teachers and children in one child care centre in Western Canada, they began to notice the impact of the walking sticks, insects that had been purchased at a pet store three years ago and had since greatly proliferated. They share how the teachers, the children, and themselves grappled with difficult ethical concerns regarding what they learned about the impact of overcrowding due to the growing population and how to co-inhabit the classroom with the insects. The children ask if they should they let them go? Would this cause damage to the local forest? They explore the question. The researchers share how this reminded them of ways that European settler-colonialism has damaged forest ecosystems. Teachers had been removing and destroying eggs (outside the children's knowledge) and struggled with this act. No easy answers are provided, but important considerations are raised.

> Rather than focusing solely on a predetermined scientific lesson about stick insects, common world pedagogies allowed us to also engage in a contextual, situated walking stick pedagogy that paid attention to the place-specific temporalities of classrooms and to what it means, specifically, to live and learn with these particular "introduced animals" in a space where ethics and the effects and affects of killing and making killable are all part of these modes of learning. (p. 1423)

Such a common worlding approach reframes childhood as collective and relational rather than individualistic and developmental (Woods et al., 2018). To learn more about this approach, the Common Worlds Research Collective is an excellent place to start (see http://commonworlds.net/).

NEW MATERIALISM

New materialism as adopted by reconceptualists asks us to consider alternative possibilities for attending to and re-composing with the interdependencies, roles, and responsibilities of childhood in a globalized context (Lenz Taguchi, 2011). In this approach it is a turn to matter, bodies, and spaces that is the focus.

New materialism as a pedagogical guide counters dominant developmental models of childhood by moving away from constructivist views of learning, which are based on the assumption that the only valid ways of knowing are those that involve "brain learning" (Lenz Taguchi, 2011; Reddington & Price, 2016). New materialism offers that learning unfolds within complex, situated relationships, where children's social locations, identity conceptions, bodies, and connections with human and more-than-human/material/physical forces shape possibilities for learning (Barad, 2007; Hultman & Lenz Taguchi, 2010; Pacini-Ketchabaw, Kind, & Kocher, 2017; Lenz Taguchi, 2011).

While narratives and policies of equity and inclusion in education have surged, much of this is rhetoric, as the main concerns of these initiatives are to revert the othered child "back" to the normal linear pattern of development. The new materialist approach is concerned with the relational interactions and encounters of the individual's experience with the world beyond mere human interaction (Reddington & Price, 2016). The focus on myriad and complex interactions between children and the non-human world offer spaces of resistance to hegemonic discourses of learning and provide possibilities of mobilizing new epistemologies based on children's encounters (Leander & Boldt, 2012). According to the new materialism, it is because of these multiple dependencies and interconnections that learning takes place. Learning, in this context, is seen as an encounter, and it occurs as a result of the mutual interconnections between "several performative agents," such as the learner and the materials used in the learning process (Lenz Taguchi, 2011). Each performative agent is dependent on, as well as acts upon, other performative agents; this is called "intra-activity" (Lenz Taguchi, 2011). Thus, learning does not take place in the isolation of the learner's mind, but is an act of reciprocity between performative agents, in a given encounter, with each affecting the other, as a result of which there is a transformation in each performative agent.

Like multi-species posthumanist approaches, the new materialism tries to do away with many of the dualisms or binaries, such as mind and body or thinking and doing, that dominate contemporary ideas about learning. Instead, it puts forward the concept of the "bodymind" (Lenz Taguchi, 2011). Thus, learning and making meaning is more than just a cognitive activity, as it involves the body as well as the mind of the learner. Learning is said to develop simultaneously in many different directions, and this can be described as "rhizomatic flows" (an idea from Deleuze) instead of linear advances, highlighting the fact that human beings are constantly learning as they interact with people, materials, and environments, and therefore there are no fixed or static positions as far as learning and learners are concerned (Lenz Taguchi, 2011). An example of this approach is provided by Hodgins (2015), who grapples with the responsibility of dealing with waste in early childhood settings by exploring moments from two collaborative inquiries in classrooms in Western Canada, one that involved paint, another that involved textiles. She draws on ideas from Haraway and Barad to attend to intergenerational ecological justice. The new materialist lens demonstrates how ECEC can be thought of beyond static forms of competency-based representation, most notably standardization, performance measures, concrete and measured evaluations of learning, and developmental progress (Leander & Boldt, 2012; O'Donnell, 2013).

To sum up, posthumanist approaches in ECEC shift us toward a consideration of children's and teachers' relationality with the world and provide for more holistic and equitable ways of thinking about and responding in the current conditions of learning and education (Hodgins, 2015; Leander & Boldt, 2012; Reddington & Price, 2016, Woods et al., 2018).

Table 10.1: Reconceptualist Theoretical Contributions to ECEC

RECONCEPTUALIST CONTRIBUTION	KEY CONCEPTS	HOW IT CHALLENGES DOMINANT PARADIGMS IN ECEC
Critical Race Theory	Children are constantly engaging in performances of race through play and peer groups. ECE settings are not neutral and race-free spaces.	Children are never too young to engage with race. ECEs must take children's race and social location into consideration to understand that some children face barriers that others do not. Multicultural approaches are usually tokenistic.
Feminist Theory	Gender identity and constructions of gender are not rigid and static but fluid. Classrooms must be places where children can experiment with gender roles.	ECE settings offer an ideal space for children to perform various gender roles by challenging the idea that gender can only be thought of in distinctly male and female categorizations.

(continued)

Table 10.1: *(Continued)*

RECONCEPTUALIST CONTRIBUTION	KEY CONCEPTS	HOW IT CHALLENGES DOMINANT PARADIGMS IN ECEC
Poststructuralism	There are no structures, only interactions between power and knowledge. Those who control power relations create structures. Those who are oppressed by these power relations are marginalized.	Rethinks how childhood is conceptualized from many identities and experiences rather than one universally constructed approach to childhood.
Queer Theory	ECE is constantly espousing heteronormative discourses in pedagogies and interactions with children and their families. Those that are non-conforming are often problematized as deviating from social norms.	Challenges heteronormative identity as a norm of childhood development. Decentres the nuclear family as a social norm and the only lived reality and experience of children and families.
Postcolonialism	Children and childhood are colonial categories in the way that colonized peoples were and are oppressed. Children are also subjugated to surveillance and domination.	Views children and childhood as autonomous and challenges the norm of pedagogies based on adult preconceived notions of children and childhood.
Posthumanism	Centres children's perspectives and experiences beyond mere encounters with materials, animals, and nature. Children have myriad experiences with the human and non-human world, and this should be centred in their learning.	Rejects Piagetian trajectories of human development that offer a one-size-fits-all approach. Children are part of humanity and not separate from it.
New Materialism	Children live in a globalized, rapidly changing interconnected and innovative world. Education has not kept pace with these changes.	Challenges the neutrality of knowledge and the narrative that children are dependent on adult control and scaffolding. Learning can only take place in relation to the child and their unique interactions with the world around them.

CONCLUSION

This chapter attests to the multiple ways that childhood developmentalist theories have permeated dominant discourses and constructions of childhood as a standardized and universal experience (Burman, 2008; Dahlberg & Moss, 2005; Nguyen, 2010). It implores readers to think otherwise about how they approach childhood through a reconceptualist lens. Reconceptualist scholars advocate for an interdisciplinary and critical idea of childhood that problematizes the ideal childhood (Taylor, 2007) and deconstructs the dualisms and constructivist, reductionary approaches to ECEC (Pacini-Ketchabaw, 2010; Nguyen, 2010). The chapter outlines several theories reconceptualist thinkers have taken up and their contributions to re-imagine childhood and the practices of ECEC through critical race theory, feminist theory, poststructuralism, queer theory, and posthumanism.

REFERENCES

Abu El-Haj, R. (2006). *Elusive justice: Wrestling with difference and educational equity in everyday practice.* New York, NY: Routledge.

Adriany, V., & Warin, J. (2014). Preschool teachers' approaches to gender differences within a child-centered pedagogy: Findings from an Indonesian kindergarten. *International Journal of Early Years Education, 22*(3), 315–328.

Alloway, N. (1995). Eight's too late: early childhood education and gender reform. *Unicorn: Journal of the Australian College of Education, 21*(4), 19–27.

Ashton, E. (2015). Troubling settlerness in early childhood education. In V. Pacini-Ketchabaw & A. Taylor (Eds.). *Unsettling the colonial places and spaces of early childhood education.* New York, NY: Routledge.

Atkinson, E., & DePalma, R. (2008). Imagining the homonormative: Performative subversion in education for social justice. *British Journal of Sociology of Education, 29*(1), 25–35.

Barad, K. (2007). *Meeting the universe halfway: Quantum physics and the entanglement of matter and meaning.* Durham, NC: Duke University Press.

Berman, R., Daniel, B. J., Butler, A., MacNevin, M., & Royer, N. (2017). Nothing or almost nothing to report: Early childhood educators and discursive constructions of colourblindness. *International Critical Childhood Policy Studies Journal, 6*(1), 52–65.

Bernhard, J. K., Gonzalez-Mena, J., Chang, H. N., O'Loughlin, M., Eggers-Pierola, C., Roberts Fiati, G., & Corson, P. (1998). Recognizing the centrality of cultural diversity and racial equity: Beginning a discussion and critical reflection on "developmentally appropriate practice." *Canadian Journal of Research in Early Childhood Education, 7*(1), 81–90.

Bhabha, H. K. (1996). Cultures in between. In S. Hall & P. Du Gray (Eds.), *Questions of cultural identity* (pp. 53–60). London, UK: Sage.

Blaise, M. (2005). *Playing it straight: Uncovering gender discourses in the early childhood classroom*. New York, NY: Routledge Taylor & Francis Group.

Blaise, M., & Taylor, A. (2012). Research in review: Using queer theory to rethink gender equity in early childhood education. *Young Children, 67*(1), 88–99.

Bloch, M. (2014). Interrogating reconceptualizing early care and education (RECE)—20 years along. In M. N. Bloch, B. B. Swadener, & G. S. Cannella (Eds.), *Reconceptualizing early childhood care and education, a reader: Critical questions, new imaginaries & social activism* (pp. 20–43). New York, NY: Peter Lang.

Bonilla-Silva, E. (2006). *Racism without racists: Colorblind racism and the persistence of racial inequality in America* (4th ed.). Lanham, MD: Rowman and Littlefield.

Boutte, G. S. (2008). Beyond the illusion of diversity: How early childhood teachers can promote social justice. *The Social Studies, 99*(4), 165–173.

Boutte, G. S., Lopez-Robertson, J., & Powers-Costello, E. (2011). Moving beyond colorblindness in early childhood classrooms. *Early Childhood Education Journal, 39*(5), 335–342. doi:10.1007/s10643-011-0457-x

Brown, S., Souto-Manning, M., & Tropp Laman, T. (2010). Seeing the strange in the familiar: Unpacking racialized practices in early childhood settings. *Race Ethnicity and Education, 13*(4), 513–532.

Burman, E. (2008). *Deconstructing developmental psychology* (2nd ed.). New York, NY: Routledge.

Butler, J. (1990). *Gender trouble: Feminism and the subversion of identity*. New York, NY: Routledge.

Campbell, S., & Smith, K. (2001). Equity observations and images of fairness in childhood. In S. Grieshaber and G. S. Cannella (Eds.), *Embracing identities in early childhood education: Diversity and possibilities* (pp. 89–101). New York, NY: Teachers College Press.

Cannella, G. (2006). *Deconstructing early childhood education: Social justice and revolution* (3rd ed.). New York, NY: Peter Lang.

Cannella, G. S., & Viruru, R. (2003). *Childhood and postcolonization: Power, education and contemporary practice*. New York, NY: RoutledgeFalmer.

Clark, K. B., & Clark, M. P. (1947). Racial identification and preference among negro children. In E. L. Hartley (Ed.), *Readings in social psychology*. New York, NY: Holt, Rinehart, and Winston.

Copenhaver-Johnson, J. F. (2006). Talking to children about race: The importance of inviting difficult conversations. *Childhood Education, 83*, 12–22.

Crenshaw, K. (2011). Twenty years of critical race theory: Looking back to move forward. *Connecticut Law Review, 43*(5), 1253–1354.

Curry, D. L., & Cannella, G. S. (2013). Foreword: Reconceptualist her/histories in early childhood studies: Challenges, power relations, and critical activism. In V. Pacini-Ketchabaw & L. Prochner (Eds.), *Re-situating Canadian early childhood education* (pp. ix–xxvi). New York, NY: Peter Lang.

Dahlberg, G., & Moss, P. (2005). *Ethics and politics in early childhood education.* New York, NY: Routledge.

Dahlberg, G., Moss, P., & Pence, P. (2013). *Beyond quality in early childhood education and care: Languages of evaluation* (3rd ed.). New York, NY: Routledge.

Dei, G. S. (2006). We cannot be colour blind: Race, antiracism and the subversion of dominant thinking. In W. Ross & V. Ooka Pang (Eds.), *Race, ethnicity and education* (pp. 25–42). Westport, CT: Praeger.

Deleuze, G. (1990/2004). *Negotiations: 1972–1990* (M. Joughin, Trans.). New York, NY: Columbia University Press. (Original work published in 1990).

Deleuze, G. (1994). *Difference and reception* (P. Patton, Trans.). New York, NY: Columbia University Press.

Delgado, R., & Stefancic, J. (2017). *Critical race theory: An introduction* (3rd ed.). New York, NY: New York University Press.

Diaz Soto, L., & Swadener, B. B. (2005). *Power and voice in research with children.* New York, NY: Peter Lang.

di Tomasso, L. (2012). *Engaging with early childhood educators' encounters with race: An exploration of the discursive, material and affective dimensions of whiteness and processes of racialization.* (Unpublished doctoral dissertation). University of Victoria, Victoria, BC.

Escayg, K. A., Berman, R., & Royer, N. (2017). Canadian children and race: Toward an antiracism analysis. *Journal of Childhood Studies, 42*(2), 10–21.

Foucault, M. (1972). *The archaeology of knowledge* (A. M. Sheridan-Smith, Trans). London, UK: Tavistock.

Genishi, C., & Goodwin, A. L. (Eds.). (2008). *Diversities in early childhood education: Rethinking and doing.* New York, NY: Routledge.

González, N., Moll, L., & Amanti, C. (2005). *Funds of knowledge: Theorizing practices in households, communities, and classrooms.* Mahwah, NJ: Lawrence Erlbaum Associates.

Graue, E. (2005). (De)centering the kindergarten prototype in the child-centered classroom. In S. Grieshaber & S. Ryan (Eds.), *Practical transformations and transformative practices: Globalization, post-modernism, and early childhood education* (pp. 39–58). Oxford, UK: Elsevier.

Grieshaber, S. (2007, 9 November). *Gender and early childhood education.* Presentation and workshop at National Taipei College of Nursing (NCTN), Taipei, Taiwan.

Grieshaber, S., & Ryan, S. (2005). Transforming ideas and practices. In S. Grieshaber & S. Ryan (Eds.), *Practical transformations and transformative practices: Globalization, post-modernism, and early childhood education* (pp. 3–16). Oxford, UK: Elsevier.

Gunn, A. C. (2011). Even if you say it three ways, it still doesn't mean it's true: The pervasiveness of heteronormativity in early childhood education. *Journal of Early Childhood Research, 9*(3), 280–290.

Hackett, A., & Somerville, M. (2017). Posthuman literacies: Young children moving in time, place and more-than-human worlds. *Journal of Early Childhood Literacy, 17*(3), 374–391.

Han, K. T. (2013). "These things do not ring true to me": Pre-service teacher dispositions to social justice literature in a remote state teacher education program. *The Urban Review, 45*(2), 143–166.

Heydon, R., & Iannacci, I. (2008). *Early childhood curricula and the de-pathologizing of childhood*. Toronto, ON: University of Toronto Press.

Hodgins, D. B. (2015). Wanderings with waste: Pedagogical wonderings about intergenerational ecological justice-to-come. *Canadian Children, 40*(2), 88–100.

Hogan, V. (2012). *Locating my teaching of gender in early childhood teacher education within the wider discourses of feminist pedagogy and poststructuralist theory*. Presentation at the Joint AARE-APERA International Conference, Sydney, Australia.

hooks, b. (1994). *Teaching to transgress: Education as the practice of freedom*. New York, NY: Routledge.

hooks, b. (2000). *Feminism is for everybody: Passionate politics*. Cambridge, MA: South End Press.

Hultman, K., & Lenz Taguchi, H. (2010). Challenging anthropocentric analysis of visual data: A relational materialist methodological approach to educational research. *International Journal of Qualitative Studies in Education, 23*(5), 525–542.

Iannacci, L., & Whitty, P. (2009). *Early childhood curricula: Reconceptualist perspectives*. Calgary, AB: Detselig Press.

Janmohamed, Z. (2005). Rethinking anti-bias approaches in early childhood education: A shift toward anti-racism education. In G. J. Dei & G. Singh Hohal (Eds.), *Critical issues in anti-racist research methodologies* (pp. 163–182). New York, NY: Peter Lang.

Knight, L. (2013). Not as it seems: Using Deleuzian concepts of the imaginary to rethink children's drawings. *Contemporary Issues in Early Childhood, 4*(2), 254–264.

Ladson-Billings, G. (1998). Just what is CRT and what's it doing in a nice field like education? *Qualitative Studies in Education, 1*(11), 102–118.

Ladson-Billings, G. J. (1999). Just what is critical race theory and what's it doing in a nice field like education? In L. Parker, D. Deyhele, & S. Villenas (Eds.), *Race is … race isn't: Critical race theory and qualitative studies in education* (pp. 7–30). Boulder, CO: Westview Press.

Langford, R. (2010). Critiquing child-centred pedagogy to bring children and early childhood educators into the centre of a democratic pedagogy. *Contemporary Issues in Early Childhood, 11*(1), 113–127.

Leander, K. M., & Boldt, G. (2012). Rereading "a pedagogy of multiliteracies": Bodies, texts, and emergence. *Journal of Literacy Research, 45*(1), 22–46.

Lenz Taguchi, H. C. (2011). Investigating learning participation and becoming in early childhood practices with a relational materialist approach. *Global Studies of Childhood, 1*(1), 36–50.

Lubeck, S. (1994). The politics of developmentally appropriate practice: Exploring issues of culture class and curriculum. In B. Mallory & R. New (Eds.), *Diversity and developmentally appropriate practices: Challenges for early childhood education* (pp. 17–43). New York, NY: Teachers College Press.

Lubeck, S. (1998). Is developmentally appropriate practice for everyone? *Childhood Education, 74*(5), 283–292.

MacNaughton, G., & Davis, K. (2009). Discourses of "race" in early childhood: From cognition to power. In G. MacNaughton & K. Davis (Eds.), *Race and early childhood education: An international approach to identity, policies and pedagogy* (pp. 17–30). New York, NY: Palgrave MacMillan.

MacNaughton, G., & Hughes, P. (2007). Teaching respect for cultural diversity in Australian early childhood programs: A challenge for professional learning. *Journal of Early Childhood Research, 5*(2), 189–204.

MacNaughton, G. (2000). *Rethinking gender in early childhood education*. London, UK: Paul Champlain.

MacNaughton, G. (2005). *Doing Foucault in early childhood studies: Applying poststructural ideas*. New York, NY: Routledge.

MacNevin, M., & Berman, R. (2017). The Black baby doll doesn't fit the disconnect between childhood diversity policy, early childhood educator practice, and children's play. *Early Childhood Development and Care, 187*(5–6), 827–839.

Matias, C. E., Vieska, K. M., Garrison-Wade, D., Madhavi, T., & Galindo, R. (2014). "What is critical whiteness doing in our nice field like Critical Race Theory?" Applying CRT and CRW to understand the white imagination of white teacher candidates. *Equity and Excellence in Education, 47*(3), 289–304.

Moss, P. (2019). *Alternative narratives in early childhood: An introduction for students and practitioners*. New York, NY: Routledge.

Nash, K. T. (2013). Everyone sees color: Toward a transformative critical race framework of early literacy teacher education. *Journal of Transformative Education, 11*(2), 151–169.

Nelson, N. (2018). Rats, death, and Anthropocene relations in urban Canadian childhoods. In A. Cutter-Mackenzie, K. Malone, & E. Barratt Hacking (Eds.), *Research handbook on childhood nature.* Springer International Handbooks of Education. Cham, Switzerland: Springer.

Nguyen, U. A. (2010). *Conflicting ideologies in early childhood education: An exploration of Reggio-inspired practice* (Unpublished master's thesis). Brock University, St. Catharines, ON.

Nieuwenhuys, O. (2013). Theorizing childhood(s): Why we need postcolonial perspectives. *Childhood, 20*(1), 3–8.

Nxumalo, F. (2016). Storying practices of witnessing: Refiguring quality in everyday pedagogical encounters. *Contemporary Issues in Early Childhood, 17*(1), 39–53.

Nxumalo, F., & Pacini-Ketchabaw, V. (2017). "Staying with the trouble" in child-insect-educator common worlds. *Environmental Education Research, 23*(10), 1414–1426.

O'Donnell, A. (2013). Unpredictability, transformation, and the pedagogical encounter: Reflections on "what is effective" in education. *Educational Theory, 63*(3), 265–282.

Osberg, D. C., & Biesta, G. J. J. (2010). The end/s of school: Complexity and the conundrum of the inclusive educational curriculum. *International Journal of Inclusive Education, 14*(6), 593–607.

Pacini-Ketchabaw, V. (2010). Introduction: Resituating Canadian early childhood education. *The Alberta Journal of Educational Research, 56*(3), 241–245.

Pacini-Ketchabaw, V. (2014). Postdevelopmental perspectives on play: Postcolonial and anti-racist approaches to research. In L. Brooker, S. Edwards, & M. Blaise (Eds.), *The SAGE handbook of play and learning in early childhood* (pp. 67–78). London, UK: Sage.

Pacini-Ketchabaw, V., & Berikoff, A. (2008). The politics of difference and diversity: From young children's violence to creative power expressions. *Contemporary Issues in Early Childhood Education, 9*(3), 256–264.

Pacini-Ketchabaw, V., Kind, S., & Kocher, L. (2017). *Encounters with materials in early childhood education.* New York, NY: Routledge.

Pacini-Ketchabaw, V., & Nxumalo, F. (2013). Regenerating research partnerships in early childhood education: A non-idealized vision. In J. Duncan & L. Conner (Eds.), *Research partnerships in early childhood education: Teachers and researchers in collaboration* (pp. 11–26). New York, NY: Palgrave MacMillan.

Pacini-Ketchabaw, V., Nxumalo, F., & Rowan, C. (2011). Nomadic research practices in early childhood: Interrupting racisms and colonialisms. *Reconceptualizing Educational Research Methodology, 2*(1), 19–33.

Pacini-Ketchabaw, V., & Pence, A. (2005). The reconceptualizing movement in Canadian early childhood education, care and development. In V. Pacini-Ketchabaw & A. Pence (Eds.), *Canadian early childhood education: Broadening and deepening discussions of quality* (pp. 5–20). Ottawa, ON: Canadian Child Care Federation.

Pacini-Ketchabaw, V., & Prochner, L. W. (2013). *Re-situating Canadian early childhood education*. New York, NY: Peter Lang.

Pacini-Ketchabaw, V., & Taylor, A. (2015). *Unsettling the colonial places and spaces of early childhood education*. New York, NY: Routledge, Taylor & Francis Group.

Pardhan, A. (2011). Influence of teacher-student interactions on kindergarten children's developing gender identity within the Pakistani urban classroom culture. *Early Child Development and Care, 181*(7), 929–948.

Popkewitz, T. S. (2003). Governing the child. In M. N. Bloch, K. Holmlund, I. Moqvist, & T. S. Popkewitz (Eds.), *Governing children, families, and education: Restructuring the welfare state* (pp. 35–62). New York, NY: Macmillan.

Popkewitz, T. S. (2007). *Cosmopolitanism and the age of school reform: Science, education, and making society by making the child*. New York, NY: Routledge.

Rautio, P. (2014). Mingling and imitating in producing spaces for knowing and being: Insights from a Finnish study of child-matter intra-action. *Childhood, 21*, 46–174.

Rautio, P., & Jokinen, P. (2015). Children's relations to the more than human world beyond developmental views. In B. Evans, J. Horton, & T. Skelton (Eds.), *Play, recreation, health and well-being. Geographies of children and young people* (Vol. 9, pp. 1–15). Singapore: Springer.

Reddington, S., & Price, D. (2016). Cyborg and autism: Exploring new social articulations via posthuman connections. *International Journal of Qualitative Studies in Education, 29*(7), 882–892.

Ritchie, J., & Rau, C. (2010). "Kia mau ki te wairuatanga": Countercolonial narratives of early childhood education in Aotearoa. In G. Cannella & L. Diaz Soto (Eds.), *Childhoods: A handbook* (pp. 355–373). New York, NY: Peter Lang.

Robinson, K. H. (2013). *Innocence, knowledge and the construction of childhood: The contradictory nature of sexuality and censorship in children's contemporary lives*. New York, NY: Routledge.

Robinson, K. H., & Diaz, C. J. (2006). *Diversity and difference in early childhood*. Maidenhead, UK: Open University Press.

Said, E. (1978). *Orientalism*. London, UK: Routledge & Kegan Paul.

Santamaria, L. J., & Santamaria, A. P. (2012). *Applied critical leadership in education: Choosing change*. New York, NY: Routledge.

Scheffel, T. L. (2009). Valuing children's roles in research on literacy engagement. In L. Iannacci and P. Whitty (Eds.), *Early childhood curricula: Reconceptualist perspectives* (pp. 143–165). Calgary, AB: Detselig Press.

Silin, J. G. (1995). *Sex, death and the education of our children: Our passion for ignorance in the age of AIDS.* New York, NY: Teachers College Press.

Skattebol, J. (2003). Dark, dark and darker: Negotiations of identity in an early childhood setting. *Contemporary Issues in Early Childhood, 4*(2), 149–166.

Slattery, P. (2006). *Curriculum development in the postmodern era* (2nd ed.). New York, NY: Routledge.

Sleeter, E. (2017). CRT and the whiteness of teacher education. *Urban Education, 52*(2), 99–110.

Strekalova-Hughes, E., Nash, K., & Erdemir, E. (2017, October). *Toward a refugee critical race theory in education.* Paper presented at the annual meeting of the Reconceptualising Early Childhood Education Conference, Toronto, Canada.

Swadener, B. B., & Lubeck, S. (1995). *Children and families "at promise": Deconstructing the discourse of risk.* Albany, NY: State University of New York.

Taylor, A. (2007). Playing with difference: The cultural politics of childhood belonging. *International Journal of Diversity in Organizations, Communities and Nations, 7*(3), 143–149.

Taylor, A. (2018). Engaging with the conceptual tools and challenges of poststructural theories. In M. Fleer & B. van Oers (Eds.), *International handbook of early childhood education* (pp. 91–115). Dordrecht, The Netherlands: Springer.

Taylor, A., & Blaise, M. (2007). What is queer theory? *International Journal of Equity and Innovation in Early Childhood, 5*(2), 1–4.

Todd, S. (2009). Educating beyond cultural diversity: Re-drawing the boundaries of a democratic plurality. *Studies in Philosophy and Education, 30*, 101–111.

Tuck, E., & Yang, K. W. (2012). Decolonization is not a metaphor. *Decolonization, Indigeneity, Education, and Society, 1*(1), 1–40.

Tzuo, P. W., Yang, C. H., & Wright, S. K. (2011). Child-centred education: Incorporating reconceptualism and post structuralism. *Educational Research and Reviews, 6*(8), 554–559.

Viruru, R. (2005). The impact of postcolonial theory on early childhood education. *Journal of Education, 35*, 7–29.

Woods, H., Nelson, N., Yazbeck, S. L., Danis, I., Elliott, D., Wilson, J., Paykack, J., & Pickup, A. (2018). With(in) the forest: (Re)conceptualizing pedagogies of care. *Journal of Childhood Studies, 43*(1), 44–59.

CHAPTER 11

Reconfiguring Early Childhood Education: Common Worlding Pedagogies

Veronica Pacini–Ketchabaw, Randa Khattar, and Meagan Montpetit

---

GUIDING QUESTIONS:

1. What are common worlding pedagogies, and how might they be embraced by early years education and care?
2. What is a learning/teaching experience that you have had with children that engaged with or in reconnaissance, experimentation, or the more-than-human?

Early childhood education considers developmental psychology, including its modernist pedagogical interventions, to be the principal framework for defining young children and the roles of those who work alongside them. Although much has been written about the limitations, risks, and dangers of a framework that asserts a white, heterosexual, male universal child (e.g., Burman, 2017; Cannella, 1998; Dahlberg & Moss, 2005), this child endures as the norm from which everything and everyone differs. Notable in this configuration is that this child subject, in a permanent process of development toward rationality, remains detached from ethico-political connotations (Lesko, 2001). Likewise, early childhood education practices obliterate any engagement that would assume deviations from developmental psychology's innocence (Burman, 2017). Departing from such apolitical and ahistorical vistas, we view early childhood education as profoundly political by engaging with common worlds frameworks.[1]

As pedagogists who are members of the Common Worlds Research Collective (http://commonworlds.net/), we co-labour with educators and children to assemble common worlds pedagogies that escape the modern territory of developmental practices. Through common worlds frameworks, we attend to our current times, our milieu. For instance, we disrupt the on-going colonization of Indigenous peoples and lands in settler-colonial societies such as Canada. We respond to the challenges of what scientists have named the Anthropocene (referring to the role of humans in climate change, species extinction, and loss of biodiversity). Engaging with common worlds frameworks, early childhood education focuses on questions like these: How might early childhood pedagogies respond creatively to our milieu within local contexts? What roles might early childhood education play, both in supporting children to respond creatively and locally to our milieu and in composing new worlds? How might early education focus on engaging with children to create life-sustaining relations informed by perspectives beyond developmental psychology theories? These questions invite us to think with our milieu without letting current conditions dictate how we must think (Stengers, 2018). In other words, common worlds frameworks refuse both to ignore and to be captured by the neocolonialism that is our milieu and insist on challenging its assumptions and privileging relations.

"Capture" in the academic world is a colonizing practice that aims to make other into same. In crafting a refrain, or refraining, as philosopher Isabelle Stengers (2008, 2011) suggests, we move from the desire to capture developmental psychology and manipulate it in ways that make it serve our particular wants, to focus instead on thinking about why developmental psychology has flourished, specifically in policy and governance. In this sense, we view developmental psychology not as an enemy of our thought, but as a partial truth that sits, often uncomfortably, with other ways of knowing. It is not developmental psychology we argue against, but the overwhelming allegiance to it that suffocates conversations and practices in early childhood education. Nor do we abdicate from discussions of it. Instead we acknowledge, as Stengers (2018) does, our debt "to the existence of others who ask different questions, importing them into the situation differently, relating to the situation in a way that resists appropriation in the name of any kind of abstract ideal" (p. 45). We resist calls for rational progress that, through demands for rationality and objectivity, silence modes of thinking that lie outside of developmental psychology (Stengers, 2018).

In this chapter, we narrate common worlds pedagogies that trace how young children and educators engage in thinking *with* the world (rather than thinking about the world) and how these pedagogies of *thinking with* create relations with potential to craft new worlds in these uncertain ecological times. The three stories that compose this chapter highlight three aspects of common worlds pedagogies: reconnaissance, experimentation, and the more-than-human. The techniques at the heart of these pedagogies cannot be easily replicated or transferred to other encounters with the world. In narrating them, we ask strange questions—strange because they do not lead to easily amenable solutions (Stengers, 2018). We begin with a brief introduction to common worlds pedagogies.

COMMON WORLDS PEDAGOGIES

Dissimilar to child-centred developmental psychology practices based on dualistic, romantic, and idealized Euro-Western notions of childhood as separate from nature (Taylor, 2013), our assembled common worlds pedagogies reconfigure children's lifeworlds within relations and within human and non-human sociality and agency. Primarily informed by Piaget's (1928) early-20th-century child developmental theories, mainstream pedagogies are resolutely committed to individually focused, child-centred learning (Blaise, 2010; Pacini-Ketchabaw, 2011). This child-centred focus encapsulates developmental psychology's creation of an autonomous and knowable child subject who reaches full potential only through the predictable transmission of universal knowledge offering a values-free and factual account of the world (Dahlberg, Moss, & Pence, 2013). Such understandings are incommensurable with the inseparable connectedness of children and the world, and they conflict with contemporary ecological understandings of human embeddedness in the environment. Common worlding pedagogies respond to the increasingly complex and challenging common worlds that 21st-century children are inheriting. They differ from the mainstream Euro-Western pedagogies that seldom support children to engage meaningfully with their complex world.

Children's common worlds comprise the full gamut of complex relationships, traditions, and legacies that children inherit in the places in which they grow up (Taylor, 2013, 2017). These include children's relationships with their immediate natural and built environments, with the other human and non-human beings that share these environments, and, in settler societies such as Canada, with complex cultural, colonial, and environmental historical traditions and legacies. This inclusive framework resists the nature/culture divide and situates childhoods within entangled human/non-human social and environmental issues and concerns. Unlike the idealized natural worlds usually associated with romantic Euro-Western traditions of nature and childhood, common worlds are the actual, messy, unequal, and imperfect worlds real children inherit and co-inhabit along with other human and non-human beings and entities (Taylor, 2013, 2017).

Common worlds pedagogies are entwined with the geological, material, discursive, historical, and political. While developmentally appropriate child-centred practices *apply* developmental psychology knowledge to replicate an existing world, common worlding pedagogies *assemble* within children's lifeworlds to configure other possible worlds. What is assembled through pedagogical work matters.

What ideas, materials, humans, and non-humans do we pay attention to/with? What discourses do we bring to children's attention? What do we highlight in our pedagogical documentation? Feminist philosopher Donna Haraway is our inspiration here. We draw on her work to weave partial connections that respond to livable political futures. Using Haraway's words, through common worlds pedagogies we *think with* children's lifeworlds because

> it matters what we use to think other matters with; it matters what stories we tell to tell other stories with; it matters what knots knot knots, what thoughts think thoughts, what descriptions describe descriptions, what ties tie ties. It matters what stories make worlds, what worlds make stories. (Haraway, 2016, p. 12)

While the process of assembling in common worlds pedagogies is intentional, it is never innocent. Stengers writes that we cannot detach ourselves from our choices as we build commons. Detachment is impossible because there is not an already-correct answer we can lean on. We are to respond and make decisions without a fixed, guaranteed outcome. Stengers (2018) challenges us "to put what are often difficult choices on the table, necessitating a process of hesitation, concentration, and attentive scrutiny" without an ideal (p. 4). In the stories that follow, we each illustrate the process of world-ing pedagogies through hesitating, concentrating, and paying attention.

COMMON WORLDS PEDAGOGIES OF RECONNAISSANCE

It's a sunny spring morning at an early childhood centre located on the trad-itional lands of the Mississaugas of the New Credit First Nation. A hunger for spring's warming presence feels palpable in both toddlers' and educators' expressions and embodied movements as they flit, flurry, and configure the contours of the landscape now uncovered from its white blanketing. Randa, from her vantage point, is drawn to an encounter on the other side of the enclosure between a child named Andrea and an educator named Ken.[2] A toque—on or off?—as the subject of initial discussion is soon replaced by Andrea's noticing of a budding greenery with a flowerette peeking through the spring's warming soil. Ken, iPad in hand to capture in digital quality the next new learning, clicks carefully as Andrea's face moves closer and closer to the plant.

Then Andrea upends the plant and offers it to Ken and Randa, looking for a reaction, it seems. She is dissatisfied or perhaps loses interest when neither reacts, Ken appearing focused on capturing the event and Randa wondering how to refrain from turning this into another moralizing moment of "teaching" how to respect or "care" for the plant. Andrea suddenly thrusts the plant onto the concrete pavement and walks off.

Randa and the educators have been discussing the relationships among movement, materials, and human bodies. For several months, as winter slowly made way for spring, we have observed the parallel movements of adult and child bodies in the toddler room. The educators are thinking about the conditions that might deepen, stretch, and intensify the aesthetics of their own experiences as they aspire to live lively lives with young children. One educator, Nicole Pierce,[3] captures this refrain:

> In the toddler program we have been noticing the children often using a material for just a few moments and then throwing it aside like gar-bage. We have noticed a lot of pushing the materials off the shields or the dumping out of baskets in a way that seems to say, "I don't want this here. I don't need this. Get it out of my way." On the other hand, we see the toddlers engage in extended, meaningful moments with materials, each

other, and us. These truly meaningful encounters take place during long periods of time, are revisited in some way almost every day, and encompass learning in all areas and on many levels for everyone involved. They seem to happen in the areas of the room with one particular focus. The paint area where we now ONLY have paint and paint accessories (though most of the accessories, brushes, trays, etc., often go unused or are simply tossed aside). In the sensory table, usually with water, where there is only water, coloured water, tubes, and various containers to scoop and pour the water with. The blocks (when the plastic animals, plastic people, etc., aren't in the way as they are usually all thrown on the floor and abandoned quickly). The other sections of the room, filled with a larger number of different types of materials, seem only to elicit this consumerist type of play—come in, take what I want from them for a minute or two, and toss them aside like garbage. So, what if we had every area set up more like the paint, the water, and the blocks? What if every material was there with intention, based on us listening to what the children really want to focus on, and we took the rest away? What if, instead of providing a thousand snacks and fast food options, we chose to provide only five-course gourmet meals? Moments of engagement meant to be savoured, with a variety of specific ingredients that blend and balance each other while making one curious as to what they might be. Would this change the way we encounter, treat, and interact with the materials, each other, and the time and space of exploration?

Part of what is heard in this reflection is a deep desire to overcome symptoms of consumerism seen in the children's apparent disregard for materials. There is, however, a deeper desire articulated here in the hope that fellow educators do not focus simply on augmenting or changing children's *behaviour*, or engage in moralizing interactions, but rather critically consider the conditions that might produce different, deeper connections to place and materials, ones that can be glimpsed through the children's and educators' altered attentiveness or sense of slowing down in the paint and water areas of the room. What is different about these areas? Are these spaces fundamentally different from other spaces in the room? How do educators and children encounter each other differently in these areas? How is memory enacted and reactivated from moment to moment? How do the children and educators know each other differently here?

Entering into experience with an always-already intent to revisit or re-know invites an openness to encountering each moment with an appetite for what is new, yet with a remembering that is also ever-present. Carlina Rinaldi (2006) sees such moments as a *reconnaissance*: "an attempt to re-visit and re-understand what has taken place by highlighting previously constructed relations, developing and challenging them, and consequently, producing new ones" (p. 131). Such reconnaissance cannot take place when the answer is known beforehand, when activities with determinable end results are planned, programmed, and implemented. Anthropologist Anna Tsing (2015) describes in visceral clarity how the elusive matsutake mushroom—both a physical presence in the world and an epistemological metaphor—can only be sleuthed out and located by uncovering the contaminated entanglements that co-exist around the hidden fungus. The end is not determined *a priori* but, as Haraway (1988) suggests, is always situated within contextualized knowledges and relationships. Reconnaissance, seen this way, must feel out the contours, edges, and indeterminate depths of the territory—always already more and different from any of its mappings (Korzybski, 1994). Stengers (2018) draws a distinction between the desire to cultivate experience as *experts*, who exist in the certainty of their own individual knowings, or as *connoisseurs*, who develop an appetite for co-labouring with others and for the indeterminacy that comes with not settling into any particular formulation of knowledge:

> Connoisseurs are not advocates of alternative knowledge, looking for professional knowledge. But their interest in the knowledges produced by scientists is different from the interest of the producers of these knowledges. It is for this reason that they can appreciate the originality or relevance of an idea but also pay attention to questions or possibilities that were not taken account in their production, but that might become important in other circumstances. (p. 9)

What might it mean to cultivate an appreciation and appetite for slowing down when thinking with pedagogies of reconnaissance? Stengers's (2018) understanding of slowing down is again helpful. She suggests that slowing down should not be seen as the monastic, privileged space of being left alone to think (p. 80) on the tops of hallowed mountains. Rather, slowing down calls for a connoisseurship in which to think collaboratively with others. It is the opposite of speed, which "demands and creates an insensitivity to everything that might slow things down: the frictions, the rubbings, the hesitations that might make us feel we are not alone in the world" (p. 81). Thinking with pedagogies of reconnaissance invites the possibility, as Stengers reminds us, of "becoming acquainted with things again, reweaving the bounds of interdependency" (p. 82) among us and others within multi-species more-than-human worlds. It invites an educational project in which we may not know how the experience will end, but that is pedagogically what Latour (2004) calls "a matter for concern."

COMMON WORLDS PEDAGOGIES OF EXPERIMENTATION

At a children's centre located in Anishinnaabeg, Haudenosaunee, and Lunaapeewak territory, a group of educators and Veronica are imagining the classroom as a space for experimentation (see Pacini-Ketchabaw, Kind, & Kocher, 2017) that affords both children and educators time to dwell with materials, slow down processes, and pay attention to particular ideas and propositions. In this way, we are composing what Stengers calls a commons as we learn to think and feel together. We are approaching our work "as it diverges, that is, feeling its borders" (Stengers, 2013, p. 184). Rather than creating a classroom for unleashing children's creative acts, we are assembling a commons to activate feeling, thinking, and imagining otherwise (Stengers, 2017). In our classroom-as-commons, we repopulate our imaginations as we learn to practise "with others, because of others, and because we accept the risk of others" (Stengers, 2017, 30:21).

For the past four months, we have experimented with creating a yarn commons. We wonder how yarn might make us hesitate, slow down, and, through this process, pay attention to worlds in-the-making. Yarn itself has become what Joel McKim and Natasha Myers (2017, p. 351) call "a medium for inquiry and for understanding" as it deepens children's and educators' engagements with other forms of life. Yarn presents itself as having a life of its own with which educators, drawing on feminist pedagogies, intersect as they design new ways of being in the classroom. Enhancing the life of yarn and playing with its rhythms and movements, the educators and Veronica knit and crocheted. We brought our creations to the children, as a gift and provocation. Small, asymmetrical, lopsided sweaters dress large wooden blocks and the backs of child-sized chairs. About ten granny squares and thirty-odd crocheted shapes with stitches missed (and a few picked up along the way) echo the sweaters across the room, lying on the floor, on tables, on shelves. We have been inspired by the words of Sylvia Kind (in Kind, Vintimilla, &

Pacini-Ketchabaw, in press) on studio processes; she describes a studio as "a space of collective inquiry that affords both children and educators time to dwell with materials, linger in artistic processes, and work together on particular ideas and propositions" (n.p.). We create spaces for experimentation.

Experimenting involves careful intervention, as Stengers (2000) explains:

> What is transmitted is not a vision of the world but a way of doing, a way not only of judging phenomena, of giving them a theoretical signification, but also of intervening, of submitting them to unexpected stagings, of exploiting the slightest implied consequence or effect in order to create a new experimentation situation. (p. 49)

The ten children embraced the staged knitted sweaters and odd-shaped crocheted pieces with curiosity and anticipation of what might be possible. Because yarn intensely stretched the children (Mori, 2003), we decided to weave and unweave ourselves into its loops. For four months, yarn became the only material we gathered around, day after day after day. Our goal became to encounter yarn in its many forms (knitted, crocheted, loose, wrapped, tied) and to follow the threads that might unravel in these encounters. Tsing (2015, p. 4) helps to explain what following materials/non-humans might produce. Writing about matsutake mushrooms, she says that following "guides us to possibilities of co-existence" otherwise. How might we live otherwise in this classroom?

Knitted pieces and bodies become entangled as children immerse themselves in the softness of yarn. Rolling, covering, twisting, tying, knotting, and wrapping, the children are reconfigured into pulsating yarn-bundles. Michele lays her head on colourful mounds of knitted pieces on the floor while Vince covers her feet and legs, hands and arms with off-white, yellow, and blue. Kyoto wraps her own arm with a large, multi-coloured granny square and carefully gathers up six knitted swaths and hands them over to Vince, saying "me too." Vince welcomes this invitation and sinks deeper into the game. Soon Michele's and Kyoto's bodies are joined with the granny squares and knitted pieces. For a while, only their faces are visible as they close their eyes and pretend to sleep. They are completely immersed. After a few minutes, they burst out in unison from underneath the covering. Now completely awake, they quickly pick up the spread-out crocheted and knitted pieces and hand them back to Vince. In silence, Michele and Kyoto lie down on the floor again. Placing one woollen piece at a time, Vince covers their entire bodies in yarn.

An educator recounts to the children vivid stories about crocheting with her grandmother: the effort, passion, achievements, pain, enjoyment, frustrations, and many mistakes. In response to the children's interest in these stories, and as a way of offering the unexpected, the educators visit the thrift store and purchase a variety of crochet hooks and colourful yarn.

One morning, the toddlers are welcomed by the educators sitting on the floor crocheting. In a fluid composition, children gather around the educators, watching intently each movement of hand, hook, and yarn. Up, down, forward, backward, decreasing and increasing stitches. Mattie brings several balls of yarn and places them in the middle of the circle that was formed around Veronica. She then picks up four crochet hooks from a basket on a nearby table and hands one hook to each of the other children sitting around Veronica. The children carefully mimic Veronica's crocheting. Yarn moves, twists, winds, tangles, loops, knots between/within/through small fingers and the hooks. We are deeply connected to the yarn. The next day, yarn and hooks in hand, we all sit to watch a YouTube video on crocheting.

It might be tempting to conclude that we were teaching these young children how to crochet. Yet this conclusion would imply conflating pedagogy with teaching and learning—which developmentally appropriate practices often do. However, these common worlds pedagogies of experimentation stay within the realm of pedagogy broadly understood "as accompanying, caring for (and about) and bringing learning to life" (Smith, 2012). These pedagogies of experimentation involve acts of care. Caring, as Thom van Dooren (2014, pp. 291–292, citing Puig de la Bellacasa, 2012) writes, "emerges as a particularly profound engagement with the world"; care involves being "affected by another, to be emotionally at stake in them in some way … to become subject to another, to recognise an obligation to look after another"; caring means that we "get involved in some concrete way, that we do something (wherever possible) to take care of another." In our caring experimentation with creating a yarn commons, these children and educators have become deeply entangled with the world. Children's and educators' movements, rhythms, and ways of being flow with the yarn and new responsibilities emerge.

MORE-THAN-HUMAN COMMON WORLDS PEDAGOGIES

It is a dark and dreary Thursday on the traditional lands of the Anishinnaabeg, Haudenosaunee, and Lunaapeewak Peoples in what is now known as London,

Ontario. In a toddler room at an early childhood centre, Meagan and an educator named Jenn comb through a collection of spare children's clothing that the centre keeps on hand. We are about to embark on our weekly planned walk with eight children. Typically, we walk to a cemetery, and while the children look forward to rejoining the squirrels, deer, turkeys, and geese we frequently share space with there, this week we have to forgo our longer walk to the cemetery because the sky threatens to pelt us with rain at any moment. We decide to head instead to a grassy hill behind the centre. Navigating a slippery downhill climb and crossing a small parking lot, we reach the grassy area we intend to engage with. Another educator had warned Jenn that she encountered a dead squirrel on the grassy hill while walking to the centre earlier that morning. Jenn and Meagan whisper our hopes that the squirrel body is no longer there. Before we can finish expressing our hushed desires to not engage with the dead animal, a child calls out, "What is *that*?" The dead squirrel has been spotted.

As the children rush to discover what mystery this grassy place is offering us, we hurry to the squirrel/child meeting place and ponder. Should we return to the child care centre playground, a benign, child-friendly place that we can see from the grassy resting spot of the squirrel, or should we remain here with the dead squirrel and the ambiguous risk it offers? We wonder what story this squirrel could tell us. Pushing through our own discomfort by resisting impulses to protect the children and respect the dead, we decide to stay with the squirrel body. Jenn takes a deep breath and responds to the children's continued "What is it?" with an honest answer: "It's a dead squirrel." Bracing ourselves to enter into risky conversations about death and life, we are bombarded with questions and theories about the squirrel's death: "How did it die?" "Maybe he ate bad food and got sick." "Maybe he missed a branch and fell." "Maybe it was chased by another animal." "His body looks squashed, maybe something heavy fell on him." "Yes, maybe it was a very big rock." The delighted children chorally repeat the word *squashed* while inching closer to the squirrel body. The squirrel appears deflated, noticeably flatter than the squirrels who currently traverse the grassy space. The flattened body hides the squirrel's tail, and its black fur is punctuated with grey patches. The squirrel's mouth is slightly agape, and a single tooth is visible. Aside from the decompression, the squirrel resembles the not-dead squirrels that also occupy this space. There are no signs of decomposition, no maggots or exposed bone.

A gentle rain starts to fall, making the grass around the squirrel body increasingly slippery and difficult for the children to navigate. As children slip and slide toward the squirrel, the grass moves under their feet and the wind sways the leaves on the overhanging tree branches. In this moment, the squirrel body seems to be the only thing not moving. Although the squirrel is no longer alive, it still matters in this moment. The squirrel, grass, rain, and children come together in a specific assemblage, one that cannot be predicted or controlled. We embrace the precariousness of squirrel/grass/rain/child assemblage. As Tsing (2015) suggests, this unpredictable encounter has the potential to transform us, and we linger with the condition of being vulnerable to more-than-human others.

Several children spot a live squirrel running through the grass and climbing trees. They wonder aloud if the squirrel is here to bring his friend home or if this other squirrel was the cause of the death. Some children try to chase the live squirrel and draw its attention to the dead one; the squirrels continue to scurry up and down trees, occasionally scooping up nuts and pieces of garbage. A child approaches the dead squirrel with a stick and begins to poke the body. When the stick meets the body, the body moves, and the child shrieks and jumps back. The rain comes down more heavily, and we decide to return to the centre. The children ask whether they can visit the squirrel later, and if the squirrel will still be there after sleep time. We offer the only answer available to us: "We don't know." The children soon begin the wet, unpredictable climb back to the centre.

More-than-human pedagogies trouble child-centred early childhood practices by engaging with the assemblages that emerge when children and the more-than-human meet. The risky encounter with the more-than-human above challenges innocent images of idyllic child-animal relations. Pedagogies of the more-than-human resist common practices of viewing the other-than-human as a tool to scaffold children's learning about scientific concepts, acknowledging instead the complex, dynamic relations that unfold in human/more-than-human assemblages (Pacini-Ketchabaw, Taylor, & Blaise, 2016). These pedagogies emphasize the laborious nature of living-with, where the dead squirrel body is not something that requires co-existence or tolerance (Puig de la Bellacasa, 2012). Instead, pedagogies of the more-than-human foreground a situational ecology of practice that embraces divergence and experiments with questions that mobilize and transform practice in early childhood education rather than asking questions that maintain current discourse and support the status quo (Stengers, 2013). By allowing the encounter with the dead squirrel body to flourish, the educators and children actively resist notions of innocent, precious child-animal relations and instead respond to Puig de la Bellacasa's (2010) question of "how to engage with care of the earth without idealising nature or de-responsibilizing human agency by seeing [human agency] as either inevitabl[y] destructive or [as] paternalistic stewardship" (p. 159). In the case of the dead squirrel body, the question emerges of caring for something one may find grotesque. This particular idea of care shifts common early childhood discourses that associate care with love, affection, and meeting physical needs to thinking with care through non-idealized, multi-layered meanings (Puig de la Bellacasa, 2012). Caring here becomes less about protecting and sheltering and more about curiosity (Haraway, 2008).

DISCUSSION

Our work is situated in urgent times. We are reminded by Stengers (2011) that no specific fate exists: the future offers neither a return to romantic visions of an unharmed world nor a utopian vision that eradicates the devastation of the current epoch. She further asserts, "there is only danger and the need to craft consequences of the fact that ours is a triply devastated world … [there is the need] to accept being situated by the question of devastation" (p. 148). In this chapter, we engaged with the trouble of worlding pedagogies for our milieu.

The pedagogies we narrated in this chapter offer more than an alternative to commonplace practices in early childhood education, more than a critique of developmental psychology. To engage with messy, non-innocent, always-partial truths is inherently difficult and relies on relaying, not simply responding to and reflecting on, dominant discourses. These pedagogies are in themselves an experiment: an experiment in crafting refrain. In refraining, Stengers (2008, 2011) suggests, we resist ideas of master narratives. We have no imperialistic desire to replace dominant developmental discourses in early childhood education with concrete ideas of our own. Rather, we envision spaces in which multiple theories sit together, sometimes in uncomfortable tension.

We acknowledge that resisting majority narratives means making uneasy connections that come at a cost and interrupt ideologies of niceness and correctness (Stengers, 2011) that often drive early childhood education. Embracing our situated stances in early childhood education through the three narratives, we sought ways of thinking and working that break from prescription and function instead within complex children's common worlds.

In other words, we approached pedagogies as an opportunity "for thinking through what is happening" in the world and milieu in which we are located (Stengers, 2013, p. 185).

Perhaps we offer these common worlds pedagogies, using Stengers's (2013) words, as "ecologies of practice" or, as she notes, as tools that are malleable, that when passed on to others have potential to change their use and application. Thus we relay these common worlds pedagogies, not as neutral, but as ways to carry the situated ways of knowing of their users. What is certain in our common worlding pedagogies is that they defy ready application.

NOTES

1. The research on which this chapter draws is supported financially by a Social Science and Humanities Research Council Partnership Development Grant.

2. Unless otherwise noted, names of children and educators in this chapter are pseudonyms.

3. Educator's real name.

REFERENCES

Blaise, M. (2010). Kiss and tell: Gendered narratives and childhood sexuality. *Australasian Journal of Early Childhood, 35*(1), 1–9.

Burman, E. (2017). Fanon's other children: Psychopolitical and pedagogical implications. *Race, Ethnicity, and Education, 20*(1), 42–56.

Cannella, G. S. (1998). Early childhood education: A call for the construction of revolutionary images. In W. Pinar (Ed.), *Curriculum: Toward new identities* (pp. 157–184). New York, NY: Taylor & Francis.

Dahlberg, G., & Moss, P. (2005). *Ethics and politics in early childhood education.* New York, NY: RoutledgeFalmer.

Dahlberg, G., Moss, P., & Pence, A. (2013). *Beyond quality in early childhood education and care: Languages of evaluation* (3rd ed.). New York, NY: Routledge.

Haraway, D. (1988). Situated knowledges: The science question in feminism and the privilege of partial perspective. *Feminist Studies, 14*(3), 575–599.

Haraway, D. J. (2008). *When species meet.* Minneapolis, MN: University of Minnesota Press.

Haraway, D. J. (2016). *Staying with the trouble: Making kin in the Chthulucene.* Durham, NC: Duke University Press.

Kind, S. (2010). Art encounters: Movements in the visual arts and early childhood education. In V. Pacini-Ketchabaw (Ed.), *Flows, rhythms, and intensities of early childhood education curriculum.* New York, NY: Peter Lang.

Kind, S. (2018). Collective improvisations: The emergence of the early childhood studio as an event-full place. In C. Thompson & C. Schulte (Eds.), *Communities of practice: Art, play, and aesthetics in early childhood.* New York, NY: Springer.

Kind, S., Vintimilla, C. D., & Pacini-Ketchabaw, V. (in press). Material choreographies: Fabric as a living language of exchange. *Innovations* (September).

Korzybski, A. (1994). *Science and sanity* (5th ed.). Baltimore, MD: Institute of General Semantics.

Latour, B. (2004). Why has critique run out of steam? From matters of fact to matters of concern. *Critical Inquiry, 30*(2), 225–248.

Lesko, N. (2001). Time matters in adolescence. In K. Hultqvist & G. Dahlberg (Eds.), *Governing the child in the new millennium* (pp. 35–67). New York, NY: RoutledgeFalmer.

McKim, J., & Myers, N. (2017). Animating molecular life: An interview with Natasha Myers. *Animation: An Interdisciplinary Journal, 12*(3), 350–359.

Mori, K. (2003). Yarn. *Harvard Review, 24*, 134–140.

Pacini-Ketchabaw, V. (2011). Developmental theories and child and youth care. In A. Pence & J. White (Eds.), *New perspectives in child and youth care* (pp. 19–32). Vancouver, BC: UBC Press.

Pacini-Ketchabaw, V., Kind, S., & Kocher, L. (2017). *Encounters with materials in early education.* New York, NY: Routledge.

Pacini-Ketchabaw, V., Taylor, A., & Blaise, M. (2016). De-centring the human in multispecies ethnographies. In C. Taylor & C. Hughes (Eds.), *Posthuman research practices in education* (pp. 149–167). Basingstoke, UK: Palgrave Macmillan.

Piaget, J. (1928). *Judgment and reasoning in the child.* London, UK: Routledge & Kegan Paul.

Puig de la Bellacasa, M. (2010). Ethical doings in naturecultures. *Ethics, Place, and Environment, 13*(2), 151–169.

Puig de la Bellacasa, M. (2012). "Nothing comes without its world": Thinking with care. *The Sociological Review, 60*(2), 197–216.

Rinaldi, C. (2006). *In dialogue with Reggio Emilia: Listening, researching and learning.* New York, NY: Routledge.

Smith, M. K. (2012). What is pedagogy? *The encyclopaedia of informal education.* Retrieved from http://infed.org/mobi/what-is-pedagogy/

Stengers, I. (2000). *The invention of modern science* (D. W. Smith, Trans.). Minneapolis, MN: University of Minnesota Press.

Stengers, I. (2008). Experimenting with refrains: Subjectivity and the challenge of escaping modern dualism. *Subjectivity, 22*, 38–59.

Stengers, I. (2011). Relaying a war machine? In E. Alliez & A. Goffey (Eds.), *The Guattari effect* (pp. 134–155). London, UK: Continuum.

Stengers, I. (2013). Introductory notes on an ecology of practices. *Cultural Studies Review, 1*(1), 183–196.

Stengers, I. (2017, February 13). *Thinking with Isabelle Stengers* [video]. Kaaitheater. Retrieved from https://vimeo.com/204158683

Stengers, I. (2018). *Another science is possible: A manifesto for slow science.* Cambridge, UK: Polity Press.

Taylor, A. (2013). *Reconfiguring the natures of childhood.* London, UK: Routledge.

Taylor, A. (2017). Beyond stewardship: Common world pedagogies for the Anthropocene. *Environmental Education Research, 23*(10), 1448–1461.

Tsing, A. L. (2015). *The mushroom at the end of the world: On the possibility of life in capitalist ruins.* Princeton, NJ: Princeton University Press.

van Dooren, T. (2014). Care. *Environmental Humanities, 5*, 291–294.

CHAPTER 12

Empathy and Rubber Sushi Are Not Enough: How Disability Can Help Us Get to Social Justice

Kathryn Underwood

GUIDING QUESTIONS:

1. Compare and contrast the continuum of social justice theories for early childhood. Why is theory important for pedagogical practice? How can disabled childhoods help us to understand these theories?

2. Consider your own interactions with children. How might disability and disability studies inform your practice? How might the continuum of theory inform your practice?

Theories of equity and social justice are taken up regularly in texts on early childhood education and care. These theories are used not only to argue for the importance of starting education for social justice at an early age, but also because it is clear that young children are enacting the power relations that are part of our larger society. The ways in which disability is implicated in equity and social justice studies in early childhood are less well understood.

Disability and how, and even whether, to teach and care for disabled children is one of the most polarizing educational discussions of the last one hundred years and is implicated in most discussions of social justice in early education. On the one hand, intervention and rehabilitation of developmental conditions is taken up as a social justice aim by health and developmental theorists (Guralnick, 2011; Odom, Buysse, & Soukakou, 2011; Shonkoff & Phillips, 2000). On the other hand, there is recognition that health and developmental theory leave out the sociological implications of disability in educational settings, which is central to disability studies in education (Erevelles, 2005). In this chapter I will present several accounts of the history of social justice theory in early childhood studies and the practice of early childhood education and care. I will then use the example of disabled childhoods to make a case that this polarization may hinder a social justice agenda. I will argue that theories that seek a more just construction of the child are warranted, and that, truly, justice must recognize that development, learning, and even recognition of norms alongside deep understanding of social, political, and historical relationships are all part of practice for social justice and change.

SOCIAL JUSTICE THEORY ON A CONTINUUM

Theories aim to explain human action, beliefs, and organization. For many of us, theory is challenging to understand because it exists in the realm of ideas rather than in the practical. Yet theory in the social sciences is critical in informing almost all social activities. In early childhood studies, we have a long history of theory that has led to significant change in practice of early childhood education and care, and in many cases to criticism of how we understand children and how we interact with them. For these reasons, it is of value to understand the theory that informs the work of early childhood education and care.

Drawing on three well-known and recognized authors who have reviewed early childhood theory and shown that a continuum of theory exists (MacNaughton & Hughes, 2007; Pacini-Ketchabaw & Berikoff, 2008; Kumashiro, 2000), I argue that a continuum is evident in most arguments for social justice that move from interactions with individual children to systemic approaches to program and policy. The positioning of this continuum is sometimes taken up as moving from the least progressive to the most progressive. Later in this chapter, I will make a case for deep understanding of the need to recognize social justice aims and actions across the continuum and informed by a wide a range of paradigms. But first, I will introduce the continuum with a summary of social justice theory in early childhood.

Pacini-Ketchabaw and Berikoff (2008), in a study of children's negotiation of racial identity, propose that social justice in childhood must be understood in the context of theoretical interpretation. In their study, they examine identity and violence through two theoretical approaches: a developmental approach and a poststructural approach, with attention to how these theories are enacted in practice through multiculturalism and anti-bias approaches. Table 12.1 is adapted from Pacini-Ketchabaw and Berikoff, work by MacNaughton and Hughes (2007), and Kumashiro's theory of anti-oppressive practice in education (2000), along with my own interpretations of the historical continuum of theory in early childhood studies. This analysis is consistent with the broader theoretical literature on social justice in early childhood. The table shows the theoretical positions as they have evolved over the last approximately 150 years, with developmental theory and poststructuralism positioned as polarized opposites, which affects the type of practices educators take up. The practices are positioned in the table so that they can be compared beside each other.

MacNaughton and Hughes (2007) recognize a range of practices that are associated with social justice and equity in early childhood. They present these theories as a continuum that begins with practices at the individual level, where teachers are "fair" through equal treatment (laissez-faire). On the left side of the table, developmental approaches in education focus on individuals and their developmental trajectories of learning. This theoretical position leads to "treating children equally [with the belief that it] produces equity and respect; anyone can succeed if given the chance; and treating people differently creates or perpetuates differences between them" (MacNaughton & Hughes, 2007, p. 201). These authors note that this view of social justice as an individual experience does not recognize the unequal social relationships that exist in societies, built on colonialism. These approaches to understanding children's learning, sense of belonging, and self-actualization perpetuate inequity in their treatment of whole groups of people, including on the basis of disability, legal status (custodial, citizenship, etc.), and race and ethnicity. These approaches for individual intervention are commonly cited as key practices for equity in early childhood education and care, some examples of which are evident in table 12.1. These approaches have been criticized because the inequality that results from broad structural discrimination is only addressed through individual intervention.

At the individual level, inequality is recognized through special provisions. In this way differences are taken up only to define "need" of help

Table 12.1: Social Justice Theory

SITE OF EXPERIENCE	DEVELOPMENTAL THEORY		POSTSTRUCTURAL AND CRITICAL THEORIES	
	AIMS	PRACTICE	PRACTICE	AIMS
Teaching and Care	Each child is understood as an individual who is either achieving (as defined by standardized outcomes) or in need of intervention in order to support that child's achievement.	Recognizes difference in order to give special provision or to ameliorate barriers to learning for individual children and to keep children safe.	Teaching and curricula have express anti-discrimination (anti-colonial, anti-racist, feminist, anti-ableist) goals, but also recognize interdependence.	Anti-oppression approaches aim to use education to challenge privilege and to change society.
Learning	Interventions are with individuals with the goal of improving skills and knowledge so individuals have agency for themselves and others.	Developing of self-esteem and group identity as well as critical thinking, knowledge, and skills for success in society.	In anti-oppression approaches, teaching to those who are "othered" recognizes the context within which that learning takes place.	Recognizes that individuals are subject to historical factors and their experiences are broader than individual identities.
Relationships	Cultural understanding and cultural competence approach (multiculturalism and anti-bias approaches).	Exposure to a broad range of experiences and cultures to develop empathy and resolve conflict, as well as address stigma.	In anti-oppression approaches, teaching about the "other" includes recognition of privilege and the context within which groups are othered.	Make visible the structural ways in which racial, colonial, and power divisions are enacted.
Belonging	All children are treated fairly by treating them the same.	Create equal opportunity by recognizing individual differences.	Listening, responding, and challenging our own views of children, their families, and the people who work in early childhood settings.	Recognition of the political, historical, and active exclusion of groups of people in our society and on the land we occupy, in order to end the colonial practice of imposing our own view of which communities one should belong to.

Source: Adapted from Kumashiro, 2000; MacNaughton & Hughes, 2007; Pacini-Ketchabaw & Berikoff, 2008.

or support. "Children or groups regarded as outside the 'norm' must learn how to succeed within it, so we need special facilities to meet these children's 'special needs' and to teach them how to become more like 'the norm'" (MacNaughton & Hughes, 2007, p. 201). The idea of particular groups being in need leads to individual intervention to ameliorate difference. Additionally, from this theoretical position, social policy, including program and curriculum policy, may be used to target barriers to individual learning, in order to create equal opportunity. In this way, developmental approaches do recognize structural sites of discrimination and oppression, but they continue to measure social justice at the individual level. In practice, social policy change alone does not address the larger social injustices that are part of the lives of children, their families, and all of the actors in education environments. Similarly, curricula such as anti-bias or multicultural approaches teach about difference but are not designed to bring change within educational environments and are unlikely to shift broader social inequality.

Curriculum, which is a plan for what and how one will take up educational practice, is a critical site for social justice. This often happens through the goal of developing cultural understanding (MacNaughton & Hughes, 2007). This approach is now very common in practice, with a focus on teaching children to both recognize other cultures and empathize with them. In Canada it is common to see educators seek to infuse empathy for other people through early childhood curricula. One approach to developing empathy is exposing children to other cultures and experiences, which usually includes having objects or toys that represent different cultural groups, including food items such as toy sushi or flatbread in drama centres in early childhood education and care programs. These items, which represent "ethnic" food, are often presented with no context for learning about culture. The challenge with these curricula is that they often do not recognize that all children do not hold the same power in a society or in relationships and that empathy and culturally stereotypical objects without education about the power and privilege that is unequal amongst individuals may reinforce privilege. In other words, we need to move beyond empathy and rubber sushi if we are going to truly recognize social justice aims in early childhood education and care.

In contrast, table 12.1 shows a different set of educational and care goals informed by poststructural and critical theories. On the right side of the table, intervention for social justice is at the structural or societal level, with the intention of changing how colonialism, racism, and discrimination are enacted. All of the theorists presented in this chapter position these approaches as more progressive and more socially just.

Kevin Kumashiro's (2000, 2002) theory of anti-oppressive education is a seminal theory in education for social justice. Kumashiro's approach has been used to examine school-based disability oppression (Beckett, 2015), LGBTQ oppression (Kearns, Mitton-Kükner, & Tompkins, 2017), anti-racism education (Niemonen, 2007; St. Denis, 2007), and Indigenous education (St. Denis, 2007). Anti-oppression teaching addresses the nature of oppression and proposes four strategies to bring about change within the context of education: educating for the other; educating about the other; education that is critical of privileging; and education that changes students and society (Kumashiro, 2000). These four strategies can be divided into individual approaches (education for and about the other) and systemic approaches (education that is critical of privilege and that changes students and society).

The anti-oppression framework is premised on the notion of the "other." Kumashiro (2000) defines the "other" as "those groups that are traditionally marginalized in society, i.e. that are *other than* the norm, such as students of color, students from under- or unemployed families, students who are female, or male but not stereotypically 'masculine,' and students who are, or are perceived to be queer" (p. 26). Kumashiro recognizes that there are other forms of oppression worth considering in anti-oppression frameworks. Since Kumashiro's earlier writing we have seen broad social movements that have brought societal attention to the specificity of anti-black racism, trans discrimination, and colonial violence against Indigenous peoples (Nagaswa & Swadener, 2017). Additionally, there is growing focus on categories of disability and ableism in discourses around violence from state structures, for example around psychiatrizing perpetrators of violence. These discourses also often define the solutions to "othering" as individual intervention. What is valued about Kumashiro's theory is that it takes up anti-oppression work with the recognition of both the oppressed and privileged, and it includes both individual and structural intervention.

Similarly, MacNaughton (2006) and MacNaughton and Hughes (2007) propose anti-discrimination as a curricular approach that builds skills for young children to actually break down or challenge discrimination in their world. The anti-discrimination approach is proposed as a way to *go further*. The anti-discrimination approach recognizes the power between children and adults. "Power relations and ideologies create and sustain in-equities and injustices between children (and adults), so we must encourage children to build self-esteem, to challenge discrimination and to champion fairness and respect diversity" (MacNaughton, 2006, cited in MacNaughton & Hughes, 2007).

While theories of social justice and the practices in early childhood education and care are presented as situated on two sides of a theoretical divide, it may be more accurate to describe these theories as situated at two ends of a continuum. The prolific childhood studies scholar Peter Moss described the need to meet "across the paradigmatic divide" (2007). In this claim, Moss recognized that there are dominant ways in which we understand childhood in Western societies, which often exclude other ways of knowing. Moss recognizes that many theories of childhood, development, and professional practice are problematic because they see the child as a subject to be acted upon. Many theories have arisen from resistance to this construction of childhood, including the new scholarship of disabled children's childhood studies (Curran & Runswick-Cole, 2013; Runswick-Cole, Curran, & Liddiard, 2018).

The literature on social justice theory is thin on disability analysis. The continuum of social justice theory, from the developmental to the poststructural, provides particular challenges for educators and children, particularly as they are "embedded, active, and constituted in the concerting of people's activities with each other" (Smith, 1999, p. 97). The challenge is that theory at both ends of the continuum and along the continuum informs the practices of professionals, institutions, and social relationships in ways that are deeply integrated into the lives of young disabled children. For this reason, theory is particularly salient in the activities that organize the ways in which young disabled children are engaged with in early childhood education and care.

DISABILITY IN EARLY CHILDHOOD EDUCATION AND CARE

Disability studies began as a critique of dominant models of understanding disability as an individual trait defined through medicine as biological, cognitive, or physical impairment (Oliver, 1996). This dominant understanding of disability is referred to as a medical or individual model and focuses on identification of impairment, and then intervention or treatment of that impairment at the individual level. These responses or treatments might be rehabilitation, charity, or special education, and they are informed by developmental theory. This pattern is evident in our early childhood education and care systems when we identify children, sometimes even before they are born, as having impairment and we seek to "fix them" (Underwood, Church, & van Rhijn, in press). This approach again is evident in the individual curricular approaches to self-actualization and teaching and learning that are presented in table 12.1.

Alternately, social models of disability, informed by poststructural theory, recognize that practices that seek to fix or assimilate are flawed and seek to instead address the attitudinal, physical, and social barriers that "disable" people. Many researchers, educators, and activists continue to define inclusion as educating disabled (or special needs) students in a regular classroom, alongside typically developing peers. This definition sets up a binary between those with disabilities and those without. In early childhood inclusion practices, this is done by seeking placement of all students in what are called "regular" classrooms or programs. The intention here is to ensure that students access the "regular" curriculum and that their presence will break down ableist attitudes of peers. Anat Greenstein (2015) calls for "social and political thinking that rejects binaries and views all people, of all embodiments, as incomplete and constantly in the process of becoming through engaging in relations with the world around them" (p. 18). In this more "radical" theory of inclusion, educators are interested not just in where children are learning (placement in a particular program), but in what it means to learn and the power that is held through the many relationships that take place in early childhood settings.

Teaching and Care

Everyone has the capacity to learn, but capabilities may or may not already be realized in the present. Capabilities are therefore the future potential that an individual has. Early childhood education and care that is grounded in social justice aims recognizes that everyone is unique in their capabilities and that the differences in capabilities are a result of individual genetic and biological factors (developmental) but also the social factors that affect human development, such as income, family structure, and access to education (poststructural) (Reindal, 2010; Sen, 1999; Terzi, 2005a, 2005b; Underwood, Valeo, & Wood, 2012). This recognition of the power embedded in our social relationships, if it is to truly take up larger social injustices, will focus practice not just for individual children, but by seeking to understand how our institutional practices shape these power relationships. This includes recognizing the long history and ongoing institutionalization of disabled people and the many forms of ableist discrimination that are ongoing in our society.

In Canada, our early childhood education and care system includes services that are supposed to serve all children, such as child care, family support and early years centres, and kindergarten. We also have a large range of early intervention services that are targeted to support the development and learning of specific children, such as therapeutic early intervention services (speech, occupational, physical, mental health, and behaviour therapy) and programs designed for specific social groups, such as Aboriginal Head Start (Underwood, 2012; Underwood, Church, & van Rhijn, in press). These specialist programs recognize that universal early childhood programs are not, in fact, designed for everyone. The question is whether these targeted approaches are more just.

Underwood, Valeo, and Wood (2012) have articulated the tension that arises in early childhood between valuing difference and ensuring access to early childhood education, care, and intervention that simultaneously support individual development and do not reinforce existing privilege. Similarly, Snoddon and Underwood (2013), in their examination of what inclusion means for deaf learners, have articulated the importance of recognizing a broad range of differences that are both individual, cultural, and contextual in how human capabilities are expressed over the life course. In both cases, these authors point out the critical learning that is possible in the early years, while recognizing the risk of social exclusion when focusing on a narrow definition of development.

Radical inclusive pedagogy is one approach that aims to address these tensions (Greenstein, 2015) between individual interests in accessing knowledge and normative curricula, with the power and privilege that is responsible for the creation of norms and the valuing of particular knowledges. Capabilities are realized both through enacting knowledge and curricular expectations but also as the future potential to know and learn. In our education system we continuously treat children with disabilities as lacking capacity. This is sometimes articulated through concepts such as learning styles that explain differences in ability but maintain the idea that abilities are fixed. This has led to ableism grounded in under-estimating people's capabilities, or low expectations. This is commonly the case with particular areas of study that are thought of as fixed fields of knowledge, such as mathematics, science, and reading and writing.

An example to illustrate this point is found in research from the 1980s by psychologist Keith Stanovich. Stanovich (1986) coined the term *the Matthew Principle* to describe a phenomenon he observed through research: the more a student excels at reading, the more opportunities that student is given to read. Conversely, the worse a student's reading skills are, the fewer opportunities they get to read. This means that, because of practice opportunities, there is a very short time period before the gap between students grows. An example in more recent times is the idea of learning styles. A learning style for a poor reader may appear different from the learning style for an advanced reader, but in fact, what we may be identifying is a difference in skills. So, a poor reader will be identified as having a learning style that does not include print material. Young children in this context start to learn early that the things they do not know how to do are things that they do not like. But what if, instead of using learning styles as labels or "categories of conditionality" (Slee, 1996), we recognized that there are many differences in what and how children learn, but at the heart of education, there is learning and development for all children? Ultimately, there is a social justice aim in identifying education practices that support learning and development for all children. What is missing from this discourse on teaching for disability justice is a comprehensive curriculum for teaching about disability discrimination. Most of the curricula that are described in the broad social justice literature are limited to teaching about accommodation of people with disabilities but not the ongoing and historical systematic exclusion of disabled people.

Learning

> The need to use labels as legitimization and explanation to the self and to other is not inherent to a "condition," but is exercised against a backdrop of a cultural discourse of normalcy or compulsory "able-bodiedness." This is a cultural discourse which assumes in advance that we all agree: able-bodied identities, able-bodied perspectives are preferable and what we all, collectively, are aiming for. (Greenstein, 2015, p. 25)

Critiques of developmental theory are particularly salient for disabled children, who are poorly represented in norm-referenced theories of development and learning. While all children develop and learn, the pace, outcomes, and ways in which human development is experienced are often measured using normative frameworks that define who is at the centre and who is an outlier.

Ultimately, normal is not a neutral category but one that is created through medical constructions of human development. Human development exists, but how it happens is unique to each individual. In order to undo the binaries that Greenstein talks about in the quote above, we need to understand how "normal" gets constructed in early childhood settings.

Differences in development are often constructed in the process of diagnosing or designating a child as disabled. This process serves an institutional function because often the diagnosis or designation is necessary for children to qualify for service provision. The reality of this situation is that professionals are given the power to determine which bodies are disabled. Disability is then a set of socially constructed categories that are deemed special because the central institutions of our society are not designed for these children in the first place.

Many studies have shown that special placements or programs, as compared to inclusive placements, are less effective developmentally for children with disability and non-normative developmental trajectories in early childhood education, care, and intervention (Dempsey & Keen, 2008; Dunst & Dempsey, 2009; Dunst, Trivette, & Hamby, 2007; Guralnick, 2011).

Education is about learning. The question is what and how much you need to learn to be "educated." As Greenstein (2015) argues, "a too-narrow definition of knowledge, which focuses heavily on language and rational thinking, fails many dis-abled students who might engage with the world in other ways" (p. 95). The continuum of theories as described in table 12.1 positions a normative developmental framework as less progressive. However, when children are engaged in defining what makes early educational experiences inclusive, they want to learn (Biklen & Burke, 2006; Comber & Kamler, 2004; Nutbrown & Clough, 2009). They do not want to be viewed as incapable, or needing help, but they do want to access the knowledge and skills that are being taught in schools and that are the norm in their schools.

Capabilities are the realization of that which one values (Sen, 1999). In the context of early childhood education and care, we need to recognize that values are constructed in the context of privilege as well as in the context of our communities. Where nations have been colonized there is a tension between valuing access into the dominant culture (assimilation) or preservation of one's own culture, and for Indigenous communities in Canada this is articulated as having ownership and control (Truth and Reconciliation Commission of Canada, 2015). Early identification and intervention that recognizes the right of families and children to both assimilate into the broad society in which they live and also preserve their identities will also recognize the need for families and children to have ownership and control over the goals embedded in early intervention. One of the reasons that developmental psychology has been so maligned is the normative frameworks that are used to identify which components of child development are most important and which ones should be "targeted" for intervention.

Relationships

Learning and development, however, cannot be disconnected from the relationships in educational settings, with peers and adults. Education should be "understood as a unique and relational *process* that supports students in constructing their subjectivities and becoming part of society, [rather than] an end *product* that needs to be effectively manufactured and sold" (Greenstein, 2015, p. 81). It is through that process that we learn, but the process of learning is also connected to places of learning, processes of socialization, and students' sense of belonging (which will be taken up in the next section).

Goodley, Runswick-Cole, and Liddiard (2015) describe the normative ways we construct human development (as well as family and sexuality), which they say is a central human activity. This normative construction can deny disabled children the vision of a very human life. At the heart of their argument is that development, family, and sexuality are part of humanity and therefore are part of what we must envision for disabled children. Through recognition of disability as a very real identity, we can see that resistance to normalization is important at the same time as recognizing there will be some kind of norm set up in the relationships children have in community. Goodley and colleagues say that central to being included as a human being are "being respected and recognized, valuing autonomy and competence, acknowledging the essential qualities of a person alongside the disruptive potential of disability to reconfigure ways of being" (Goodley et al., 2015, p. 781). Belonging to humanity and community is central to understanding equity, alongside learning and development, in the early years.

One way to understand differences in development is by recognizing the many contexts within which human development is experienced. These include the contexts of political, social, and economic freedoms, as well as specific environmental, relational, social, and familial differences (Sen, 1999; Underwood, Valeo, & Wood, 2012). In addition to shaping differences in how individuals develop, these contexts also affect the values individuals hold, which is important in recognizing that each individual may have many capabilities but not all of those capabilities are valued by the child. If the context allows for the capabilities that one values to be realized as functional skills or abilities, we can say that the child has freedom (Sen, 1999). Further, while our institutions construct developmental difference as a risk, it is also part of human identity. Material equality, which may arise from skills-based learning, does not lead to social and relational equality. Social and relational equality are connected to the ways in which people treat each other and to the skills people have to engage in social relationships. These social relationships may include finding community and social connections amongst other people with disabilities and shared differences.

Belonging

In addition to learning, early childhood education and care settings are sites of social development and an entry point into the larger society. Because early childhood education and care programs are often not inclusive of the services that best support disabled children's development, their belonging to the social group in these settings is compromised. As an example, Snoddon and Underwood (2013) note that deaf children lack access to signed language instruction in ECEC settings, which hinders their learning and also their social belonging within Deaf communities. So learning and belonging are interconnected.

In early childhood education and care programs, the physical and emotional care associated with toileting, feeding, dressing, and sleep are entwined with the care that is part of human relationships and belonging. In both the physical care and the care of belonging, "caregiver and care recipient are loaded with meanings of powerful and powerless" (Phillips, 2007, p. 15, cited in Wood, 2015). In this context, the interdependence of all human relationships is juxtaposed with the dependent care associated with disability (Wood, 2015). The physical care of disabled children is often used to exclude, as when children are required to be toilet-trained to participate in a program. But also, emotional care is normative, with children who have "behaviour" problems being regularly excluded from early childhood programs. Both childhood and disability are human categories associated with dependence. However, "normal" childhoods are often defined as a state of becoming self-actualized and independent, while disabled childhoods are defined as needing special supports and in a perpetual state of dependence. The fact that early childhood environments are not designed for independent participation on the part of disabled children, or to recognize the inherent interdependence of the human condition, calls for a more nuanced recognition of how anti-oppression efforts should be taken up at the individual level.

If we can instead recognize that *all* children are inter-dependent, with each other and with the adults who care for them, and design our early childhood education and care programs to expect differences in the type of care each child will need, we can then begin to recognize that identity formation and group belonging are at the heart of participation. In our understanding of care, we must also take up intersectional identities. For disabled students, there may be many communities with whom they share a sense of belonging. In schools, we segregate on the basis of disability, in ways that we never would for other social groups. This leads us to consider, in special education settings, which identities are being constrained and which social relationships are we denying students? For other social groups, the choice to congregate for educational purposes has been one way of reclaiming educational space, for example in Africentric schools or First Nations schools. But these kinds of spaces have also been created to entrench privilege, as in gifted programs and alternative schools (Parekh, Brown, & Conley, 2016).

How do we address the need for students to find community, and how do educational institutions ensure that students have the right to congregate for cultural, social, and political activities? Annamma, Connor, and Ferri (2013) describe the disability movement's parallels with racial groups who initially were congregated through racial apartheid and then self-congregated for political purposes, and who, through these movements, began to form re-imagined cultural, social, and political identities. Segregated schools have also been the site of cultural, social, and political action. Depending on the school, these movements have sometimes been centred on the mothers and other family members who fought for their children. In other cases, as with the Deaf community, cultural production in these schools has been central to the identity of the group (Murray, Snoddon, de Meulder, & Underwood, 2018). For all young children, while inclusive practice can support developing normative skills for participation in the community, economy, and family, it can also hinder participation in a disability community.

Inclusive education needs to recognize that belonging is not just about social participation in one's classroom, but also belonging to multiple identity groups at the same time. Belonging is about finding places where one feels like oneself, but also having the acceptance that comes from regular participation in the social institutions that hold power in a society. Baglieri and colleagues (2011) note that "in most instances, all of us self-regulate (and therefore self-normalize) in the pursuit of social acceptance" (p. 2127). As Nutbrown and Clough (2009) found, "identity and self-esteem are the two most important issues to be addressed though curriculum and early years pedagogy if children are to successfully experience a sense of inclusivity and belonging in their early years settings" (p. 202). It is therefore critical to recognize the many types of belonging that young children seek and value.

DISCUSSION

Disability identity is intertwined with institutional process at the site of diagnosis and documentation. This is unique to disability. It is not that other identities are not taken up or defined in educational settings, but no other social category is more connected to institutional documentation. For young disabled children, their development is the site of both identity and control by social and political structures. What this means is that in critical theory and practice with social justice aims, if human development is relegated to the low end of the social justice continuum, then children with disabilities can be pushed out of the social justice conversation. Their identity and the practices associated with their identity become practices that are named racist, colonial, and oppressive. And ironically, the practices associated with teaching disabled children are also used to enact racial and class discrimination, with much higher rates of poor racialized students in segregated programs. In order to consider how disability is taken up at the systemic level in education, we can look at the legislation that seeks to make our social institutions more equitable. Both human rights and accessibility legislation are examples of this approach to changing structural inequality.

The UN Convention on the Rights of Persons with Disabilities (CRPD) (2006) identifies the right to be included in education. This right is mirrored in national and local human rights legislation in many countries, including in Ontario, where the right to be included is protected by the Human Rights Code, which outlines the "duty to accommodate." At the same time, the CRPD identifies the right to early intervention. This right is listed as a right under "health," not education, but it is the only reference to early childhood in the CRPD. In practice, this means that many early childhood education and care programs do not recognize that intervention is, in fact, part of the educational process for young disabled children. In fact, oddly, education that is effective for young children with disabilities is often classified as early intervention, but it may be better understood to be education.

Byrne notes that a human rights framework can both support and hinder an inclusion agenda when the language is unclear and when it situates disabled children within a deficit-based "special needs" framework (2013, p. 233). Byrne further criticizes approaches that simply aim to integrate disabled students into a world/institution that is not designed with them in mind and that reinforces an individual-deficit approach. Inclusion is a right, but assimilation and accommodation that do not value disabled people as human beings with capabilities is not justice. Capabilities in this context include learning of skills that may not be evident competencies if we see disabled students through a deficit lens. Capabilities also include intersectional identities, belonging, and relationships with educators, peers, family, and the multiple communities with whom an individual or group belongs. We must also not forget that these communities of belonging can include disability communities.

While, in the province of Ontario, the Human Rights Code clearly protects disabled people from exclusion and favours inclusion in early childhood education and care, forcing professionals to comply through legislation can lead to a superficial form of inclusion. Institutions may be able to show that they are doing what they are told to, but they may not, in fact, be engaging in a true relationship with children and their families, something that is recognizable as care. This tension is the difference between compliance and care. Byrne says, "Not only do children with disabilities have a right to receive an education without discrimination on the grounds of disability and to express their views on educational matters affecting them, but to be provided with assistance to ensure that access to education is 'effective'" (2013, p. 235).

It is useful to consider the limitations as well as the power of legislation. The power of legislation is in its ability to use the courts as a mechanism to force institutions to do things. However, there are limitations to the efficacy of legislating equity. In particular, it is necessary to engage with development and individual-level intervention if we are to include disability as a valued identity. I would argue that the degree to which disability as a construct is entrenched in early childhood education and care means that an understanding of disability is at the heart of social justice practice. This type of justice will require curriculum and teaching that embrace disability as an identity that is grounded in pride, not "need" and special services. It will also mean that social justice theorists start to include the historical and systematic oppression of disabled people in their analyses of social justice education and education for social justice.

CONCLUSION

Given the goal of this text as a reader for students who are learning to be educators, the chapter takes up the question *what is the role of early childhood educators in social justice practice?* This question leads us to other questions that have been raised by theorists and educators, such as: Who is social justice education for? Can educators teach about experiences and social positions that they do not embody themselves? Can or should educators aim to equalize opportunity from within their programs? These questions are taken up in the work of scholars examining disability, race, gender, sexuality, poverty, and class. Drawing on these scholars, we can see a continuum of theoretical positions for understanding equity. At one end of the continuum are individual approaches with a focus on human difference as the underlying cause of differences in human development, capability, and oppression through socially constructed order. At the other end of the continuum is the broader systemic-level context for anti-oppression and the possibilities for early childhood education and care to catalyze meaningful social change.

In the documents that are used to plan education for children with disabilities (i.e., individual program plans, individual education plans, and the report card), there are no provisions to ensure disabled children are valued. Further, none of the legislation ensures the right to learn in addition to being free from discrimination. Because education settings, including early childhood education and care, have as their core purpose development and learning, and because children with disabilities are defined by their non-normative development and learning, they are at great individual risk within institutions. For this reason, understanding both developmental and post-structural theories of social justice is critical for engaging in education practice that takes disabled childhoods into account.

In the social justice theories presented in this chapter, the individual and developmental theorists are positioned as furthest on the continuum from anti-oppressive, anti-colonial, and anti-racist approaches. Recognizing disabled childhoods illustrates that it is socially just to ensure that learning and development are recognized as both possible and ultimately a right of all children, including those who are disabled. However, this call for recognition of developmental approaches does not preclude recognizing the relational aspects of learning and the right of young children and their families to belong to a society and to multiple identity groups. Ultimately, I argue that all of these approaches must be taken up simultaneously if we are to achieve socially just early childhood education and care programs.

REFERENCES

Annamma, S. A., Connor, D., & Ferri, B. (2013). Dis/ability critical race studies (DisCrit): Theorizing at the intersections of race and dis/ability, *Race Ethnicity and Education, 16*(1), 1–31.

Baglieri, S., Bejoina, L. M., Broderick, A. A., Connor, D. J., & Valle, J. (2011). [Re] claiming "inclusive education" toward cohesion in educational reform: Disability studies unravels the myth of the normal child. *Teachers College Record, 113*(10), 2122–2154.

Beckett, A. E. (2015). Anti-oppressive pedagogy and disability: Possibilities and challenges. *Scandinavian Journal of Disability Research, 17*(1), 76–94.

Biklen, D., & J. Burke (2006). Presuming competence. *Equity and Excellence in Education, 39*, 166–175.

Byrne, B. (2013). Hidden contradictions and conditionality: Conceptualisations of inclusive education in international human rights law. *Disability & Society, 28*(2), 232–244.

Comber, B., & Kamler, B. (2004). Getting out of deficit: Pedagogies of reconnection. *Teaching Education, 15*(3), 293–310.

Curran, T., & Runswick-Cole., K. (Eds.). (2013). *Disabled children's childhood studies: Critical approaches in a global context.* UK: Palgrave-MacMillan.

Dempsey, I., & Keen, D. (2008). A review of processes and outcomes in family-centered services for children with a disability. *Topics in Early Childhood Special Education, 28*(1), 42–52.

Dunst, C. J., & Dempsey, I. (2009). Family–professional partnerships and parenting competence, confidence and enjoyment. *International Journal of Disability, Development, and Education, 54*(3), 305–318.

Dunst, C. J., Trivette, C. M., & Hamby, D. W. (2007). Meta-analysis of family-centered help giving practices research. *Mental Retardation and Developmental Disabilities Research Reviews, 13*, 370–378.

Erevelles, N. (2005). Understanding curriculum as normalizing text: Disability studies meet curriculum theory. *Journal of Curriculum Studies, 37*(4), 421–439.

Goodley, D., Runswick-Cole, K., & Liddiard, K. (2015). The DisHuman child. *Discourse: Studies in the cultural politics of education, 37*(5), 770–784.

Greenstein, A. (2015). *Radical inclusive education: Disability, teaching and struggles for liberation.* New York, NY: Routledge.

Guralnick, M. J. (2011). Why early intervention works: A systems perspective. *Infants & Young Children, 24,* 6–28.

Kearns, L., Mitton-Kükner, J., & Tompkins, J. (2017). Transphobia and cis-gender privilege: Pre-service teachers recognizing and challenging gender rigidity in schools. *Canadian Journal of Education, 40*(1).

Kliewer, C., Biklen, D., & Kasa-Hendrickson, C. (2006). Who may be literate? Disability and resistance to the cultural denial of competence. *American Educational Research Journal, 43*(2), 163–192.

Kumashiro, K. K. (2000). Toward a theory of anti-oppressive education. *Review of Educational Research, 70*(1), 25–54.

Kumashiro, K. K. (2002). *Troubling education: Queer activism and antioppressive pedagogy.* New York, NY: RoutledgeFalmer.

MacNaughton, G. (2006). *Respect for diversity: An international overview.* Bernard van Leer Foundation: The Hague.

MacNaughton, G., & Hughes, P. (2007). Teaching respect for cultural diversity in Australian early childhood programs: A challenge for professional learning. *Journal of Early Childhood Research, 5*(2), 189–204.

Moss, P. (2007). Meetings across the paradigmatic divide. *Educational Philosophy and Theory, 39*(3), 229–245.

Murray, J., Snoddon, K., de Meulder, M., & Underwood, K. (2018). Intersectional inclusion for deaf learners: Moving beyond general comment no. 4 on article 24 of the UNCRPD. *International Journal of Inclusive Education.* Retrieved from https://doi.org/10.1080/13603116.2018.1482013

Nagaswa, M. K., & Swadener, B. B. (2017). Be/longing: Reciprocal mentoring, pedagogies of place, and critical childhood studies in the time of Trump. *Global Studies of Childhood, 7*(2), 207–221.

Niemonen, J. (2007). Antiracist education in theory and practice: A critical assessment. *The American Sociologist, 38*(2), 159–177.

Nutbrown, C., & Clough, P. (2009). Citizenship and inclusion in the early years: Understanding and responding to children's perspectives on "belonging." *International Journal of Early Years Education, 17*(3), 191–206.

Odom, S. L., Buysse, V., & Soukakou, E. (2011). Inclusion for young children with disabilities: A quarter century of research perspectives. *Journal of Early Intervention, 33*(4), 344–356.

Oliver, M. (1996). *Understanding disability: From theory to practice.* Basingstoke, UK: MacMillan.

Pacini-Ketchabaw, V., & Berikoff, A. (2008). The politics of difference and diversity: From young children's violence to creative power expressions. *Contemporary Issues in Early Childhood, 9*(3), 256–264.

Parekh, G., Brown, R. S., & Conley, C. (2016). *Institutional racism and classism enacted through special education programming: An exploratory study of the Toronto District School Board's Home School Program.* Presented at the Toronto District School Board's Structured Pathways Conference, Toronto, ON.

Parekh, G., & Underwood, K. (2015). *Inclusion: Creating school and classroom communities where everyone belongs. Research, tips, and tools for educators and administrators.* (Research Report No. 15/16-09). Toronto, ON: Toronto District School Board.

Phillips, J. (2007). Changing gendered notions of care: Is caring still a feminist issue? In *Care* (pp. 73–89). Cambridge, UK: Polity Press.

Reindal, S. M. (2010). What is the purpose? Reflections on inclusion and special education from a capability perspective. *European Journal of Special Needs Education, 25,* 1–12.

Runswick-Cole, K., Curran, T., & Liddiard, K. (Eds.). (2018). *Handbook of disabled children's childhood studies: Building understandings.* UK: Palgrave-MacMillan.

Sen, A. (1999). *Development as freedom.* Oxford, UK: Oxford University Press.

Shonkoff, J. P., & Phillips, D. A. (Eds.). (2000). *From neurons to neighbourhoods: The science of early child development.* Washington, DC: National Academy Press.

Slee, R. (1996). Clauses of conditionality: the "reasonable" accommodation of language. In L. Barton (Ed.), *Disability and society: Emerging issues and insights.* London, UK: Longman.

Smith, D. (1999). *Writing the social: Critique, theory, and investigations.* Toronto, ON: University of Toronto Press.

Snoddon, K., & Underwood, K. (2013). Toward a social relational model of deaf childhood. *Disability & Society, 29*(4), 530–542.

Stanovich, K. E. (1986). Matthew effects in reading: Some consequences of individual differences in the acquisition of literacy. *Reading Research Quarterly, 22,* 360–407.

St. Denis, V. (2007). Aboriginal education and anti-racist education: Building alliance across cultural and racial identity. *Canadian Journal of Education, 30*(4), 1068–1092.

Terzi, L. (2005a). A capability perspective on impairment, disability and special needs: Towards social justice in education. *Theory and Research in Education, 3,* 197–223.

Terzi, L. (2005b). Beyond the dilemma of difference: The capability approach to disability and special education needs. *Journal of Philosophy of Education, 39,* 443–459.

Truth and Reconciliation Commission of Canada. (2015). *Honouring the truth, reconciling for the future: Summary of the final report of the Truth and Reconciliation Commission of Canada.* Retrieved from www.trc.ca

Underwood, K. (2008). *The construction of disability in our schools: Teacher and parent perspectives on the experience of labelled students.* Rotterdam, Netherlands: Sense.

Underwood, K. (2012). Mapping the early intervention system in Ontario, Canada. *International Journal of Special Education, 27*(2), 126–135.

Underwood, K., Church, K., & van Rhijn, T. (in press). Responsible for normal: The contradictory work of families. In S. Winton, Carpenter, & G. Parekh (Eds.), *Critical perspectives on education policy and schools, families and communities.* Charlotte, NC: Information Age.

Underwood, K., Valeo, A., & Wood, R. (2012). Understanding inclusive early childhood education: A capability approach. *Contemporary Issues in Early Childhood, 13*(4), 290–299.

United Nations. (2006). *Convention on the rights of persons with disabilities.* Retrieved from http://www.un.org/disabilities/convention/conventionfull.shtml

Vibert, A. B., Portelli, J. P., Shields, C., & Laroque, L. (2002). Critical practice in elementary schools: Voice, community, and a curriculum of life. *Journal of Educational Change, 3,* 93–116.

Viruru, R. (2005). The impact of postcolonial theory on early childhood education. *Journal of Education, 35*(1), 7–29.

Wood, R. (2015). To be cared for and to care: Understanding theoretical conceptions of care as a framework for effective inclusion in early childhood education and care. *Child Care in Practice, 21*(3), 256–265.

CHAPTER 13

Nurturing the Seeds of Indigenous Early Learning and Child Care in Canada

Jessica Ball

GUIDING QUESTIONS:

1. What progress has been made in establishing and supporting Indigenous early learning and child care in Canada, and what are the associated strengths and challenges?
2. How can knowing the historical context of Indigenous families in Canada inform your work with First Nations, Métis, or Inuit children you may work with in your practice?
3. What can you do to encourage Indigenous perspectives on early learning and child care?

LANDSCAPES OF INDIGENOUS CHILDHOOD IN CANADA

We in Canada live in a land of Indigenous inspiration. Inuit, First Nations, and Métis cultural traditions support strong extended families as the foundation of survival, growth, and development of children, communities, and intergovernment relations (Anderson & Ball, 2019). Recognition of oneness with the natural world has been taken as axiomatic for millennia, as has the need to nurture the spirit of each child through ritual and everyday practices of connection with family and the land (Greenwood, 2006).

We in Canada also live in a land of Indigenous[1] aspirations for children. As the century of residential schools drew to a close in 1986 (Milloy, 1999), First Nations, Inuit, and Métis peoples envisioned the dawn of a new day for a turnaround generation: children and young people who are proud of their culture, skilled in the ways of their people, and ready to succeed in education, work, family, and social participation (Blackstock, Prakash, Loxley, & Wien, 2005). This vision has been accompanied by a sustained call for investments in Indigenous early learning and child care (IELCC/ECCD)[2] (Royal Commission on Aboriginal Peoples, 1996; Truth and Reconciliation Commission of Canada, 2015). In 1996, the Royal Commission on Aboriginal Peoples recommended that

> federal, provincial, and territorial governments co-operate to support an integrated early childhood funding strategy that (a) extends early childhood education to all Aboriginal children regardless of residence; (b) encourages programs that foster the physical, social, intellectual and spiritual development of children, reducing distinctions between child care, prevention and education; (c) maximizes Aboriginal control over service design and administration; (d) offers one-stop accessible funding; and (e) promotes parental involvement and choice in early childhood education options. (Vol. 3, pp. 422–423)

Since the early 1990s, many Indigenous communities have created early childhood programs with the goal of supporting the vigorous growth of children "from seed to cedar" (British Columbia Aboriginal Child Care Society, 2017) and of fortifying their family and community ecologies. But seedlings struggle to thrive in soil that provides insufficient nourishment. Across the country, community-based IELCC initiatives are dogged by deficits in some of the key ingredients for flourishing: fully qualified personnel, adequate facilities and learning resources, sustained funding for salaries and facilities maintenance, and working links with relevant programs and sectors.

Over many years of participating as a non-Indigenous ally[3] in the growing movement to develop a robust system of comprehensive early childhood services for Indigenous children, I have been both inspired and dismayed. In this chapter, I reflect on what I have seen of the landscape for IELCC in

Canada, including conditions for children that continue to produce and amplify their vulnerability,[4] as well as promising practices[5] that draw on Indigenous cultural values of holism and connection. I highlight key challenges that persistently jeopardize IELCC efforts in communities, and I outline ways that governments at all levels could nurture the seeds of Indigenous renewal. I argue that a comprehensive national IELCC strategy can be an organizing framework for delivering on promises made by provincial, territorial, and federal governments[6] and called for by the Truth and Reconciliation Commission of Canada (TRC) to ensure equity of opportunities for Indigenous children to experience development outcomes and quality of life comparable to non-Indigenous children.

Reconciliation with Indigenous peoples will never be more than empty words without universal access by Indigenous children to high-quality early childhood care and development programs. These programs must be based on local cultural understandings, goals, and practices and afford opportunities to learn one's heritage language. They must involve local community self-determination[7] as one means toward cultural safety, cultural continuity, and decolonization in education, health, and child and family services. Community-led programs must be supported by sustained government funding that allows for varying local resources and for access to meaningful training for early childhood educators and for specialists across a range of services to ensure quality and timely intervention.

A DEPLETED FOUNDATION CANNOT SUPPORT GROWTH

In Canada, massive, recurring colonial government assaults on Indigenous Peoples have shaken the foundations of Indigenous child, family, and community wellness. Since contact, programs to deplete the very soil that sustains Indigenous peoples have included engineered epidemics, appropriation of land, suppression of hunting rights and cultural expression, the reservation system, residential schools, forced removals of children for adoption, and government failure to fulfill its responsibilities, resulting in ongoing deprivations and indignities (Milloy, 1999; Pettipas, 1994; Truth and Reconciliation Commission of Canada, 2015). Many Indigenous children live in the shadow of these colonial legacies and experience their devastating sequelae in every aspect of life. Although some conditions for First Nations, Métis, and

Inuit children have been improving, significant gaps remain in nearly every domain, affecting opportunities for equity, dignity, and quality of life for Indigenous children (First Nations Information Governance Centre, 2012).

Some Indigenous children in Canada are thriving. However, demographic and health statistics show that, as a population, First Nations, Inuit, and Métis children face serious health and social disparities compared to their non-Indigenous counterparts. They are far more likely to live in poverty than non-Indigenous children.[8] Based on data gathered in 2016 by Statistics Canada, one in two First Nations children living on reserves live in poverty, as do 22 to 32 percent of other Indigenous children (Macdonald & Wilson, 2016). Poverty is associated with many conditions that produce wellness deficits and are common in Indigenous communities. For example, Indigenous children are far more likely than non-Indigenous children to live in overcrowded, deteriorated homes with high levels of indoor air pollution, lack of access to clean water[9] and to fresh fruits and vegetables, lack of stimulation, and exposure to maternal depression and domestic violence. They are less likely than non-Indigenous children to participate in any type of early learning or child care program[10] or to receive timely access to health care for early childhood illnesses and clinical ancillary services for development disorders. Young Indigenous children are much more likely than non-Indigenous children to die before their first birthday, most often due to respiratory disease (Kovesi, 2012); develop obesity and diabetes during childhood; and suffer dental decay, hearing loss, and chronic respiratory diseases, particularly tuberculosis, asthma, and respiratory tract infections (Irvine, Kitty, & Pekeles, 2012).[11] A disproportionate number of Indigenous children start school with hearing loss, speech and language delays and disorders, tooth decay, and cognitive, behavioural, and emotional problems (First Nations Information Governance Centre, 2012). Indigenous children are more likely to repeat a grade in primary school, leave school without completing a diploma, have a child of their own during adolescence, and raise their own children while being unemployed and living in poverty. These findings are compounded by other factors, including the negative impacts of residential schools on parenting, cultural vitality, and community wellness. Almost half of First Nations children living on reserves live with a lone parent.[12] Almost half of all children in foster care in Canada are Indigenous, including 4,300 Indigenous children under four years old (Statistics Canada, 2017b). Former Indigenous Services Minister Jane Philpott cites poverty as the main driver behind the disproportionate number of Indigenous children in the child welfare system, which she describes as a "humanitarian crisis" in Canada (as cited in Barrera, 2017).[13]

These environmental conditions and early health and developmental problems are antecedents of chronic disease, mental health and addiction problems, inability to participate fully in work and social life, and multigenerational parenting challenges. The costs of these long-term outcomes far exceed the costs of implementing a national strategy for IELCC that brings sectors together to address outstanding needs.

Leaders of First Nations, Inuit, and Métis organizations have all called upon every sector and level of government to contribute to restoring the foundations for dignity, wellness, and prosperity of Indigenous children. Comprehensive early childhood services, including early learning and child care programs, are a prominent component of this agenda. The board president of the British Columbia Aboriginal Child Care Society, Mary Teegee, has declared the following:

> We call upon the federal, provincial, territorial, and First Nations governments to make young Aboriginal children and early childhood development, education and care a priority in any reconciliation agenda. The destructive impacts of residential schools have been felt through generations and contribute to the gap in wellness and quality of life between Aboriginal peoples and other Canadians. By providing high quality, culturally relevant early childhood education for our children we can help to limit the impacts of Canada's Residential School legacy in the youngest generation. (British Columbia Aboriginal Child Care Society, 2015, para. 2)

There is little doubt that high-quality early childhood programs can contribute significantly to children's wellness and long-term outcomes, especially for disadvantaged children (Heckman, 2006; Irwin, Siddiqui, & Hertzman, 2007; World Health Organization, 2007). Poverty reduction and a robust system of IELCC that brings sectors together are arguably among the highest priorities for federal, provincial, and territorial governments to support the flourishing of Canada's youngest Indigenous citizens.

FORTIFYING THE FOUNDATION BY CENTRING IELCC

Importance of IELCC

The need to fortify the foundation for young Indigenous children and their families is emphasized in the TRC *Calls to Action* recommendation 12: "We call upon the federal, provincial, territorial, and Aboriginal governments to develop culturally appropriate early childhood education programs for Aboriginal families" (Truth and Reconciliation Commission of Canada, 2015). The current government of Canada asserts that "all Canadian children deserve a real and fair chance to succeed, and that early learning and child care provides a solid foundation for future success. For Indigenous families and children, access to culturally appropriate, high-quality, fully inclusive, flexible and affordable early learning and child care is critical" (Government of Canada, 2017, paras. 1–2). Through Employment and Social Development Canada, the federal government has committed to engage with Indigenous organizations and partners to develop an Indigenous Early Learning and Child Care Framework. This framework is being developed on a separate and parallel track to the Federal–Provincial/Territorial Framework for Early Learning and Child Care to reflect the unique cultures and needs of First Nations, Inuit, and Métis children. It involves Indigenous and Northern Affairs Canada, Health Canada (HC), the Public Health Agency of Canada (PHAC), and Status of Women Canada. The framework is guided by the following key principles: co-development and partnership; comprehensive and inclusive dialogue; responsiveness to needs; focus on outcomes; and family-centredness.

Quality

Research shows that positive outcomes demonstrated for early childhood care and development (ECCD) depend on programs being of high quality (Yoshikawa et al., 2013). Criteria for determining quality vary across perspectives and constituencies. In general, quality IELCC emphasizes an environment where Indigenous people care for and educate their children within rich linguistic and cultural surroundings (Greenwood, de Leeuw, & Fraser, 2007; Greenwood & Shawana, 2003; Preston, Cottrell, Pelletier, & Pearce, 2012). Indigenous leaders in IELCC tend to agree that quality programs transmit an Aboriginal worldview, respect for others and for Earth's gifts, Indigenous language(s), and skills to prepare children to contribute positively to society. According to BC Aboriginal Child Care Society (2005), quality programs are inclusive of all children and reach out to involve Elders and family members. They use culturally appropriate, holistic curricula and assessment tools and favour multi-age groupings of children. They value personnel and volunteers and provide opportunities for them to develop skills and network with others working in the field. They value research as a means to build knowledge about IELCC and to be accountable to communities. They comply with regulations developed or accepted by Indigenous child care administrative bodies to ensure children's health and safety.[14]

Indigenous Pedagogy

Indigenous pedagogy emphasizes creating safety for children through direct care, psychosocial support, listening to and observing children, storytelling, giving ample time for children to respond, and engaging children in experiential learning, including hands-on and land-based activities. Indigenous educator Archibald (2008) describes Aboriginal education as an enculturation of self-reliance, observation, discovery, and respect for nature. Indigenous-authored guides for creating IELCC programs (e.g., McLeod, 2000) and observations of Indigenous early childhood programs highlight traditional crafts, songs, music, and dance, harvesting on the land, discovery of natural materials, including plants and animals used in traditional foods, and decoration with cultural images and objects (Ball, 2012b). Indigenous scholar Brant Castellano (2016) discusses the contributions of Elders to teaching and learning:

> Elders' teachings are concerned with personal development of apprentices as well as with knowledge acquisition. Moral precepts for personal behaviour and ethical precepts governing relationships are codified in principles such as kindness, honesty, sharing, and strength in Anishinaabe tradition (RCAP, 1996, Vol. 1, 654) or the Good Mind that is fundamental to achieving peace, power, and righteousness in personal experience and community relations, as prescribed in the Iroquois Great Law of Peace (Newhouse, 2008). (pp. 88–89)

Relational Practice

Indigenous pedagogy in early childhood programs engages in relational practice centred on the family and not only on the child. Programs typically respond to the dynamics of the family unit and reach out to a range of family members (Preston et al., 2012). Indigenous parents are often young: three times more adolescent First Nations women give birth compared to non-Indigenous adolescent women (Statistics Canada, 2016). Young mothers and fathers benefit from having a culturally safe, comfortable, accessible place to bring their babies and receive parenting support. Grandparents often assume parenting responsibilities, either to support young families or through custom adoption. Through family-centred IELCC programs, grandparents raising young children can find social support, resources such as a toy-lending library, nutrition supplements, information, and respite. Grandparents may also find that they can contribute knowledge of cultural practices and enjoy sharing these with children and younger caregivers. In IELCC, children may receive quality stimulation, access to hygiene, and nutrition. A study of the BC Aboriginal Infant Development Program (Gerlach, Browne, & Suto, 2016) found that its practices seek to mitigate child health inequities, racism in caregivers' encounters with child health service providers, and impacts of structural social factors on families' lives. They facilitate cultural connections and networks of belonging and support for children and their caregivers. The study also found that the program defers a normative, mainstream "ECD agenda" while affording priority to caregivers' self-identified priorities.

Holism

The concept of holism is central to Indigenous approaches to child and community development. Indigenous philosophies and practices consistently emphasize the interconnectedness among people across time past, present, and future, including the inseparability of the child from extended family and community units and the broader ecology, including the natural and spiritual worlds. Cree/Métis psychologist Joe Couture (2011) quotes traditional sources as declaring, "There are only two things you have to know about being Indian. One is that everything is alive, and two is that we're all related.... The centred and quartered Circle[15] is the sign of wholeness, of inclusiveness of all reality, of life, of balance and harmony between man and culture" (p. 36). Culturally fitting approaches to supporting young children encompass the host of factors that affect their wellness, development, and readiness to journey through the stages of life.

Integrated and Intersectoral Approaches

Integration is a goal of many Indigenous child- and family-serving agencies. Integrated approaches bring different types of services under the roof of one program serving a group of children and families. Intersectoral coordination may involve multiple programs within one or more sectors (e.g., child care, a nursing station, mental health and addictions counselling, justice, sanitation, and housing) co-located in the same or nearby facilities. Co-location makes referral, service delivery, and follow-up readily accessible to families and efficient for service practitioners, increases the chance of coordinating supports for children and their families, and provides opportunities for interprofessional service learning and memory. Service delivery based on relationships of familiarity increases participation by community members in programs such as parent support groups, mental health and substance abuse counselling, health education, preventive health services, and cultural and community events. This in turn enables early identification of health challenges as they emerge in children or their family members. It promotes social inclusion of children and families who may otherwise be isolated. These approaches can also optimize requirements for cultural safety and have capacity development and motivational impacts on communities (Ball, 2005). A series of *Lancet* articles documents how effective ECCD programs provide "direct learning experiences to children and families, are targeted toward younger and disadvantaged children, are of longer duration, high quality, high intensity, and are integrated with family support, health, nutrition, or educational systems and other services (Engle et al., 2007, p. 229).

Prevention

Intersectoral coordination is a touchstone of the vision articulated by 11 national organizations in the report *Many Hands, One Dream* (Blackstock, Bruyere, & Moreau, 2006). Considering rates of child welfare involvement and placement in foster care that are 10 times greater for Indigenous compared to non-Indigenous children (Blackstock, Cross, George, Brown & Formsma, 2006), universal access by Indigenous families to integrated and intersectoral IELCC programs is even more urgent. High-intensity, holistic IELCC is a form of primary prevention for all children living in conditions known to produce risks to wellness such as poverty, unsuitable housing, low food security, and domestic conflict (Grantham-McGregor et al., 2007; Walker et al., 2007). It is a form of secondary prevention for children who are identified as at risk and more likely to be removed from home or community by child welfare services.

GERMINATING THE SEEDS OF IELCC

Research has illustrated how early childhood services can become the nucleus of community life and a hub for delivering a range of services and supports for all family members. For example, a promising practice that became known as the "hook and hub" approach was demonstrated by three groups of First Nations on reserves in BC (Ball, 2005; Ball & Le Mare, 2011; Ball & Simpkins, 2004). These communities perceived early childhood as the most opportune period to promote health and prevent chronic disease and identified high-quality early childhood programs run by community members as the optimal starting gate to introduce a range of programs, services, and community supports to primary caregivers. They began with a partnership with the University of Victoria to deliver two years of postsecondary education in child and youth care, including course requirements for early childhood educator certification. A cadre of community members were thereby prepared to deliver licensed day care, early learning, and after-school care programs for infants and young children, including those with special needs. Starting with community kitchens and a drop-in program for babies, they gradually added these new programs as families identified their needs and showed their receptivity. Multi-service centre activities reach out to family members with a range of health promotion and disease prevention activities, such as injury prevention; workshops in preparing nutritious, affordable meals including traditional foods; dental and other home hygiene practices; facilitating speech and language development at home; positive discipline; land-based and intergenerational learning activities; counselling for mental health and addictions; referrals; and navigator assistance in connecting with services beyond the community.

Another example is the Laichwiltach Family Life Society in BC, which started as a small support group for First Nations women experiencing family violence and also provided child care. This formative step generated impetus to apply to PHAC to become a host site for Aboriginal Head Start (AHS). Soon after, provincially funded Aboriginal Infant Development and Aboriginal Supported Child Development programs were added. The organization grew to become a multi-service centre that is First Nations–operated and governed by a board comprising eight contributing First Nations (Ball, 2012c). It is described by families as a lifeline connecting them to one another and to services within and beyond the centre. These promising program models capitalized on the common experience that children, especially babies, can be catalysts for mobilizing people and resources toward actions that promote wellness.

Aboriginal Head Start

AHS is the most extensive federally funded program for young Indigenous children in Canada (Ball, 2012a). There are two AHS programs, both primarily reaching Indigenous children three to five years old with three to four half-days per week of community-based programs. AHS in Urban and Northern Communities (AHSUNC) was created in 1995 and constituted a federal investment of $174.1 million during the five-year period 2011/12 to 2015/16. Conceived as an early childhood intervention, it serves First Nations children living off reserve, as well as Inuit and Métis children, with a target of enrolling the most vulnerable. Through contribution agreements with community organizations (which are mostly Indigenous), funding is provided by PHAC's Health Promotion and Chronic Disease Prevention Branch and led by the Centre for Health Promotion. The "sponsor," or host organization, designs and delivers the program. In 2016, there were 134 AHSUNC sites, most of which have been in existence since the programs' creation in 1995. Annual enrollments are generally stable at about 4,750 children per year (Public Health Agency of Canada, 2011), reaching roughly 4 percent[16] of all Indigenous children zero to six years old living off reserve across Canada (Findlay & Kohen, 2014).

AHS On-Reserve (AHSOR) was created in 1998 and constitutes a federal investment of $47.37 million annually. It is operated by Health Canada, except in BC, where the First Nations Health Authority in BC delivers this program since they have taken over federal responsibilities for First Nations health in the province. AHSOR is one component of the Healthy Child Development Cluster, which is a network of federal programs that address early learning and healthy development of First Nations children living on reserve. These include day care funded by Employment and Social Development Canada's First Nations and Inuit Child Care Initiative and Indigenous Services Canada. AHSOR serves about 14,000 First Nations children on reserve (excluding BC) annually. From 2011 to 2015, in five provinces (excluding the Atlantic provinces and BC), 84 percent (356 out of 425) of First Nations had an AHSOR program. Since 2011, communities as well as national and regional offices of the Healthy Child Development Cluster of programs, including AHSOR, have improved integration and coordination of programs and services and reduced community program silos (Health Canada & Public Health Agency of Canada, 2014). Integration and coordination at the community level was occurring through efforts such as referrals, co-location of programs, and pooling of resources. The First Nations and Inuit Health Branch of Health Canada supported integration and coordination by providing greater community support at the regional level through a reorganization of its governance structure.

Using a community empowerment model, both the AHSOR and AHSUNC programs address a federally mandated set of program domains: education; promotion of Aboriginal culture and language; health promotion; nutrition; parent involvement; and social support. Most programs are free of charge to participants but require some kind of voluntary participation. A decentralized approach to specific program design decisions and curricula enables each community to deliver a program that meets local needs, draws on local assets, and supports the community's vision for children's care and early learning. AHS programs have the flexibility to develop in ways that are family-centred, family-preserving, and delivered within a community development framework. In addition to centre-based programming, many AHS programs reach out to families and the broader community. For example, some sites offer a home visiting component that provides information, guidance, and counselling to parents, and learning activities for children. Other program activities may include parenting and skill development workshops for family members and cultural events for the whole community. Anecdotal reports often describe how AHS programs help families of participating children to access food, warm clothing, income assistance, and needed health, mental health, and social services. AHS programs may be delivered in a variety of settings and may be provided alongside or integrated with other early childhood initiatives. For example, some programs provide nutrition supplementation by integrating AHS with federal nutrition programs. In First Nations on reserves, AHS may be co-located with day care programs funded through Indigenous and Northern Affairs Canada as well as Employment and Social Development Canada. To serve Inuit and First Nations off reserves, AHS may be co-located with day care funded by provincial/territorial and local programs.

Based on limited available evidence,[17] both AHSUNC and AHSOR have demonstrated effective implementation and impacts. The most recent review by PHAC (2017) found increased school-readiness skills, including improved language, social, motor, and academic skills, cultural literacy, and exposure to Aboriginal languages. A study of 10 AHSUNC sites in the Northwest Territories found high satisfaction among parents with the program's effects on their children and decreased grade repetition among AHS attendees (Western Arctic Aboriginal Head Start Council, 2006). A case study of Waabinong AHSUNC in Ontario (Mashford-Pringle, 2012) found that within the first three months of attending AHSUNC, children showed improved early learning skills, health routines, and nutrition. Their parents and other caregivers reported reduced tobacco consumption and increased visits to physicians, dental care, and Aboriginal social support workers; 10 percent returned to school and 11 percent moved from part-time to full-time employment. There was also an increase in the use of other social programs, including the Ontario Early Years Centres. Less information is available on the implementation process and impacts of the AHSOR program. However, program reviews by HC and PHAC have reported generally positive impacts despite significant implementation challenges (Health Canada & Public Health Agency of Canada, 2014). One study reported increases in children's access to daily physical activity and access to dental and health care (Barrieau & Ireland, 2003). Statistics Canada (2017a) found that children who had participated in AHSUNC had more positive health and education outcomes in both elementary and intermediate/high school years. The study also found that AHSUNC successfully reaches high-risk Indigenous populations. Children who have attended these programs experience significantly greater socio-demographic challenges, such as living with a single parent, having a parent or grandparent who attended residential school, living in the north, and being in a lower income household than children in non-Indigenous-focused early childhood programs. But children who participated in AHSUNC achieve similar health and education outcomes as their peers who are not faced with the same adversity. In others words, participating in AHSUNC, with its strong focus on Indigenous culture and language, helps to close disparity gaps and promote resilience for Indigenous children.

AHS has stimulated growth of community capacity to deliver culturally based programs in communities. Non-formal reports often identify AHS as the most positive program in Canada for Indigenous families with young children. Receiving funding to develop an AHS program, or renewed funding to sustain existing programs, is often identified as a top priority in many communities. However, the AHS program's ability to increase its reach in terms of the numbers of sites it operates and children and families it serves is hindered by key resource limitations. The program has not had an increase in funding since its inception in 1995, while sites have seen a reduction of resources available to them, due to, for instance, increases in the cost of food, gas, and salaries and in the number of children in need of special education, as well as continuing difficulties with staff recruitment and retention. These issues have the potential to affect program quality.

Other Government Supports for Community Initiatives

Other prominent examples of programs providing critically needed supports for young Indigenous children include the federally funded Community Action Program for Children (CAPC) and the Canadian Prenatal Nutrition Program (CPNP), both funded by PHAC. These are both community-based programs that create partnerships within communities and strengthen community capacity to achieve project objectives. CAPC[18] promotes healthy development of young children (zero to six years), including Indigenous children, who face challenging life circumstances. Programming offered by CAPC projects varies by location; however, they generally offer child health and development activities, parenting skills programs, nutritional support and collective kitchens, physical activity programs, outreach, and home visits. CPNP[19] provides support for maternal/infant health, including improvements in birth weights and support for breastfeeding. CPNP services First Nations families living off reserves, as well as Inuit and Métis families. A separate stream of the program administered through HC serves Inuit and First Nations women living on reserves.

In addition to federally funded initiatives, each province and territory funds early childhood programs, including some that are specifically dedicated to young Indigenous children and their families. Examples include the Aboriginal Supported Child Development Program for vulnerable children in BC, the Aboriginal Infant Development Program for all Indigenous infants and toddlers in BC, and the Aboriginal Healthy Babies, Healthy Children program in Ontario.

The programs highlighted here are bright lights in an otherwise gloomy landscape for young Indigenous children overall. Serious challenges limit the quantity, quality, sustainability, and expansion of early childhood initiatives in First Nations, Inuit, and Métis communities, discussed subsequently.

CANADA'S CHILLY CLIMATE FOR IELCC FLOURISHING

Canada lags behind other advanced economies in spending on the early childhood education sector and lacks a national strategy to ensure access to quality programs either for all children or for children in an identified risk category or equity group.[20] The current "catch-as-catch-can" collection of ELCC programs with come-and-go funding creates a weak medium in which to grow early childhood programs. This situation is vastly bleaker in Indigenous communities, where demand for early childhood spaces is far greater than supply. To improve access, community leaders must deal with precarious funding, a fragmented service system, inadequate facilities, lack of trained personnel in communities, and other challenges.

Insufficient and Precarious Funding

BC Aboriginal Child Care Society board president Mary Teegee comments, "One of the greatest hurdles we face in sharing knowledge and training services is insufficient, insecure funding. The TRC recommendations help remind the public and leadership that in order 'close the gap' adequate, sustained funding is necessary" (British Columbia Aboriginal Child Care Society, 2015, para. 5). Funding formulas across federal, provincial, and territorial governments tend to be based primarily on population data, without considering contextual exigencies. Funding levels need to account for local conditions, including remoteness, human resources, infrastructure, and the demographic and health profiles of children and parents in a catchment area. For example, adolescent parents, parents with addiction problems, and grandmothers raising children require more supports. Children in communities with low food security need nutrition supplementation within IELCC programs. Communities with high birth rates, such as First Nations on reserves,[21] need to build ahead for a rapidly expanding population of infants and young children.

A Fragmented Service System

In 2002, the Romanow Report was the first national report to devote specific attention to Aboriginal health. The report concluded that the dismal state of Indigenous Peoples' health, well-being, and quality of life calls for a

multi-jurisdictional, integrated, and intersectoral approach to wellness, especially for those residing in rural and remote settings and on reserves (Commission on the Future of Health Care in Canada, 2002). Yet there have been
chronic failures to move ahead with a coordinated service approach. National
coordination among stakeholders in Indigenous early childhood education
was identified as a strategic gap in a review of the AHSUNC program (Public Health Agency of Canada, 2017). It was noted that filling this gap could
increase the program's potential to achieve several intended outcomes, including children's transitions to mainstream education systems.

Political, conceptual, and practical quagmires include professional turf
wars, silo mentalities within fragmented bureaucracies, resource and staffing
limitations, unequal and inadequate community funding, competition for
funding, and reluctance to share both authority over health care expendi-
tures and accountability for health outcomes. Non-action is also attributable
to the dominance of Western medical models of health that focus on individuals rather than families or communities as the unit of service delivery
and that target proximal determinants, such as individual health choices,
rather than targeting more difficult but often more potent distal determinants of health. Responsibility rests with organizations such as First Nations
and Inuit Health Branch within HC, PHAC, and other organizations and
partners in federal, provincial, and territorial governments to influence policy and funding to create the intersectoral partnerships necessary to impact
the more distal, though potent, determinants.

Inadequate Program Facilities

The critical need for renovation and more construction of facilities, especially
in rural and remote communities, hinders expansion, quality, and sustainability of early childhood programs. For example, during recent visits to remote First Nations, I found that programs were restricted in the numbers of
children they could serve, numbers of days they could operate, and/or types
of activities they could support because of inadequate facilities. Some had
rusted, leaky pipes, causing mold that provoked respiratory illnesses in the
children and forced facilities to close. Many had operated out of portables
for years because the community could not secure funding to construct or
renovate a permanent facility. Many had no potable water. Most had no safe
playground or outdoor play equipment. None provided snacks because nutrition comes under a different funding stream, and many provided no drinking
water because the community water filtration system was broken. In some

communities, funding is sufficient to employ a qualified early childhood educator from outside the community, but the community cannot provide safe and suitable accommodation for a non-resident employee.

Training Gaps

Accessible, culturally informed, relevant postsecondary education for early childhood educators to work in IELCC programs has been a long-standing and well-known gap. While the government of Canada invests substantially in AHS and First Nations and Inuit Child Care, there has never been sufficient investment in accessible, culturally relevant professional education in early childhood education. Community members working in AHS programs often comment on how they have received "enough certificates of completion from weekend workshops and two- and three-week trainings to wallpaper a bedroom," but these short-term, one-off training events do not build toward a recognized credential. Most provinces require a postsecondary certificate or diploma from an accredited institution in order to offer a licensed program. Organizations that provide funding or other resources often have licensing as an eligibility criterion. Across Canada, many community-based programs are operating on various forms of temporary permission until a fully qualified early childhood educator can be found. Without licensing, programs are often restricted as to the number of children who can attend at any one time.[22]

IMPROVING THE ECOLOGY FOR IELCC FLOURISHING: KEY STRATEGIES

Increased, Sustained Funding

Increased long-term, streamlined funding commitments are needed at every level of government to support expansion of IELCC to meet the demands of a rapidly growing population of Indigenous citizens and respond to the *Calls to Action* by the TRC. For example, the AHSUNC evaluation reported by PHAC (2011) noted that resource leveraging and partnerships at the site level are strengths of the program. However, short-term funding agreements and implementation of the National Strategic Fund in AHSUNC have been challenging. Government funding formulae must consider varying conditions, resources, technology, and needs and goals of communities rather than applying a universal formula.

Intersectoral Coordination

IELCC programs must respond to the multiple needs of Indigenous families and communities, bringing together supports that promote wellness and not only day care or early learning. HC and PHAC and other branches of federal, provincial, and territorial governments must capitalize on the potential for IELCC programs to impact both proximal and distal determinants of wellness by integrating programs and help self-selected communities make IELCC the nucleus of multi-service hubs. IELCC programs could be focal points for integrated health promotion / disease prevention services, including health education, nutrition, dental hygiene, physical activity, emotional self-regulation / mental and spiritual wellness, coping skills, early identification, referral, early intervention, and follow-up. IELCC programs could be strategically coordinated with the formal education sector, especially junior and senior kindergartens, the health sector, child welfare services, the housing sector, economic and social development, and sanitation. The combination of these inputs to children's ecologies shapes children's quality of life and wellness.

Training

Postsecondary institutions need to be funded to create partnerships with Indigenous communities in order to deliver postsecondary certificate and diploma courses in early childhood education. These courses need to seek input about local Indigenous cultures and aspirations for children and respond to local needs, resources, and circumstances, such as seasonal and demographic fluctuations. A well-documented example is the First Nations Partnership Program, spearheaded by the Meadow Lake Tribal Council in Saskatchewan in the early 1990s in partnership with the University of Victoria. The partnerships approach provided community-based, culturally grounded, accredited postsecondary education in early childhood education, yielding certificate, diploma, and degree-level professional education in early childhood education for more than two hundred students in 56 First Nations land-based communities (Ball & Pence, 2006).

Community Decision-Making

Self-determination is a goal of most Indigenous communities, enabling all aspects of community life to be inspired by Indigenous knowledge and fortified by community governance and participation. Federal, provincial, and territorial governments must work with Indigenous leaders and champions of IELCC to empower local planning, governing, operation, and evaluation of community-based IELCC programs.

National Indigenous Children's Commission

A mechanism is needed for monitoring the extent to which Canada is honouring its commitments to Indigenous children in the Constitution, in the Government of Canada's Jordan's Principle, and in various international declarations and conventions. A legal framework and an independent national Indigenous children's commission could monitor conditions for young Indigenous children, including cross-jurisdictional and intersectoral cooperation. These strategies were recommended in a 2007 Senate report (Standing Senate Committee on Human Rights, 2007). Such a commission could track progress on key targets; identify opportunities to fill gaps; coordinate federal, provincial, and territorial policies that affect children's access to needed services, including access to quality IELCC; and bring legal action where necessary. Exploratory studies cited in this chapter suggest how investments in a coordinated, strategic program of research on *implementation and process* as well as *outcomes* of IELCC can inform government policy and program decisions and ensure accountability to the calls to action of the TRC.

CONCLUSION

This chapter has reflected on progress made, key challenges, and strategies that can help to strengthen the foundation for Indigenous-inspired, -operated, and -sustained IELCC programs in Canada. Highlighting AHS and smaller, more local innovations demonstrating a hook and hub approach, the chapter points to some fertile ground in an otherwise impoverished landscape for Indigenous children in Canada. Examples of IELCC rooted in Indigenous pedagogy and aspirations for children show how programs can respond to the unique settings, needs, and strengths of Indigenous children and families, with the hope of better outcomes for this turnaround generation (Ball, 2012c) of young Indigenous people.

Canada's lacklustre performance with regard to ameliorating Indigenous child poverty and the dismal conditions into which many Indigenous children are born is abundantly evident. Closing the many equity gaps affecting outcomes for Indigenous children requires policy change across multiple sectors. A relatively low-hanging fruit in terms of costs and feasibility is a policy and associated funding that ensure universal access by Indigenous children to IELCC.

Children are not only our future: they are here *now*. Assembly of First Nations[23] National Chief Perry Bellegarde and First Nations Child and Family Services Society[24] executive director Cindy Blackstock frequently call upon Canadians to recognize that *children only have one childhood*. These national leaders argue that the time is *now* to get things right for young Indigenous children so that we don't have to apologize to yet another generation of Indigenous people. Quality holistic, culturally grounded IELCC can support Indigenous aspirations to nurture healthy children able to thrive within strong families and communities.

NOTES

1. Currently in Canada, Indigenous people represent themselves politically as belonging to one of several major groups: First Nations (status Indians on reserve, status Indians off reserve, and non-status Indians), Inuit, and Métis. These groupings reflect Section 35 of Canada's Constitution Act, as well as the federal Indian Act, which defines the term *status Indian*. From a cultural perspective, Aboriginal people in Canada comprise more than 50 distinct and diverse groups, each with its own distinct language and traditional land base.

2. Since about 2010 in Canada, concurrent with the downward expansion of formal schooling to junior and senior kindergarten, there has been increasing emphasis on "early learning" to ensure "school readiness." This narrowing of scope (perhaps as an advocacy strategy) is reflected in a shift from early childhood care and development (ECCD) to early learning and child care (ELCC). Many Indigenous organizations have adopted the term *Indigenous early learning and child care* (IELCC).

3. I am a third-generation settler of European descent. I am grateful to have spent much of my childhood in the forests and on the riverbanks of the Musqueam First Nation in Vancouver, BC, and to have raised my children on the unceded territories of the W̱SÁNEĆ Peoples near Victoria, BC. Beginning in 1996, I have been honoured by invitations from Indigenous organizations and communities to partner in projects aimed at improving conditions for Indigenous children and families.

4. We typically speak of children and families as vulnerable or developing non-normatively, as if these are individual differences. I argue for a shift in assessing the locus of atypicality and vulnerability to environments for children and the degree to which they are non-normative and productive of risks.

5. I argue that the notion of best practices is simultaneously seductive and illusory. No practice is the best for every child or community, and almost no practice model has been evaluated to prove conclusively it is better than a comparison practice and warrants being hailed as the best.

6. Canada has been slow to honour its commitments to remedial action following previous national investigations and proclamations, including the Royal Commission on Aboriginal Peoples (1996) and the pursuant Aboriginal Action Plan (Minister of Indian Affairs and Northern Development, 1997), an apology in 2008 by the prime minister for Indian residential schools (Government of Canada, 2008), and several international policy declarations and conventions (Blackstock, Cullen, D'Hondt, & Formsma, 2004). Most recently, the Canadian Human Rights Tribunal found that the government of Canada has persistently failed to implement Jordan's Principle, which requires intergovernment cooperation to ensure First Nations children's access to needed services (First Nations Child & Family Caring Society of Canada, 2017).

7. Section 35 (1) of the Constitution Act of 1982 recognizes Aboriginal and treaty rights and affirms First Nations' inherent right to self-government, including the creation of laws and systems for the provision of lifelong learning for First Nations populations. First Nations expect the Crown not only to recognize their jurisdiction to lifelong learning, but also to "fulfill their Constitutional, Treaty and international obligations to First Nations peoples by supporting the design and implementation of First Nations comprehensive learning systems with adequate and sustainable resourcing" (Assembly of First Nations, 2010, p. 20).

8. Disaggregation of Statistics Canada data on child poverty in 2016 finds the worst poverty experienced by status First Nation children (51 percent, rising to 60 percent for children on reserve). The second-worst poverty rate is experienced by other Indigenous children and disadvantaged groups (ranging from 22 to 32 percent). Children who are non-Indigenous, non-racialized, and non-immigrant experience a poverty rate of 13 percent, which is similar to the global average calculated by Organisation for Economic Co-operation and Development (OECD, 2017).

9. As of 2017, 85 First Nations communities on reserves were under government advisories not to drink water from faulty treatment systems (Lukawiecki, 2017; Morales, 2006).

10. In 2009, less than 18 percent of Indigenous children had access to any early learning program (Leitch, 2008). Investments have not changed significantly since this estimate, suggesting that access has not improved.

11. Inuit children have the world's highest rate of hospitalization for lower respiratory tract infections—an average of 306 admissions per 1,000 infants—and over 800 per 1,000 for infants with heart defects (Egeland, Faraj, & Osborne, 2010, p. 8).

12. Over one-third (34 percent) of Indigenous children aged zero to four years live with a lone parent. This is the case for 38.9 percent of First Nations, 25.5 percent of Métis, and 26.5 percent of Inuit children zero to four years old (Statistics Canada, 2017c).

13. In 2016, Indigenous children zero to four years old account for about 50 percent of all foster children, although they constitute only 7.7 percent of all children aged zero to four years in Canada (Statistics Canada, 2017c).

14. Cultural vitality can be conceived as a social determinant of wellness. Robust, culturally grounded identity can function as a moderating factor, limiting the negative impacts of difficult-to-control distal factors that erode Indigenous children's life chances. Several studies have illustrated how revitalization, maintenance, and active use of Indigenous languages and cultures may be linked to improved education outcomes for Aboriginal children (Royal Commission on Aboriginal Peoples, 1996), improved mental health and lower suicide risk (Hallett, Chandler, & Lalonde, 2007), and overall health (Borré, 1994; Healey & Meadows, 2008; Minore & Katt, 2007).

15. The Circle refers to the Medicine Wheel. The Medicine Wheel is the representation of all things connected within the circle of life. It is told that there are over one hundred relevant traditional teachings given of the Medicine Wheel. Each teaching holds its own meaning and purpose. The Medicine Wheel usually focuses on the significance of the numbers 4 and 7. Commonly, the Medicine Wheel teaches seven aspects within each of the four quadrants, which represent life in specific stages: the four directions, the four elements of life, the four medicines, the four seasons, the four states of well-being, the four colours of humans, and four stages of life (Anishnaabeg Bimaadiziwin, n.d.).

16. The greatest reach is in the Northwest Territories (12.2 percent) and Quebec (11.5 percent).

17. Performance measurement of AHS has mostly involved federally mandated program reviews every five years. There is an outstanding need for regional and national studies of the implementation processes and impacts of AHSUNC and AHSOR using sound longitudinal research design and culturally relevant, robust outcome measurement, as well as case studies to understand factors affecting successful innovations, for example, in cultural components, Indigenous language revitalization, integration, and intersectoral coordination.

18. In 2015, there were 415 CAPC projects serving more than 223,000 vulnerable children and parents/caregivers in more than three thousand communities across Canada (Government of Canada, 2015b).

19. In 2015, there were 276 CPNP projects serving 51,000 pregnant women and parents/caregivers in more than two thousand community across Canada (Government of Canada, 2015a).

20. Canada, at all levels of government, currently spends 0.3 percent of its GDP in early childhood education, the lowest among 14 OECD countries and far below the UNICEF benchmark of 1 percent of GDP.

21. The birth rate for First Nations women is 2.4, compared to 1.58 for all Canadian women.

22. In a typical scenario, I visited a community recently where there were 70 children whose parents tried to enroll them; 40 were admitted, and each child is allowed to attend the program for one three-hour period per week. Although, in this setting, the facility is adequate for a full cohort of 40 children, the program is restricted to having five children at any one time because the program leader lacks a credential in early childhood education.

23. http://www.afn.ca/

24. https://fncaringsociety.com/caring-society-staff-information

REFERENCES

Anderson, K., & Ball, J. (2019). Foundations: First Nation and Métis families. In G. Starblanket & D. Long (Eds.) with Olive P. Dickason, *Visions of the heart: Issues involving Indigenous peoples in Canada* (5th ed., chapter 9). Toronto, ON: Oxford University Press.

Anishnaabeg Bimaadiziwin. (n.d.). *Medicine wheel.* Retrieved from http://ojibweresources .weebly.com/medicine-wheel.html

Archibald, J. (2008). *Indigenous storywork: Educating the heart, mind, body, and spirit.* Vancouver, BC: UBC Press.

Assembly of First Nations. (2010). *It's our vision, it's our time: First Nations control of First Nations education.* Retrieved from https://www.afn.ca/uploads/files/ education/3._2010_july_afn_first_nations_control_of_first_nations_education_ final_eng.pdf

Ball, J. (2005). Early childhood care and development programs as hook and hub for inter-sectoral service delivery in Indigenous communities. *Journal of Aboriginal Health, 1,* 36–49.

Ball, J. (2011). Lessons from community-university partnerships with First Nations. In H. Goelman, J. Pivik, & M. Guhn (Eds.), *New approaches to early child development: Rules, rituals, and realities* (pp. 69–94). New York, NY: Palgrave Macmillan.

Ball, J. (2012a). Federal investments in strengthening Indigenous capacity for culturally based early childhood education and care. In N. Howe & L. Prochner (Eds.), *Recent perspectives on early childhood education and care in Canada* (pp. 337–366). Toronto, ON: University of Toronto Press.

Ball, J. (2012b). Identity and knowledge in Indigenous young children's experiences in Canada. *Childhood Education, 88*(5), 286–291.

Ball, J. (2012c). *Lifeline: Creating a community service hub for Aboriginal children and families.* Victoria, BC: Author. Retrieved from http://www.ecdip.org/reports/

Ball, J. (2012d). "We could be the turn-around generation": Harnessing Aboriginal fathers' potential to contribute to their children's well-being. *Paediatrics and Child Health, 17*(7), 373–375. Retrieved from https://www.ncbi.nlm.nih.gov/pmc/articles/PMC3448537/

Ball, J., & Le Mare, L. (2011). Lessons from community-university partnerships with First Nations. In H. Goelman, J. Pivik, & M. Guhn (Eds.), *New approaches to early child development: Rules, rituals, and realities.* New York, NY: Palgrave Macmillan.

Ball, J., & Moselle, K. (2013). *Healthy Aboriginal child development and health promotion/chronic disease prevention.* Unpublished scoping paper prepared for Health Canada, First Nations and Inuit Health Branch, Interprofessional Advisory Program Support Directorate. Retrieved from http://www.ecdip.org/

Ball, J., & Simpkins, M. (2004). The community within the child: Integration of Indigenous knowledge into First Nations childcare process and practice. *American Indian Quarterly, 28*, 480–498.

Ball, J., & Pence, A. (2006). *Supporting Indigenous children's development: Community-university partnerships.* Vancouver, BC: UBC Press.

Barrera, J. (2017, November 2). Indigenous child welfare rates creating "humanitarian crisis" in Canada, says federal minister. *CBC News.* Retrieved from http://www.cbc.ca/news/indigenous/crisis-philpott-child-welfare-1.4385136

Barrieau, A., & Ireland, D. (2003). *Aboriginal Head Start On Reserve program: Summary of the evaluation.* Ottawa, ON: Health Canada.

Blackstock, C., Bruyere, D., & Moreau, E. (2006). *Many hands, one dream: Principles for a new perspective on the health of First Nations, Inuit, and Métis children and youth.* Retrieved from https://fncaringsociety.com/sites/default/files/manyhands-principles.pdf

Blackstock, C., Clarke, S., Cullen, J., D'Hondt, J., & Formsma, J. (2004). *Keeping the promise: The Convention on the Rights of the Child and the lived experiences of First Nations children and youth.* Ottawa, ON: First Nations Child and Family Caring Society of Canada.

Blackstock, C., Cross, T., George, J., Brown, I., & Formsma, J. (2006). *Reconciliation in child welfare: Touchstones of hope for Indigenous children, youth, and families.* First Nations Child & Family Caring Society of Canada and National Indian Child

Welfare Association. Retrieved from https://fncaringsociety.com/sites/default/files/Touchstones_of_Hope.pdf

Blackstock, C., Prakash, T., Loxley, J., & Wien, F. (2005). *Wen:de: We are coming to the light of day.* Ottawa, ON: First Nations Child and Family Caring Society of Canada. Retrieved from http://cwrp.ca/sites/default/files/publications/en/WendeReport.pdf

Borré, K. (1994). The healing power of the seal: The meaning of Inuit health practice and belief. *Arctic Anthropology, 31,* 1–15.

Brant Castellano, M. (2016). Elders' teachings in the twenty-first century: A personal reflection. In D. Long & O. Dickason (Eds.), *Visions of the heart: Issues involving Aboriginal peoples in Canada* (4th ed., pp. 80–98). Don Mills, ON: Oxford University Press Canada.

British Columbia Aboriginal Child Care Society. (2005). *Elements of quality child care from the perspectives of Aboriginal Peoples in British Columbia.* West Vancouver, BC: Author. Retrieved from http://www.acc-society.bc.ca/files_2/documents/Quality-Statementshort-final.pdf

British Columbia Aboriginal Child Care Society. (2015). *BCACCS calls for action on the Aboriginal early childhood education TRC recommendation* [press release]. Retrieved from http://www.acc-society.bc.ca/files_2/documents/NR_BCACCSED-joinsthecallforactionontheTRCrecommendations_000.pdf

British Columbia Aboriginal Child Care Society. (2017). *From seed to cedar: A campaign to support Indigenous early learning and child care (IELCC).* Retrieved from http://seedtocedar.com/

Commission on the Future of Health Care in Canada. (2002). *Building on values: The future of health care in Canada. Final report.* Retrieved from http://publications.gc.ca/collections/Collection/CP32-85-2002E.pdf

Couture, J. (2011). The role of native Elders: Emergent issues. In D. Long & O. Dickason (Eds.), *Visions of the heart: Canadian Aboriginal issues* (3rd ed., pp. 18–34).
Don Mills, ON: Oxford University Press Canada.

Crengle, S., Freemantle, J., Gallaher, G., McAullay, D., McShane, K., & Taualii, M. (2009). *Indigenous children's health report: Health assessment in action.* Toronto, ON: The Centre for Research on Inner City Health.

Egeland, G. M., Faraj, N., & Osborne, G. (2010). Cultural, socioeconomic, and health indicators among Inuit preschoolers: Nunavut Inuit Child Health Survey, 2007–2008. *Rural and Remote Health, 10*(1365). Retrieved from https://www.rrh.org.au/public/assets/article_documents/article_print_1365.pdf

Engle, P. L., Black, M. M., Behrman, J. R., Cabral de Mello, M., Gertler, P. J., Kapiriri, L., … International Child Development Steering Group. (2007). Strategies to avoid the loss of developmental potential in more than 200 million children in the developing world. *Lancet, 369*, 229–242.

Findlay, L., & Kohen, D. (2014). *Aboriginal children aged 0–6 living off reserve in Canada: Demographic trends at the community level.* Technical report for Public Health Agency of Canada. Ottawa, ON: Statistics Canada.

First Nations Child and Family Caring Society of Canada. (2017). *Jordan's principle.* Retrieved from https://fncaringsociety.com/jordans-principle

First Nations Information Governance Centre. (2012). *First Nations Regional Health Survey 2008–2010: National report on adults, youth and children living in First Nations communities.* Ottawa, ON: Author. Retrieved from https://fnigc.ca/sites/default/files/docs/first_nations_regional_health_survey_rhs_2008-10_-_national_report.pdf

Gerlach, A. J., Browne, A. J., & Suto, M. J. (2016). Relational approaches to fostering healthy equity for Indigenous children through early childhood intervention. *Health Sociology Review, 27*(1), 104–119.

Government of Canada. (2008). Prime minister offers full apology on behalf of Canadians for the Indian residential schools. Press release, Retrieved from http://pm.gc.ca/eng/media.asp?id+2149

Government of Canada. (2015a). *Canada Prenatal Nutrition Program (CPNP).* Retrieved from https://www.canada.ca/en/public-health/services/health-promotion/childhood-adolescence/programs-initiatives/canada-prenatal-nutrition-program-cpnp.html

Government of Canada. (2015b). *Community Action Program for Children (CAPC).* Retrieved from https://www.canada.ca/en/public-health/services/health-promotion/childhood-adolescence/programs-initiatives/community-action-program-children-capc.html

Government of Canada. (2017). *Indigenous early learning and child care.* Retrieved from https://www.canada.ca/en/employment-social-development/programs/indigenous-early-learning.html

Grantham-McGregor, S., Cheung, Y. B., Cueto, S., Glewwe, P., Richter, L., Strupp, B., & International Child Development Steering Group. (2007). Developmental potential in the first five years for children in developing countries. *Lancet, 369*, 60–70.

Greenwood, M. (2006). Children are a gift to us: Aboriginal-specific early childhood programs and services in Canada. *Canadian Journal of Native Education, 29*(1), 12–28.

Greenwood, M., de Leeuw, S., & Fraser, T. (2007). Aboriginal children and early childhood development and education in Canada. *Canadian Journal of Native Education, 30*(1), 5–18.

Greenwood, M., & Shawana, P. (2003). Whispered gently through time: First Nations quality child care. *Native Social Work Journal, 4*(1), 51–83.

Hallett, D., Chandler, M. J., & Lalonde, C. E. (2007). Aboriginal language knowledge and youth suicide. *Cognitive Development, 22*, 392–299.

Healey, G. K., & Meadows, L. M. (2008). Tradition and culture: An important determinant of Inuit women's health. *Journal of Aboriginal Health, 4*, 25–33.

Health Canada & Public Health Agency of Canada. (2014). *Evaluation of the healthy living (2010–2011 to 2012–2013) and healthy child development clusters (2008–2009 to 2012–2013)*. Retrieved from https://www.canada.ca/en/health-canada/corporate/about-health-canada/accountability-performance-financial-reporting/evaluation-reports/evaluation-healthy-living-2010-11-2012-13-healthy-child-development-clusters-2008-09-2012-13.html

Heckman, J. J. (2006). Skill formation and the economics of investing in disadvantaged children. *Science, 312*(5782), 1900–1902.

Irvine, J., Kitty, D., & Pekeles, G. (2012). Healing winds: Aboriginal child and youth health in Canada. *Paediatrics and Child Health, 17*(7), 363–364.

Irwin, L. G., Siddiqi, A., & Hertzman, C. (2007). *Early child development: A powerful equalizer.* Final report for the World Health Organization's Commission on the Social Determinants of Health. Geneva, Switzerland: World Health Organization.

Kovesi, T. (2012). Respiratory disease in Canadian First Nations and Inuit children. *Paediatrics and Child Health, 17*(7), 376–380.

Leitch, K. K. (2008). *Reaching for the top: A report by the advisor on healthy children and youth.* Ottawa, ON: Health Canada.

Lukawiecki, J. (2017). *Glass half empty? Year 1 progress toward resolving drinking water advisories in nine First Nations in Ontario.* David Suzuki Foundation & The Council of Canadians. Retrieved from https://davidsuzuki.org/wp-content/uploads/2017/09/REPORT-progress-resolving-drinking-water-advisories-first-nations-ontario.pdf

Macdonald, D., & Wilson, D. (2016). *Shameful neglect: Indigenous child poverty in Canada.* Ottawa, ON: Canadian Centre for Policy Alternatives. Retrieved from https://www.policyalternatives.ca/shameful-neglect

Mashford-Pringle, A. (2012). Early learning for Aboriginal children: Past, present and future and an exploration of the Aboriginal Head Start Urban and Northern Communities Program in Ontario. *First Peoples Child & Family Review, 7*(1), 127–140.

McLeod, D. (2000). *Developing culturally focused Aboriginal early childhood education programs: A handbook.* West Vancouver: BC Aboriginal Child Care Society.

Retrieved from http://www.acc-society.bc.ca/files_2/documents/Developing-CulturallyFocusedAECEProgramsweb.pdf

Milloy, J. S. (1999). *A national crime: The Canadian government and the residential school system, 1879 to 1986*. Winnipeg, MB: University of Manitoba Press.

Minister of Indian Affairs and Northern Development. (1997). *Gathering strength: Canada's Aboriginal Action Plan*. Retrieved from http://publications.gc.ca/collections/collection_2012/aadnc-aandc/R32-189-1997-eng.pdf

Minore, B., & Katt, M. (2007). Aboriginal health care in Northern Ontario: Impacts of self-determination and culture. *Institute for Research on Public Policy Choices, 13*(6), 1–22.

Morales, S. N. (2006). A glass half empty: Drinking water in First Nations communities. In J. White, D. Beavon, & S. Wingert (Eds.), *Aboriginal policy research: Setting the agenda for change* (Vol. 3, pp. 161–185). Toronto, ON: Thompson Educational. Retrieved from https://ir.lib.uwo.ca/cgi/viewcontent.cgi?article=1320&context=aprci

Organisation for Economic Co-operation and Development. (2017). *Child poverty*. Retrieved from http://www.oecd.org/els/CO_2_2_Child_Poverty.pdf

Pettipas, K. (1994). *Severing the ties that bind. Government repression of Indigenous religious ceremonies on the prairies*. Winnipeg, MB: University of Manitoba Press.

Preston, J. P., Cottrell, M., Pelletier, T. R., & Pearce, J. V. (2012). Aboriginal early childhood in Canada: Issues of context. *Journal of Early Childhood Research, 10*(1), 3–18. Retrieved from http://ecr.sagepub.com/content/10/1/3.full.pdf+html

Public Health Agency of Canada. (2011). *Aboriginal Head Start in Urban and Northern Communities: A national analysis of the program's geographic reach*. Ottawa, ON: Author.

Public Health Agency of Canada. (2017). *Evaluation of the Aboriginal Head Start in Urban and Northern Communities program: 2011–2012 to 2015–2016*. Office of Audit and Evaluation, Health Canada, & Public Health Agency of Canada. Retrieved from https://www.canada.ca/content/dam/hc-sc/documents/corporate/transparency/corporate-management-reporting/evaluation/2011-2012-2015-2016-aboriginal-head-start-urban-and-northern-communities-program/ahsunc-apacu-eng.pdf

Royal Commission on Aboriginal Peoples. (1996). *Report on the Royal Commission on Aboriginal Peoples* (Vols. 1 & 3). Ottawa, ON: Ministry of Supply and Services Canada.

Standing Senate Committee on Human Rights. (2007). *Children: The silenced citizens: Effective implementation of Canada's international obligations with respect to the rights of children*. Ottawa, ON: Author. Retrieved from https://sencanada.ca/content/sen/committee/391/huma/rep/rep10apr07-e.pdf

Statistics Canada. (2016). *First Nations, Métis, and Inuit women*. Ottawa, ON: Author. Retrieved from http://www.statcan.gc.ca/pub/89-503-x/2015001/article/14313-eng.htm

Statistics Canada. (2017a). *Aboriginal Head Start in Urban and Northern Communities: Closing the gap in health and education outcomes for Indigenous children in Canada*. Ottawa, ON: Government of Canada, Public Health Agency of Canada. Retrieved from https://www.canada.ca/content/dam/hc-sc/documents/services/publications/healthy-living/aboriginal-head-start/closing-the-gap-fact-sheet-en.pdf

Statistics Canada. (2017b). *Aboriginal peoples in Canada: Key results from the 2016 census*. Ottawa, ON: Author. Retrieved from http://www.statcan.gc.ca/daily-quotidien/171025/dq171025a-eng.pdf

Statistics Canada. (2017c). *Diverse family characteristics of Aboriginal children aged 0 to 4*. Census in brief. Ottawa, ON: Author. Retrieved from http://www12.statcan.gc.ca/census-recensement/2016/as-sa/98-200-x/2016020/98-200-x2016020-eng.cfm

Truth and Reconciliation Commission of Canada. (2015). *Calls to action*. Winnipeg, MB: Author. Retrieved from http://www.trc.ca/websites/trcinstitution/File/2015/Findings/Calls_to_Action_English2.pdf

Walker, S. P., Wachs, T. D., Meeks Gardner, J., Lozoff, B., Wasserman, G. A., Pollitt, E., … International Child Development Steering Group. (2007). Child development: Risk factors for adverse outcomes in developing countries. *Lancet, 369*, 145–157.

Western Arctic Aboriginal Head Start Council. (2007). *Ten years of Aboriginal Head Start in the Northwest Territories 1996 to 2006*. Yellowknife, NWT: Author.

World Health Organization. (2007). *Early child development: A powerful equalizer*. Geneva, Switzerland: Author. Retrieved from http://www.who.int/maternal_child_adolescent/documents/ecd_final_m30/en/

Yoshikawa, H., Weiland, C., Brooks-Gunn, J., Burchinal, M., Espinosa, L., Gormley, W. T., … Zaslow, M. (2013). *Investing in our future: The evidence base on preschool*. Washington, DC: Society for Research on Child Development. Retrieved from https://www.fcd-us.org/the-evidence-base-on-preschool/

CHAPTER 14

There Are Relationships beyond the Classroom: A Nature Kindergarten

Enid Elliot

GUIDING QUESTIONS:

1. What are the benefits and challenges of learning and teaching out-side and in the natural environment?

2. How might you infuse elements and ideas of forest kindergarten theory and practice, and local Indigenous narratives and knowledge, into your own work with children?

It was September, and twenty-two children came out onto the school field with their new black rain pants swishing, grins on their faces and a bounce or two in their steps. A sunny day with the hint of a small breeze; the grass was a bit prickly due to having had a dry summer. Eyeing each other a little shyly and listening to the teacher's instructions to make a circle, the children put their little backpacks in a pile in the centre of what would be the circle and sat down. Introductions happened, and the teacher and early childhood educator began to build a community that would spend half of each day outside. After a year and a half of planning, the Sooke School District's Nature Kindergarten had started.

FOUNDING A NATURE KINDERGARTEN

Moving beyond the walls of the classroom into a natural landscape can offer children and educators different opportunities for learning than what might be available in a more customary classroom setting. The air, the earth, and the life found in the forests, creeks, beaches, or parks can offer teachings not found within a traditional classroom. Being outside, children experience the weather, the terrain, and the air; there are multiple invitations to engage in relationships unique to their particular place.

In British Columbia, the Sooke School District is on southern Vancouver Island within the traditional territory of the Coast Salish First Nations, the Kwsepsum (Esquimalt), Lekwungen (Songhees), Scia'new (Beecher Bay), and T'Sou-ke (Sooke) peoples. The school district opened a Nature Kindergarten in 2012 and has had students engaged in the forest and creeks adjoining Royal Roads University, the Esquimalt Lagoon, and the beaches of the Juan de Fuca Strait, all just west of the provincial capital of Victoria. This is a place of forests, rocky coastlines, sandy beaches, lakes, and meadows and has been loved, used, and appreciated over the past thousands of years by the Coast Salish peoples. Douglas fir, cedar, and Garry oak meadows offer narratives and knowledge unique to this part of the world. By being immersed in the living, breathing world, the children find educational opportunities that engage them at a local level in the lands where they live.

The idea for the Sooke Nature Kindergarten was inspired by the forest preschools from Northern Europe, where children and educators spend most of the day outside, whatever the weather, and which have been part of the Scandinavian tradition (Denmark, Sweden, and Norway) since the 1950s (Knight, 2009). A philosophy of *friluftsliv* is common to both Norway and Sweden. This "philosophical lifestyle is based on experiences of the freedom in nature and the spiritual connectedness with the landscape. The reward of this connectedness with the landscape is this strong sensation of a new level of connectedness with the landscape" (Gelter, 2000, p. 78). The founders of this approach believed that by engaging outdoors in their local natural setting, children would begin to understand and experience connections to their place (Robertson, 2008; Williams-Siegfredson, 2012). Having children outside engaged in the natural spaces where they lived was an appealing idea, and by the 1990s programs spread to the UK and Germany (Knight, 2009).

The initiators of the Sooke project, Frances Krusekopf, a principal in the school district, and I (Enid Elliot), an early childhood educator and researcher (Elliot & Krusekopf, 2017; Hoyland & Elliot, 2014), had both been intrigued and inspired by the Scandinavian models of forest schools when we met for coffee in January 2011 to discuss our mutual interest in this type of education. These Scandinavian programs were relatively common educational options in Northern Europe, but at the time were little known in Canada. We felt inspired to create a similar program in our community on southern Vancouver Island, where many schools have some direct access to forests, beaches, or a natural green space. Krusekopf felt the time was right and that the Sooke School District would be supportive of the idea.

Establishing a program within the BC provincial school system presented its own challenges. We needed to include in our educational vision and thinking a provincial curriculum that details the academic content for kindergarten and how this would be accommodated. Not only was an educational vision and curriculum fit needed, but we would also need to plan for the logistics of safety, teacher qualifications, the logistics of the day, the parent registration process, and other details.

Hearing of the plan to begin this type of program, interested individuals and organizations within our community gathered to help support and plan. While initially we were a small group from the school district and the local college and universities, the word spread, and soon people were asking to join the committee. We welcomed anyone who was interested. Besides a belief in the *idea* of a Nature Kindergarten, each person brought a unique perspective and orientation to our discussions. A diverse and dynamic group came together; the advisory committee was drawn from different segments of the community, including First Nations educators and environmentalists, early childhood educators and classroom teachers, academics, biologists, naturalists, and park interpreters. Each brought a unique idea of what a Nature Kindergarten might look like, each idea tinted with a person's personal experiences and passions. While this sort of program was not widely known in Canada, the idea of the Nature Kindergarten caught on quickly.

The Sooke school superintendent and school board provided space, as well as a teacher and an early childhood educator as staff, and took the risk to implement this novel program. In response, parents and children enthusiastically embraced the first year of the program (Elliot, 2014; Gordon, 2013) and have continued to do so in the following years. Many parents realized that they wanted something more, something different for their children than they had experienced in school (Gordon, 2013). Parents cited different reasons for choosing the Nature Kindergarten; some knew their child would fare better being able to move more freely, while others felt it was a good beginning for school and others wished they had had a similar program when they began school. Within the next couple of years, programs began in different areas of British Columbia and Canada, and the expansion of Nature Kindergartens grew to become a small movement (Elliot, 2014).

While our interest was primarily focused on the educational possibilities and opportunities of these programs (Elliot & Krusekopf, 2017), we were aware of the growing public concern about children's lack of engagement with nature and lack of exercise, as more and more of children's time is seemingly spent on computer games or other forms of digital entertainment (e.g., Gordon, 2013; Knight, 2009; Lohr, 2007). We were also aware of the concern that children were having little time for unstructured play in natural contexts in which they could explore their abilities of negotiation, imagination, and problem-solving (Scottish Government, 2013) because they were spending inordinate amounts of time with digital devices (Andrew-Gee, 2018). The time seemed to be right for a program of this type to be proposed.

PRINCIPLES FOR THE PROGRAM

Creating an educational vision to guide the teacher and early childhood educator in this program in their exploration of forests, creeks, and bushes meant finding and articulating a perspective and a guiding philosophy. The planning team needed to consider where the program's emphasis might lie and what skills would be key for the two educators, as they would be the ones who would truly find the form the program would take. The advisory group spent much time discussing logistics and ideas related to taking children outside for much of the day, regardless of weather. A set of principles emerged from the advisory group's discussion, which were meant to guide the educational experience.

- *Connecting Deeply with Nature: Environmental Stewardship*—teachers and students would nurture their relationship with nature by fostering a "Sense of Wonder," curiosity, and inquiry and by encouraging a sense of responsiveness, caring, and commitment to the environment and by supporting an understanding of ecology and sustainability.
- *The Environment as Another Teacher*—the value that all living things and systems are in connection with us; this concept is central to the program. Spending significant periods of time in the outdoors

should support children's growing awareness of their intertwined connections with natural landscapes and phenomena. Moving freely in outdoor spaces, learning by looking into and with nature rather than at it, developing self-confidence in natural landscapes, engaging with the sensuality of nature, engaging in unstructured and spontaneous play, and enjoying the sensory awareness of being engaged outside can all provide a rich learning situation.

- *Learning Collaboratively as a Part of a Community*—through a growing sense of place, children would begin to appreciate their connections within their local community, which includes family, neighbours, friends, and nearby nature. The students would learn and teach with a kindergarten teacher, early childhood educator, and community members such as First Nations Elders, Capital Regional District parks educators, Royal BC Museum curators, grandparents, and parents and build a sense of belonging and community by developing a sense of attachment to their "larger community" (Berry, 1988).

- *Physical and Mental Health*—with consistent and sustained interaction with the natural environment, children's physical and mental well-being can benefit, as being in a green setting fosters mental health and provides multiple opportunities for movement (Kuo, 2010). Exploring their physical abilities, children can find opportunities for taking risks and becoming comfortable in their bodies.

- *Aboriginal Ways of Knowing/Local Traditional Knowledges*—the forest the children would be entering each morning has been a special place of gathering and engagement for several Coast Salish First Nations, the Kwsepsum, Lekwungen, Scia'new, and T'Sou-ke (Turner, 2005; Turner & Hebda, 2012).

These principles were developed in order to guide the development, implementation, and evaluation of our program. Sharing them with the broader community to get their ideas and feedback was an important step in our process. Even before the Sooke Nature Kindergarten started, other schools and educators became interested in what we were doing. The process of articulating our key ideas provided opportunities for discussion among the advisory group, as well as with our wider community and the community of interested educators.

For example, we immediately got feedback on our proposal to include "Aboriginal ways of knowing"; several people within the local Indigenous community suggested our wording gave the impression that we were assuming a universal Aboriginal understanding of nature. Each Aboriginal band and First Nation has narratives, histories, and knowledge unique to their land. We were grateful for this feedback and changed the term to "local traditional knowledges." Through this, we began to understand that we needed to focus on sharing with the children the narratives that belong to the particular place in which they would be playing and learning. This aspect of our vision was complex and had multiple layers; even before the program started, we were learning to think carefully about what it might entail.

Another aspect we investigated deeply was the idea of the living, breathing world as a teacher. The world beyond humans has much to share with us, and local Indigenous narratives can help share understandings of that world with children that open their minds and hearts to hear and observe the teachings embedded in place (Hill & Wilkinson, 2014; Johnson, 2013). Hill and Wilkinson (2014) call land the first teacher and say "information is not simply transferred from educators to students, but is discovered and shaped by their interpersonal interactions both with and within the environment" (p. 184). Children learn, care, and connect in their own ways; different narratives and perspectives can provide guideposts to their understanding and encourage ways of seeing.

Being outside can inform a different pedagogy, as it provides opportunities for children to have more space for movement, expression, and exploration, not contained by a classroom's walls and ceiling. Engaging children wholly, body, mind, and spirit, we hoped they would see themselves as members of a community connected deeply to the place where we all live. As the children were a part of the ecosystem of south Vancouver Island, we hoped that the experience of Nature Kindergarten would allow the students' sense of community to expand into the "larger community" of which Thomas Berry speaks: the community of land, rocks, moss, and salamanders.

As the children's relationships with voles, mushrooms, or trees deepened, they could be open to the life and narratives embedded in their local landscape. Styres (2011) comments:

> Exploring the same land each day provides an ever changing/unchanging terrain. Land as pedagogy can be easily adapted to any geographical space (including urban centres) because it is land in all of its abstract and concrete fluidity, interrelatedness and shifting realities that informs pedagogy. In this way the past is renewed in (re)membering our connection to the land, how land informs pedagogy as well as how storied experiences are expressed through personal, community, national and global narratives. (p. 728)

BUILDING SAFETY AND COMMUNITY

Encouraging the children to take responsibility for themselves and each other was part of our risk management plan. Our belief was that children are capable of caring for themselves and each other. As the children arrived that first September, they were new to each other, to the idea of school, and to working together as a group; so, the first month was spent learning to pay attention to the educators when they called and how to stay safe in the group. Learning that the educators would care for them and help them stay safe began a process of building trust within the group. Children chose the calls that the educators would use to signal either for children's attention or to gather together. They learned how to behave if they sighted a predator (there are cougars and bears in the school's habitat), what to do if they stepped on a wasps' nest, and how to negotiate how high they felt safe climbing or what to do if they got lost in the forest. To promote children's responsibility to care for themselves, each child was given a kit of Band-Aids, Kleenex, a "space blanket," and emergency food to carry in their backpacks, as well as dry socks and extra mittens. Being in charge of a component of their own safety encouraged children to understand their own limits rather than limits imposed on them, and to learn that each person's safety depended on everyone's safety. Focusing on safety by caring for their own and others' well-being was a first step to building a community.

Learning that the teachers would care for them physically helped build their trust in their educators, which in turn could create an attachment with them that would provide security for the children (Elliot, 2007). This took on real meaning for the children, as they were aware of the presence of cougars and bears in the forest and the fact that they were potential prey. After several months during the first year, I was sitting beside a child in the forest and she shared she had had a nightmare about a cougar eating her. While there had been no cougar sighted up to that point in the year (and none in the subsequent years, although they are around), I realized that the children had continued to be aware of the possibility of meeting a predator. While by springtime they were feeling comfortable in the forest, they were conscious that they were part of an ecosystem in which they could be considered prey.

BECOMING A COMMUNITY OF LEARNERS

Within a community of safety, trust hopefully develops at an emotional, as well as physical, level. Building emotional trust was an ongoing project, and it was important to learn that it was safe to express one's self and that respect was both given and expected by educators. Within this community, self-regulation meant being responsive to the group and its particular dynamics. Each child found a place within the class as the class became a community. A child who insisted on barking all morning was told by the children that she could be a fairy dog, and fairy dogs "don't bark." Rather than being told to be quiet because her barking was annoying, the children found a way for her to still be a dog, but a quiet one.

While the teachers helped the children cohere into a group, being outside with feet on the earth and surrounded by fresh air lent support to the teachers' efforts. Each day as the children entered the site where they would spend the morning, they went to the spot where they regularly sat for five to ten minutes (a shorter time in the beginning and longer as the year progressed). Each child had found their place to sit in quiet within the site. One child, who could not easily sit quietly, found a spot by a log that he could repeatedly climb and jump from as the other children sat quietly. This disturbed no one, as the forest floor cushions jumps and his movement took place in fluid and shifting surroundings where his movement was part of the ongoing gestalt.

In the forest or on the shore, there is space to be a dog or a restless child. The educators tried to recognize what children needed and respond appropriately. Movement was not necessarily curtailed but channelled in ways that supported a child and the group's well-being. Trees invited different moves and encouraged children to pay attention when they climbed in the branches. As trust grows, relationships can become stronger as the children listen to each other and to the educators. They learned with each other and with the place within which they were located; they were connected within a web of relationships. Over time, their attachments to the more-than-human world seemed to grow deeper and stronger.

Over the course of one year, a group of the children watched an anthill grow and change. Every morning, they walked by it to see what there was to notice about the ants and their home. As the fall advanced, they wondered why the anthill grew quieter. "Perhaps they are afraid of the ghosts in the woods," they wondered near Halloween time. Over the year of observation, theorizing and listening to stories and information about ants, the children learned that activity lessens in the colder months. They also learned which ants protected the colony or found food or cared for the babies. When, one morning in the spring, they found that someone had put a log and stones on the anthill, they were indignant, knowing that logs and stones were not good for the ant home. The children were angry and made signs to warn others that this was the ants' home and to be careful. A smaller group of children went to the other classes in their school to share their understanding of ants and ask for their help in protecting the ants' home. The children's interest and curiosity had motivated their learning; the familiarity of daily observation had encouraged the children to become advocates for the ants. The teachings from the ants, land, and educators had provoked the group into taking action.

EMBODIED KNOWING AND CONNECTEDNESS

Being outside in the forest or at the seashore has layers of learning, experiencing, and teaching, and while the landscape appears to remain the same over time, it also changes with the seasons and weather. A familiar trail has surprises along the way as one learns to look carefully and see small changes or gifts. After the first autumn rain, mushrooms appeared along an oft-taken trail. In January, the striking yellow and distinctive odour of the skunk cabbage in bloom appeared. One morning, a child with sharp eyes spotted a dead vole; it was grey, blending into the soil and barely an inch or two long. She ran with it to the teachers, and together they looked it up in their guidebooks to see if they could find out what its name was. They found it, a long-tailed vole, and quickly discovered it was not alone, but had a maggot burrowing inside it.

The surprises and gifts are endless. While the class moves into their site each morning, they find the trees and the rocks that they found the day before. Simms (2008) reminds us that "we are cradled among places that stay put" (p. 38). This constancy provides security to children, just as does the behaviour of the teachers who remain consistent and strive to keep them safe. Bowlby (1978) noted that the mother can provide a secure base from which the infant explores, comfortable in the knowledge she is available to him or to her if she is needed. Expanding on Bowlby's ideas of attachment, we can consider the role of place as providing a place of security for the children. Children head into the forest or venture along the shore, and they find the earth feels firm and familiar to their feet and the trees are still standing guard. Place does shift and change; rain creates puddles where the ground was dry, mushrooms appear, the moss turns brown in the summer heat, but still the place welcomes a child back and offers the sanctuary of the cedar tree that stays put, or the pleasure of the water in Bee Creek, which runs through the forest found adjacent to Royal Roads University.

Through their senses, children's bodies and minds become attuned to a place. They learn where to expect the turns in the path, but soon understand there are many changes and new additions to be discovered on that path. Knowing the landscape helps the children become sensitive to the changes and shifts in the setting. They learn to spot the red fungus that has appeared overnight, or new buds on the red currant bush, or animal scat that wasn't there yesterday. The wind and air change with the seasons and so does the rain. Whether they can articulate it or not, their bodies learn to know when to keep moving to stay warm, or how to move on a wet, slippery log that is easier to walk along when it's dry, or the satisfaction of jumping in a puddle even if their socks get wet. Through their bodies they develop a sense of "embodied connectivity" (Rose & Robin, 2004).

Understanding worms is different when you have observed their appearance after a rain and held them in your hand. At that point, they are not just a science fact from a textbook, but a living creature that invites you to know it. Each creature has its habits and ways of being. Earthworms wiggle out with lots of rain. Salamanders are difficult to find and hold. One child became an expert salamander finder; he understood on a five-year-old level that inside decaying wood or under a log, he might find the Western red-backed salamander, and with quick eyes and quicker hands, he found and caught several at a time (and, with encouragement, let them go). What was it he understood about salamanders? What drove him to try to find them? He seemed to feel a kinship with the salamanders and held them gently and with pride.

TEACHING/LEARNING WITHIN THE LARGER COMMUNITY

Multiple relationships exist outside in the wider world. The trees, the natural materials, and the life found outside the classroom form community with the children and educators. Thomas Berry (1988) reminds us that "the natural world is the larger sacred community to which we belong." In a Nature Kindergarten, the children and the educators are immersed in a larger community that offers teachings and relationships, and they can learn to pay attention to the invitations found along the paths they take. The children learned to ask questions and the educators learned alongside the children, finding answers or asking more questions. The teachers' roles shifted as they explored the forest and beaches near their school together. Not knowing the name of a dead owl, they asked a local bird expert; wondering about Bee Creek and the life it held, they listened with the children to the volunteers who cared for and cared about Bee Creek. They approached their pedagogy as "contextualized, grounded in organic and dynamic relationships" (Styres, 2011, p. 721).

The educators were engaged with the children in observing the ants. They listened to children's ideas and theories, asking questions and then offering resources and further knowledge to build on their thinking. Children began to incorporate into their theories the information and stories offered by the educators. Sharing time and space with the ants meant the ants became part of the children's world, included in their community. Information was useful; engaging in the anthill observations and understanding that the ants had homes and "children" and needed food helped the children connect to the ants. As Ingold (2000) reminds us,

> information, in itself, is not knowledge, nor do we become any more knowledgeable through its accumulation. Our knowledgeability consists, rather, in the capacity to situate such information, and understand its meaning, within the context of a direct perceptual engagement with our environments. And we develop this capacity, I contend, by having things shown to us. (p. 21)

Upon sighting a bird's nest, one kindergarten boy told me, this past school year, "that is my first time of seeing a bird's nest in the real." Imagine the excitement and satisfaction when something seen in a book or heard about becomes three-dimensional. Seeing the nest gave him a different understanding of nests, where they might appear, how they really look, and how they are nestled in the trees. With luck, he will see more nests over his life and come to a richer appreciation of them than he would have if he just read about them in books, and perhaps he will be more motivated to look. This knowledge found locally in the land, and the creatures and materials found there, gives substance to the world. "Eye and ear, nose and mouth, skin and hand are engaged and nourished by their encounter with the things of the world" (Simms, 2008, p. 20).

While we speak of the impacts on both children and educators on seeing the world in its sensual form, the world is, in turn, impacted by the children. If the world is a "symphony of relationships" (Weber, 2017, p. 29), then children also leave echoes behind. Twenty children in a forest site help the decomposing logs disintegrate faster than they might without the children climbing and playing. Having entered into a relationship with the ants, the children could educate other children on the importance of respecting anthills.

Encounters with salamanders, ant colonies, and cedar trees all provide relationships and offer teachings. There is so much to wonder about when travelling in the forest. There are multiple stories to share—why worms come out in the rain, why cedar is a powerful ally, the history of immigrants and settlers—about plants and people.

WHAT WE MIGHT LEARN FROM INDIGENOUS PEDAGOGIES

Elders and knowledge keepers have visited and shared knowledge and teachings with the kindergarteners. Thanking the cedar tree for its protection and power, Elders have emphasized the importance of reciprocity, shared with the children that the gifts that trees and plants share with us must be recognized and gratitude given. Children heard which trees would be used for canoes, how cedar bark was used for clothing, and what plants were useful for healing. An Aboriginal support worker supported the class's interests with stories, information, and Elder visits to enhance the children's interests and share simple words for welcome and thanks. The support worker could enrich the children's interests with a story or an invitation to a local Elder and/or knowledge keeper. When the children expressed interest in whittling, a carver came in to share his work. Exploring the nature of water, the children heard of the importance of honouring water and how important water is to the life in our world. Elders brought in teachings that reflected a view of the living, breathing world that respected and honoured all its inhabitants (Greenwood & de Leeuw, 2007).

These small stories are tentative beginning steps to include a place-based wisdom that is embedded in the particular world the children find outside their classroom. Learning to thank the site that they visit each day, knowing that cedar can be powerful, or that a certain plant is useful for finding their way home enrich the children's understandings of the natural world and life.

Indigenous scholar Gregory Cajete (1994) writes of an Indigenous model of knowledge that "sees the world as an intimate relationship of living things" (p. 13). Speaking of education, he reminds us that we understand something by knowing it with mind, body, emotion, and spirit. Certainly the children observing the ants in their colony over the year had come to understand the ants through mind, body, and emotion. They felt a connection with the life found in the colony as they observed the ants' movements while they felt the air and weather, talked about it, and empathized with the ants having their home disturbed. It became more than a hill of dirt. With that connection to the ants and other materials and life in the forest, the children learned to appreciate and see the life found outside the classroom. They are beginning to know, as Kimmerer (2013) reminds us, that the world is "a neighbourhood of nonhuman residents" similar to what Berry (1999, 2006) means when he speaks of our "larger community."

Indigenous scholars (Johnson, 2013; Styres, 2011; Watts, 2013) remind us that many Indigenous cultures see the world as filled with spirit. Kimmerer (2013) speaks of her Potawatomi culture/language as knowing that "rocks are animate, as are mountains and water and fire and places" (p. 55). In the Nature Kindergarten, children spoke of a rock growing when walking down a trail in a heavy downpour or noting that the sky was waving to us when the clouds parted one day. In a discussion about the nature of water, children observed that water moved, grew, transformed, and could hold one. They carried on a discussion over the year about whether water was alive.

On finding a dead owl, the children gathered around it and wondered what kind of owl it was, how it had died, and if its family missed it. The Aboriginal support worker shared with the children that among her community there was an understanding that seeing an owl could mean the death of something, like a bad habit or a fear of something. The children talked about what bad habit they might give up and went on to wonder if the owl was happy when it died.

Children are reminded of their responsibility in their relationships with the land and living things. They are given power and shelter by the cedar tree, water gives life to people, and we all share the air. Children learn to thank their site before they leave it and talk about the importance of gratitude and being aware of one's responsibility. Immersed in the environment outside, children who feel their connection can also begin to feel a responsibility. Wading in Bee Creek in the springtime, a child saw a dead shrimp and worried that their wading had caused the shrimp's death. The class discussed their possible responses to the concern the next day before heading out to the creek. They wondered if they tiptoed or walked along the edges if that might prevent stepping on one of the shrimps. When they arrived at the creek, though, the pull of the water was overwhelming, and they rushed right in, but they had discussed the ethical situation and had a beginning awareness of their responsibility. As Thomas Berry (1999) writes, "everything has a right to be recognized and revered. Trees have tree rights, insects have insect rights, rivers have river rights, and mountains have mountain rights" (p. 5).

We can find inspiration in Indigenous narratives and the knowledge of the plants, animals, and other landforms that are part of our local landscape. There are stories to remind us of our responsibility to care for the world outside the classroom and be grateful for all it offers us. The children's learning is enriched with the knowledge that is shared from the local First Nation.

THE WAY FORWARD

Going beyond the classroom walls can provide exciting educational opportunities for young children. Taking away the walls encourages both educators and children to pay attention to the larger world in which we live and breathe. Educators are challenged to engage with the children in the world they find outside and make space for the power of the natural world to instruct. Stepping into the world beyond the walls, we move into a living system in which we are a small part. Perhaps we can re-imagine our connections with the world and with education by taking away the walls and finding the place where we live.

REFERENCES

Andrew-Gee, E. (2018). Your smartphone is making you stupid, anti-social and unhealthy. So why can't you put it down? *Globe and Mail*. Retrieved from https://http://www.theglobeandmail.com/technology/your-smartphone-is-making-you-stupid/article37511900/

Berry, T. (1988). *The dream of the earth*. San Francisco, CA: Sierra Club Books.

Berry, T. (1999). *The great work: Our way into the future*. New York, NY: Bell Tower.

Berry, T. (2006). *Evening thoughts: Reflecting on Earth as sacred community*. San Francisco, CA: Sierra Club.

Bowlby, J. (1978). *Attachment* (2nd ed., Vol. 1). London, UK: Penguin Books.

Cajete, G. (1994). *Look to the mountain: An ecology of Indigenous education*. Durango, CO: Divaki Press.

Elliot, E. (2007). *"We're not robots": The voices of infant/toddler caregivers*. Albany, NY: SUNY Press.

Elliot, E. (2014). Envisioning a nature kindergarten. *Green Teacher, 103*, 38–42.

Elliot, E., & Krusekopf, F. (2017). Thinking outside the four walls of the classroom: A Canadian nature kindergarten. *International Journal of Early Childhood, 49*(5) 1–15. doi: 10.1007/s13158-017-0203-7

Gelter, H. (2000). Friluftsliv: The Scandinavian philosophy of outdoor life. *Canadian Journal of Environmental Education, 5*(1), 14.

Gordon, A. (2013, 5 June). Star dispatches: Forest kids: Why the modern classroom is moving outside. *Toronto Star.* Retrieved from https://http://www.thestar.com/news/insight/2013/06/05/star_dispatches_why_the_modern_classroom_is_moving_outside.html

Greenwood, M., & de Leeuw, S. (2007). Teachings from the land: Indigenous people, our health, our land, and our children. *Canadian Journal of Native Education, 30*(1), 48–53.

Hill, G., & Wilkinson, A. (2014). Indigegogy: A transformative Indigenous educational process. *Canadian Social Work Review, 31*(2), 175–193.

Hoyland, T., & Elliot, E. (2014). Nature kindergarten in Sooke: A unique collaboration. *Canadian Children, 39*(2), 39–44.

Ingold, T. (2000). *The perception of the environment: Essays on livelihood, dwelling and skill.* London, UK, and New York, NY: Routledge.

Johnson, L. M. (2013). Plants, places, and the storied landscape: Looking at First Nations perspectives on plants and land. *BC Studies, 79*, 85–101.

Kimmerer, R. W. (2013). *Braiding sweetgrass: Indigenous wisdom, scientific knowledge and the teachings of plants.* Canada: Milkweed.

Knight, S. (2009). *Forest schools and outdoor learning in the early years.* London, UK: Sage.

Kuo, F. (2010). Parks and other green environments: Essential components of a healthy human habitat. In *Research Series.* National Recreation and Parks Association

Lohr, V. (2007). Benefits of nature: What we are learning about why people respond to nature. *Journal of Physiological Anthropology, 26*(2), 83–85.

Robertson, J. (2008). *I ur och skur: "Rain or shine" Swedish forest schools.* Creative Star Learning Company.

Rose, D. B., & Robin, L. (2004). The ecological humanities in action: An invitation. *Australasian Humanities Review, 31–32.*

Scottish Government. (2013). *Play strategy for Scotland: Our vision.* Edinburgh, UK: Author.

Simms, E. M. (2008). *The child in the world.* Detroit, MI: Wayne State University Press.

Styres, S. D. (2011). Land as first teacher: A philosophical journey. *Reflective Practice, 12*(6), 717–731.

Turner, N. (2005). *The earth's blanket: Traditional teachings for sustainable living.* Vancouver, BC/Toronto, ON: Douglas & McIntyre.

Turner, N., & Hebda, R. (2012). *Saanich ethnobotany: Culturally important plants of the WSÁNEĆ people*. Victoria, BC: Royal BC Museum.

Watts, V. (2013). Indigenous place-thought and agency amongst humans and non-humans (First Woman and Sky Woman go on a European world tour!). *Decolonization: Indigeneity, Education and Society, 2*(1), 20–34.

Weber, A. (2017). *Matter and desire: An erotic ecology* (R. Bradley, Trans.). Hartford, VT: Chelsea Green.

Williams-Siegfredson, J. (2012). *Understanding the Danish forest school approach: Early years education in practice*. Oxford, UK: Routledge.

CHAPTER 15

Young Children Using Digital Technology: The Case of Belle

Laura Teichert

GUIDING QUESTIONS:

1. How do children use digital technology in their lives?
2. How do you feel about children's use of technology and media from a young age? Do you support it, not support it, or are your feelings somewhere in the middle? Explain.

INTRODUCTION

Digital technology has proliferated across much of Western society, and young children are quickly becoming daily users of digital devices. Children from six months to six years are reported to use screens every day for recreation, school work, or reading (Rvachew, 2016) and are living media-rich childhoods (Kucirkova, Littleton, & Kyparissiadis, 2018; Marsh et al., 2005; Rideout, 2011, 2013; Rideout, Vandewater, & Wartella, 2003). In the two years between 2011 and 2013, Common Sense Media noted dramatic increases in young children's access to mobile media devices (e.g., iPads). For example, in 2011, only 8 percent of families surveyed accessed an iPad, but by 2013, 40 percent of families used iPad technology. Although traditional screen time (e.g., TV, DVD) for children between birth and eight years declined, mobile screen time saw a threefold increase in that two-year period. In some American families, children owned their own mobile device (e.g., iPad) before they entered kindergarten and engaged in media multitasking (i.e., using an iPad to play a game while watching TV) (Kabali et al., 2015). In Canada, Media Smarts reported one quarter of fourth-grade students owned their own smartphone, while 30 percent of grade four to six children have a Facebook page, despite being younger than the minimum age of 13 years.

Tensions continue to exist about whether digital technology is necessary in young children's lives. The Canadian Paediatric Society (2017) issued a policy statement urging parents and caregivers to limit young children's daily screen time: one hour or less for children between two years and five years and no screen time for children under two years. Yet young children continue to access and use digital technology in their homes and early years classrooms (Harwood et al., 2015; Laidlaw & Wong, 2016; Marsh, Hannon, Lewis, & Ritchie, 2017; Plowman, McPake, & Stephen, 2013; Wohlwend, 2015). Therefore, it is important to understand what digital technology and digital tools young children access and how they use digital technology and digital tools in their everyday lives. I use the term *digital tools* as an umbrella term that encapsulates the many different digital technologies used in society. In line with Marsh's (2004) characterization of "techno-literacy" (p. 52), I include both new technologies and older technologies in this term. Therefore, I refer to digital tools as devices that require computerized technology to operate. This chapter focuses on digital technology in the early years by focusing on examples of how one four-year-old girl used digital technology in her home.

MULTIMODALITY AND DIGITAL PLAY

The technological developments of the 21st century brought a shift to communication patterns in Western society. A key component of this shift was the acknowledgement of the role of non-print ways (or *modes of communication*) people represent meaning. Using the term *multimodality*, theorists view literacy as meaning-making that involves multiple modes of "visual, gestural, spatial, and other forms of representation" (Perry, 2012, pp. 58–59). Jewitt (2008) called these multiple modes of communication "new multimodal ensembles" (p. 241) that humans draw from to represent and communicate meaning. Kress (2000) referred to this process as "means of expression" (p. 182) and included music (i.e., sound) and technology in the many modes humans use to create meaning and understand their worlds. In an educational context, this shift changes both "what is to be learned … and how it is to be learned" (Jewitt, 2008, p. 241). Kress and Van Leeuwen (2001) suggested that four domains of practice guide the "question of meaning" (p. 4) within multimodal communication: discourse, design, production, and distribution. Discourse refers to the socially constructed knowledge developed within a specific context that governs how social actors appropriate meaning—for example, understanding the difference between speaking in a job interview and speaking with friends. Design is the "conceptual side of expression" (p. 5) and employs "semiotic resources" (p. 5) in all modes and combinations of modes to communicate meaning. This requires individuals to understand which modes of communication best express their meaning, whether it be one mode (e.g., writing) or multiple modes (e.g., movement and music). Production involves organizing the expression and the "material articulation of the semiotic event" (p. 6) or the manufacturing of the "semiotic artefact" (p. 6). This results in something material, such as a book or a webpage, a product that may be shared. And finally, there is distribution, which may not affix meaning, but facilitates the "pragmatic functions of preservation and distribution" (p. 7), such as the necessary dynamic between musical performers and the technicians who record their music digitally.

Play-based theories of early learning dominate curricula in Canada (e.g., BC's Early Learning Framework [Government of British Columbia, 2008, 2018]; Ontario's Kindergarten Program [Ontario Ministry of Education, 2016]). Vygotsky (1978) argued that play is one of the stimuli for the child's internal development processes, as play provides children with learning opportunities. Play allows the child to explore cultural symbol systems, including reading, writing, gesture, visual, and sound, and it is through play that "the child achieves a functional definition of concepts or objects" (p. 99). For example, a child uses a toy smartphone and imitates the behaviours of adults using the device in the real world. This may include pretend phone calls or pretend text messaging. Play provides spaces for children to engage with multiple modes of expression and to try on new ways of communicating with those around them.

Today, children's play environments are a "complex series of interactions between consumption, digital media and meaning making" (Edwards, 2011, p. 204). Edwards (2011) contended that play that involves digital technology and media sits beside traditional play and is not inferior to it. Edwards (2013) used the term *converged play* to refer to play that was related to children's popular cultural artifacts and texts and argued that traditional and converged play are not oppositional but interrelated. She argued converged play also leads to imaginative play and supports children's connection with reality, which provides children with learning opportunities to make meaning from relevant cultural tools in their local communities. Similarly, Marsh, Plowman, Yamada-Rice, Bishop, and Scott (2016) adapted Hughes's (2002) definitions of play type to reflect contemporary children's digital realities and defined digital play using Hughes's traditional play types. For example, Hughes described symbolic play as "when children use an object to stand for another object, [for example] a stick becomes a horse" (p. 246), while Marsh and colleagues extended this definition into the digital sphere by defining symbolic play as "when children use a virtual object to stand for another object [for example] an avatar's shoe becomes a wand" (p. 246). In total, Marsh and colleagues redefined 16 types of play to include digital activities. They also argued that contemporary children now navigate between online and offline spaces, and although the tools used in some play activities have changed, the type of play children engage in remains the same. Therefore, contemporary children engage in play activities that incorporate adult-world digital devices and "pretend their way into [digital] literacies by 'playing at' using computers, iPads, or cellphones as they try on technologically savvy user identities" (Wohlwend, 2010, p. 145). Digital play is now observed in young children's classrooms and homes and can be viewed as an important part of children's budding understanding of the important cultural tools of their communities.

In the next section, I address the research examining young children's access and use of digital technology in early childhood classrooms and in their homes.

REVIEW OF RESEARCH

Digital Tools in Early Childhood Classrooms

There still exists a tension in early childhood classrooms about the appropriateness of digital technology for young learners. Research continues to document early childhood educators' concerns about screen time and digital technology's place in play-based classrooms. For example, Wolfe and Flewitt (2010) described early childhood educators who worried that a technology-dominated childhood had the potential to damage "family time" and communication. Finch and Arrow (2017) reported early childhood educators who believed parents used digital devices as "baby-sitting" tools

(p. 12), while multiple scholars have reported early childhood educators who felt children spent enough time with digital technology in their homes and therefore did not need further opportunities with these devices in their classrooms (Finch & Arrow, 2017; McTavish, Anderson, Anderson, Laidlaw, & Wong, 2017). Despite these concerns, researchers and educators have built early years pedagogies that incorporate digital tools into play-based early years classrooms, most notably Karen Wohlwend's (2013) *Literacy Playshop* curriculum, which positions children as multimedia producers rather than passive recipients of media messages. In the study, Wohlwend and her research team established a moviemaking centre in three preschool and kindergarten–grade one classrooms in a midwestern American city. The moviemaking centre included a video recorder and dramatic play toys, which the children could use to create movies. They found children explored, experimented, and refined their video-recording abilities over the course of the project; that the final product of recording was secondary to the children's desires to simply play with the technology; and that children had "few expectations for the content of their films" (p. 39). They also found that the moviemaking centre provided children many opportunities to collaborate and negotiate shared meaning-making as they decided who held the video camera or what story they would film. Teachers scaffolded the children's narrative understandings by introducing storyboards and other narrative organizers, as well as facilitating classroom discussions, or "critical conversations," about "heroes, villains, and power" (p. 9) presented in many of the popular-culture and movie characters children borrowed from as they explored in the moviemaking centre. Similarly, Roberts-Holmes (2014) described an early childhood classroom in South West England that embraced digital technology in its classrooms by hiring a digital media consultant to assist educators and children in creating mini-movies with touchscreen PCs. Roberts-Holmes noted educators believed the movie-making project increased children's motivation and developed children's "positive learning dispositions" (p. 6). Like Wohlwend (2013), Roberts-Holmes also noted the collaborative way children developed and negotiated their movies and cooperated when using the touchscreen PCs. In addition to movie-making projects, other studies of early years classrooms have documented children's informational search abilities (Spink, Danby, Mallan, & Butler, 2010); how young children transferred digital skills from one digital device to another (Levy, 2009); young children's phonemic awareness and early literacy development using digital devices (McLean, 2017; Northrop & Killeen, 2013);

and how digital tools allowed children to engage in "communicative practices and meaning making through play" (McLean, 2017, p. 247).

Tablet technology instigated a shift in early years digital pedagogy because of the technology's ease of use, flexibility, and portability (Geist, 2012). The iPad was first introduced by Apple in 2010 and affords young learners "greater multimodal meaning-making and … productive consumption of media text" (Rowsell & Harwood, 2015, p. 138). Tablet technology allowed young children the opportunity to move from passive viewers of digital content to producers and creators of media texts. Researchers have documented young children in roles of director and author of digital content (Laidlaw & Wong, 2016); children as producers of digital photographs and film creation (Harwood et al., 2015); children who used specialized applications that allowed them to take photographs and record their verbal explanations or to upload videos they recorded (McGlynn-Stewart et al., 2017); how children used puppet applications collaboratively to create a shared narrative (Wohlwend, 2015); and how children extended their inquiry learning by accessing information from tablets (Finch & Arrow, 2017; Harwood et al., 2015). In addition to creating and producing digital content, researchers have noted the ways children have developed social skills while using digital technology in their early years classrooms. Children learned to problem-solve software difficulties independently (or with the help of peers), rather than solely rely on their teachers (Harwood et al., 2015; McLean, 2017). Children learned to self-regulate while waiting to use the limited number of tablets available in their classrooms and to share with their classmates (Harwood et al., 2015). The portability of tablet devices allowed children to move around classrooms to interact and collaborate with friends, such as playing apps together or creating media texts (Rowsell & Harwood, 2015; Wohlwend, 2015). Tablet technology allowed children to easily view and share each other's work (Laidlaw & Wong, 2016) and to move from digital spaces to non-digital spaces with ease (Rowsell & Harwood, 2015). Tablet technology also shifted teachers' abilities to immediately respond to children's queries and allowed teachers to create responsive learning communities (Harwood et al., 2015).

Digital Tools in the Home

Many children's first experiences with digital technology come from interactions in their homes. Marsh's (2004) seminal study defined children's early engagement with digital tools as "techno-literacy" (p. 52). At the time, Marsh argued literacy skills were no longer limited to paper-based activities and that children accessed texts from multiple modes and highlighted the "importance of visual, aural, and corporeal ways of meaning-making" (p. 52), not just print. She used a questionnaire and interviews to ask parents about their children's literacy practices in the home in relation to a variety of media: books and comics, environmental print, TV and film, computer games, mobile phones, and music. From participants' answers, Marsh outlined children's emergent techno-literacy practices and the role(s) parents (and other significant adults) played in scaffolding children in learning to use these technological devices. She found that parents supported and encouraged young children's techno-literacy practices, and these practices played a role in families' relationships in the home. For example, the area around the TV was often set up for "celebrating and extending the children's relationship with the screen" (p. 58), such as keeping dress-up clothes or toys nearby so children could easily access these props when re-enacting screen content. She also noted that children were not simply passive viewers but played with narratives and images viewed on the screen through re-imagined storylines and imitation of on-screen behaviour. As well, she found that 14 of the 26 families in her study owned a video game console and in those 14 homes, men introduced children to video games and supported children's learning of both the game and devices (e.g., operation of a joystick). Men were more likely to collaborate with children in video game play, whereas women were more likely to participate in print-literacy activities (e.g., read a storybook).

Other seminal work in this field came from a group of scholars in Scotland. Over the last decade, this group documented what digital tools three- to five-year-old children used, how they used them, and how their parents mediated these uses (McPake, Plowman, & Stephen, 2013; McPake, Stephen, Plowman, Sime, & Downey, 2005; Plowman, McPake, & Stephen, 2008). They described children as "encountering technologies in the home" (Plowman, Stevenson, Stephen, & McPake, 2012, p. 33) because encounters were unplanned or fleeting and not predictable patterns. Findings from their three longitudinal studies found that by the time children entered kindergarten, they had encountered a variety of digital devices, such as mobile phones, TVs, video game consoles, DVD players, and MP3 music players, and that children enjoyed using technology in their homes and were acquiring a range of technical competencies with a variety of digital devices (Plowman et al., 2012; Stephen, McPake, Plowman, & Berch-Heyman, 2008). Most of the children lived in homes with mobile phones (98 percent), interactive TV (75 percent), and a computer with Internet access (69 percent) (Plowman et al., 2008). Children surfed websites independently and with adult supervision, and many children could independently operate mobile phones (Plowman et al., 2008). New technology was a favoured source of entertainment, but children continued to engage with traditional toys and enjoyed outdoor physical activity (Stephen et al., 2008). They noted children viewed digital technology as part of their "everyday environment and understood their [the device's] purposes" (McPake et al., 2013). Children drew from digital technology and media in play activities, such as dressing up like their favourite character or re-enacting scenes (Plowman & McPake, 2013) or using old and discarded digital tools (e.g., computers, supermarket scanners, or laptops) in their homes as play props during imaginative play and games (McPake et al., 2013). As well, digital technology provided young children opportunities to engage in relevant communicative practices before being able to write or type, for example, by sending an emoji or photograph to family members on a mobile phone (McPake et al., 2013; Plowman & McPake, 2013).

In addition to these well-known studies, other researchers explored young children's uses of digital technology in their homes. O'Hara (2011) reported what digital tools four- and five-year-old children could operate in their homes. He found children could operate personal computers (PCs) and various video game consoles; operate two or three remote controls in conjunction with one another; use zoom, widescreen, and fast forward options on DVD players (skipping segments of videos they found boring); turn on PC monitors and properly shut down computer systems; locate desired games on the PC; navigate children's websites; and drag and drop files accurately. An important finding by O'Hara was that access to digital tools did not necessarily mean children used the digital tool. For example, 20 families reported owning a scanner, but only four parents reported that their child had any experience using the device. Gillen and colleagues (2018) documented how children between birth and age three years used digital technology in their daily lives. Their qualitative study of 11 families across Europe found digital technology was used in a variety of ways and integrated into "the rhythm of the day" (p. 5). The authors found children learned technical skills (i.e., how to operate the device) while developing literacy skills and discovering content they enjoyed. How frequently children used digital technology varied. Low levels of young children's digital engagement involved "just watching TV/Youtube" (p. 5), while young children using digital technology more frequently also played "games or apps on tablets or smartphones" (p. 5) or engaged in Skype calls with relatives.

Entertainment is often reported as one of young children's purposes for using digital technology. Friedrich, Teichert, and Devadas (2017) observed children use digital tools to entertain themselves. Children used digital tools to watch cartoons, sing along to music videos, or play games; for example, one participant accessed music videos in Thai, Burmese, and Chinese. Children were also observed extending their knowledge on a topic by using Google or accessing content-specific websites (e.g., a science website intended for children). Four-year-old Kelly, in Stephen, Stevenson, and Adey's (2013) study, used her Puppy Grows and Knows Your Name electronic toy dog in imaginative and creative play. Kelly constructed an evolving story of "a family of toys going to a ballet class" (p. 159). Huh (2015) noted that children pretended to be their favourite digital-game characters while engaged in non-digital play. For example, one of the children in her study, Chan, pretended to be a "super strong" (p. 164) robot, a character from his favourite digital game, while he used a plastic squirt gun to water his mother's tomato plant. He also recreated scenes from this game while playing with his friends in rough and tumble play, climbing on the couch while pretending to be characters from the game.

Plowman and colleagues (Plowman et al., 2008; Plowman et al., 2012) identified levels of competencies in four main areas of learning with technology within the home: operational learning; extending knowledge and understanding of the world; developing dispositions to learn; and understanding the role of technology in everyday life. Below I describe each learning area and provide an example of this learning from the literature.

Operational learning encompasses learning how to control and use devices and getting the technology to do the things you want it to do, (e.g., loading the correct web browser or operating a mouse). Davidson's (2010) conversation analysis of a brother and sister playing a CD-ROM game, *A Day with the Wiggles*, is an example of children's operational learning of computer practices. Davidson documented how the four-year-old brother and six-year-old sister played the game, and found that the game's repetitive structure oriented family members to assist the children without actively playing the game alongside them. The parents attended to their children when requested and assisted immediately without having to watch the children play. Family members used previous knowledge to talk about the game with the children. From a sociocultural perspective, the gestures and talk by the father and older sister scaffolded the four-year-old boy's understanding of the game and helped him navigate the game. Through social interaction, he learned to read symbols in certain ways and to act on these symbols.

Extending knowledge and understanding of the world described the role of technology in finding out about people, places, and the natural world. In a study with different participants, Davidson (2009) described six-year-old Matthew's informational search practices with a computer in his home. In one episode, Matthew, with the help of his father, used Google to search for lizards. His father supported Matthew's searching practices by guiding him (entering keywords into the search engine), using gesture (pointing at images on the screen), and using verbal cues (asking questions, replying and/or reinforcing Matthew's comments, praising Matthew's knowledge), a process Vygotsky referred to as operating within the zone of proximal development (ZPD) (1978). Interestingly, Matthew did not rely solely on Google for acquiring information about lizards. He combined his Google search with a print book about reptiles. His mother assisted him in locating the name of the lizard he wanted to search, the green basilisk lizard, in his book. On his own, he copied the words from his book into the Google search bar. By using both digital and print tools, Matthew was able to accomplish his task and extend his knowledge of lizards.

The phrase *dispositions to learn* describes children showing greater concentration and persistence and gaining self-confidence while becoming more competent users of digital technology. Levy (2009) documented 12 three- to six-year-old children using a variety of texts (digital and non-digital) in both their home and school settings in order to examine how children read digital texts and how this compared to reading paper-based texts. She found that before entering formal schooling, the children acquired "transferable literacy" (p. 84); that is, the children developed skills that allowed them to "operate unfamiliar technologies with fluency" (p. 84). For example, one participant, Shaun, had little contact with computers at home and mostly played games with the TV, mobile phones, and hand-held game consoles; yet he transferred those skills to the computers at school, and his teacher reported that with little instruction, he could "do loads on the computer" (p. 84), such as play games and search computer files. Levy also described how many of the children in her study could apply their previous knowledge of computers to a new screen context and with little help "access a range of texts with independence" (p. 85), such as transferring the knowledge of a desktop mouse to a laptop trackpad.

Understanding the role of technology in everyday life considers how children develop a "cultural awareness" (Plowman et al., 2008, p. 309) of digital technology's role in their family life. Children may demonstrate this awareness by asking to send family members who live at a distance a text message or picture, using vocabulary related to digital tools, such as "load Internet" or "iPhone" (Plowman et al., 2008). Children come to understand the role of digital technology in everyday life through both observation of adults and through adult scaffolding (Bruner, 1983, 1986). In her study, Wong (2015) described how five-year-old Andrew used the iPad and could independently take photographs, enter passwords, and spell "Lego" when using search engines. While at child care, Andrew used the iPad to video record his play with friends. At home, the iPad contributed to Andrew's motivation and independent learning as he simultaneously engaged with Lego instructions, print books, and YouTube videos reviewing Lego. Despite his limited traditional reading and writing skills, the iPad allowed Andrew to produce and design literacy texts. For example, Andrew, with the help of his father, planned, rehearsed, recorded, and uploaded his own Lego review to YouTube. His engagement with the Lego reviewer community on YouTube inspired and motivated him to create his own Lego review, and the iPad allowed him to accomplish this task.

In the next section, I describe the ways one four-year-old child used technology and digital tools in her home as one realization of technology and multimodality in one Canadian home.

BELLE: USING DIGITAL TECHNOLOGY IN HER HOME

Methods and Participant

The child reported on in this chapter is one participant of a larger case study examining young children's engagement with digital tools in their homes before and as they transitioned into kindergarten. The study used three primary sources of data, collected over 12 months: two semi-structured interviews with focal mothers (one at the beginning of the study and one to conclude the study), participant observations in the participants' homes, and media capture function[1] shared via mobile phone. Following Plowman and Stevenson (2012), focal parents were asked to provide a digital image (with descriptive text) once a month to me via mobile phone. The purpose of this data collection method was to understand how families used digital technology in their everyday lives in the absence of the researcher.

Belle[2] was an only child and lived in a rented one-bedroom apartment with her mother, Lindsay. She was four years old when the study began and celebrated her birthday in June 2015. From the age of 12 months, Belle attended child care five days a week while her mother worked. The child care centre followed a play-based curriculum that centred on different themes throughout the year. The centre fostered academic development through activities such as circle time, shared book reading or read alouds, and learning the letters of the alphabet. Belle was interested in digital technology and used digital tools as Lindsay allowed. She also enjoyed reading stories and re-enacting narratives from her books. She engaged in dramatic play with her stuffed animals, Disney princess dolls, and an assortment of kitchen and restaurant dramatic play toys (e.g., tea party set, grocery set).

Belle's home contained a number of digital tools: TV with cable and a DVD player, Leap Pad 2 Mini,[3] iPad, Leap Frog Me Reader,[4] Leap Frog Violet[5] (toy dog), audiobooks, a laptop, and "Naya," Belle's battery-operated horse. Lindsay owned a BlackBerry smartphone and a landline telephone. Lindsay did not regulate Belle's digital technology use, but she did not particularly encourage it either. Belle was allowed to use all devices in the home under Lindsay's supervision, but Lindsay encouraged other activities before giving Belle digital tools. For example, Lindsay described a beading craft they had begun doing together (a children's kit that provided beads and accessories for necklaces and/or bracelets) (Fieldnote, March 29, 2015) and cooking together (Fieldnote, September 6, 2015). Lindsay placed an emphasis on physical activity and was concerned Belle did not get enough exercise during the week. Since Lindsay wanted Belle to be physically active, when she and Belle were home, rather than promote activities using a digital tool, Lindsay promoted physical activity, such as going to the park or swimming pool. She also enrolled Belle in ballet, a once-a-week class that lasted 45 minutes, and gymnastics before that. However, due to the popularity of the sport and the limited number of spaces, she was only able to register Belle into lessons during the summer months. Lindsay also enrolled Belle in swimming lessons "but not in the winter" due to the weather (Informal conversation, March 29, 2015). When Belle did engage with digital technology in her home, she did so in three ways: to entertain herself, to learn, and to transmediate from digital to non-digital spaces.

Entertainment

In general, Belle engaged in activities in her home because they entertained her; she found them fun and enjoyable. Her digital choices were no different.

She played with digital tools she enjoyed using, such as her Leap Pad Mini 2, which allowed her to play games and read stories, or the iPad, which she used to play games, watch Netflix, and gain information on topics she was interested in. As Belle simply explained, she chose these activities because "they're fun!" (Fieldnote, May 17, 2015). Over the course of the study, Belle's digital interests shifted from Netflix programs, such as *Mia and Me*, and Disney movies to iPad app games called *Clumsy Ninja*, *Cat Hotel*, and *Blossom Blast*. After Christmas holidays, Belle was most excited about the gift her grandfather gave her, as I documented in my fieldnotes:

> Belle excitedly told me about a karaoke machine she received from her grandfather for Christmas. The machine was a Disney product and featured the movie *Frozen*. Belle told me she used it at her grandfather's house and could "sing and dance" along to the music. She explained the *Frozen* karaoke machine played four songs, "even Let It Go," and that two songs had words and two songs were "just instruments." Lindsay explained the karaoke machine did not come with a screen, but was "fairly certain" the machine connected to a computer or iPad and displayed lyrics. She also thought you might be able to use any CD with the machine and therefore access a greater variety of music. (Fieldnote, January 17, 2016)

This digital tool combined two of Belle's interests: the Disney movie *Frozen* and music. Belle was eager to entertain herself and sing along to familiar songs.

Digital entertainment for Belle also translated into opportunities to explore and create meaning in her world. I now provide an example of how Belle learned and developed skills using digital technology in her home.

Learn

Belle owned a Leap Pad Mini 2 and mostly used the device as an electronic reading tool (i.e., an e-book). The Leap Pad Mini 2 was a handheld device that allowed her to manually input and load a variety of game cartridges. Each game cartridge contained many different activities, such as read-aloud stories, word games, colouring activities, and quest games (in which the user has to accomplish tasks before advancing to the next level in the game). It also came with a plastic pen Belle could use to tap the screen. Reading aloud was an activity Belle enjoyed and often asked me to read print-based storybooks to her during my observations. She most frequently accessed the read-aloud function and word games available on her Leap Pad Mini 2.

The device offered two options for reading aloud: electronically reading the story to Belle or Belle reading the story herself and using the pen to tap unfamiliar words, which were then read aloud by the device. Belle used her Leap Pad Mini 2 to help her learn to read. I observed her use this digital tool during three separate observations, two of which I describe. The first time Belle showed me her Leap Pad Mini 2, she input her *Tangled* cartridge and showed three features, first the colouring game:

> Belle first showed me how she could colour in her *Tangled* game. Belle used her Leap Pad pen to tap the colouring icon. Once the page loaded she asked me which image I wanted to colour. I chose the picture of Rapunzel with a flower. Belle tapped a colour wheel to select a colour and then tapped a section of the picture. The colour appeared on the page. She continued this process until all sections of the picture contained colour. (Fieldnote, March 29, 2015)

She next showed me how the Leap Pad Mini 2 read stories aloud to her:

> On the main menu page Belle tapped the book icon. This feature read the story aloud to Belle. She sat on the couch and held the Leap Pad while the audio recording of the story played. (Fieldnote, March 29, 2015)

The final feature Belle showed me was a word game:

> After hearing the story, Belle returned to the main menu and selected a game. It was a word game. The Leap Pad displayed two or three words (the game increased in difficulty as it progressed) on the screen, and an audio recording asked Belle to select a particular word (by tapping the word on the screen with her pen), for example, "cat." If Belle selected the correct word the game congratulated her. If she selected the incorrect word the Leap Pad read the word out loud while flashing the word on the screen. (Fieldnote, March 29, 2015)

On another occasion, I observed Belle select the read-aloud function in her new *Sophia the First* game cartridge:

> Belle held the device and read aloud along with the Leap Pad. The *Sophia the First* story progressed when Belle tapped the small book icon on the bottom of the right page. Belle sounded out unfamiliar words and then

tapped the screen to hear the correct reading. She did this until she completed the story. (Fieldnote, September 6, 2015)

The American Academy of Pediatrics (2011) argued that children who live in homes with heavy media use spend "between 25% (for three to four-year old) and 38% (for five to six-year old) less time being read to or reading [independently]" (p. 3) and are less likely to read compared to peers with low media use in their homes. Because many educators saw shared book reading as an important site for children's language and literacy development, as well as for acquiring or constructing concepts, information, or knowledge (Kucirkova, Snow, Grover, & McBride-Chang, 2018), any decrease in reading time was seen as potentially detracting from children's learning. Yet Belle's use of the Leap Pad Mini 2 increased her opportunities to engage in shared book reading in the home and assisted her development of letter-sound correspondence and word recognition, as the device isolated letter sounds or identified unknown words for Belle when she tapped the word.

Transmediate from Digital to Non-Digital Spaces

Over the course of the study, it became apparent that Belle's digital interests influenced her non-digital activities. Belle borrowed characters, action sequences, or narrative arcs from favoured TV programs or movies in her non-digital play (e.g., dramatic play with dolls). Suhor (1984) referred to this process as "transmediation" and described it as understanding one sign system and moving it into another sign system in order to create meaning. Belle's transmediation practices were most evident in the ways she borrowed characters and storylines from the Netflix TV program *Mia and Me*.[6] The following is an example of how Belle borrowed elements of *Mia and Me* to inspire her non-digital play:

I observed Belle transmediate *Mia and Me* from a digital space to a non-digital space:

I arrived at Belle's apartment for my observation, and Belle was finishing her dinner. She watched *Mia and Me* on Netflix with the iPad propped up by a support so she could watch "hands-free" as she ate dinner. Lindsay cleared the dishes and cleaned the kitchen while Belle finished. Once she was done eating, Belle left the table and began to draw on her blackboard with chalk. She drew a unicorn. She told me this was Uncha, the baby unicorn from *Mia and Me*. She then drew Mia riding Uncha and departed from the storyline of the episode she just watched and created a new narrative arc. As she drew her picture on the blackboard she narrated the action of her story (the new narrative arc). Belle decided Mia was the only person who could ride unicorns (in addition to communicate with them) and drew wings on Uncha so that Uncha could fly (unicorns do not have wings on the TV program). Once her chalk drawing was completed, Belle recorded her new narrative in a small notebook that contained images, alphabet letters and short words. (Fieldnote, September 6, 2015)

In another example, Belle showed me a picture she had drawn earlier in the week that was inspired by *Mia and Me*. Belle drew a book that resembled Mia's *The Legend of Centopia* book. Belle was inspired to retell her favourite scene in the TV program and explained that that story was contained in her book. Belle drew symbols to match the runes from that episode and explained, "When I clip the book like this [pages together], it takes me to another world like Mia" (Informal conversation, September 6, 2015). In *Mia and Me*, the oracles in the book are upside down. Photo 15.1 shows Belle using a mirror to unlock the oracles in the book she created.

Photo 15.1: Belle Unlocking Oracles

Marsh (2004) described children who were "active meaning-makers" (p. 56) when viewing TV. She observed that when children began watching a TV program or a movie, they temporarily sat quietly, but as the movie or TV show progressed, they engaged in a number of activities, such as talking about the programming, talking to the characters, or dancing and/or singing along with programming. This is consistent with Belle's engagement with *Mia and Me*. She watched an episode, or parts of an episode, and used the storyline to create a new episode on her chalkboard. Belle did not simply retell the original story but extended the plot by allowing Uncha to have wings and for Mia to ride Uncha in Centopia. Wohlwend (2009) noted the ways young children transmediated their digital interests into paper-based activities in a primary classroom. She observed a kindergarten boy construct his own "iPod using materials that were 'to hand' in his classroom" (p. 126). The young boy used pompoms, pipe cleaner, yarn, and paper to construct his "dial and an LCD screen display that read 'Thomas and Friends'" (p. 126). Wohlwend also described the action and negotiation between two young boys playing a print-based version of a two-player video game, *Digimon Rumble Arena*.

CONCLUSION

The Canadian Paediatric Society (2017) warns that young children are passive viewers of digital technology and that digital tools take away from more meaningful activities. The case of Belle shows that this view of young children using digital technology is not always accurate. While Belle is only one child, the findings are consistent with the last decade of research in the field of early digital literacy (e.g., Gillen et al., 2018; Laidlaw & Wong, 2016; Marsh et al., 2005; Marsh, Hannon, Lewis, & Ritchie, 2017; Plowman et al., 2008, Plowman et al., 2012; Plowman & McPake, 2013). Belle was an "active meaning-maker" (Marsh, 2004) who used digital tools in her home for entertainment, learning, and transmediation. First and foremost, Belle used digital technology as a method to entertain herself while at home. She enjoyed watching Netflix TV programs, watching movies, playing app games on the iPad, and singing karaoke on her *Frozen* karaoke machine. These activities were not always done passively; rather, Belle frequently danced and played while she enjoyed digital programming. She transmediated (i.e., moved from a digital mode to a non-digital mode) as she watched *Mia and Me*; she recreated and extended episode storylines on her chalkboard and created her own book of oracles. As well, digital devices allowed Belle to supplement her early literacy skills. Belle enjoyed storybooks and being read aloud to, and her Leap Pad Mini 2 allowed her to practise her reading skills while her mother engaged in household chores or was otherwise occupied in the home. Most importantly, Belle's use of digital technology did not displace other activities more positively associated with childhood, such as shared book reading with her mother, socio-dramatic play with her dolls and stuffed animals, and playing board games. Digital tools were one mode Belle drew from to make meaning in and of her world. This research highlights the way educators can build from children's digital interests in their classrooms to move children from passively using digital technology to being producers and creators of media content.

NOTES

1. Media capture function refers to images and text shared between mobile phones. I asked parents to send me one image (e.g., photograph) with descriptive text in a text message or email between in-home visits.
2. Belle is the child's self-selected pseudonym.
3. Leap Pad devices are similar to handheld video game consoles. The device allows users to interchange cartridges to play different games and activities. Each cartridge is based on a story, which the reader can read at their own pace, or a child can listen to a narration of the story. A pen allows the user to touch the screen to identify and assist the user in decoding the unknown word (i.e., it slowly reads each syllable in the word). Leap Pad allows the user to touch the screen to complete objectives in games and activities.
4. Me Reader is an audiobook collection. Each book comes with a CD so that users may read along with while the audiobook is playing.
5. Leap Frog Violet is a battery-operated dog that comes with five books. The title of each book identifies the skill developed in each book: *Pattern*, *Narrative*, *Concept*, *Rhyming*, and *Learn About*. Violet, the stuffed dog, has a number of buttons on its face and paws, which are to be pushed as the book is read. Violet reads the book and asks comprehension questions, which prompt the user to touch particular buttons on Violet.
6. *Mia and Me* is the story of a girl named Mia who attends a prestigious boarding school in Florence, Italy, as an exchange student. Her parents recently passed away in an accident. Her father was a successful game maker, and Mia's aunt gives her a game he made before his death. The game is in the form of a large book called *The Legend of Centopia* (a book he read to her when she was younger), which is

full of mystical rune writing that gives Mia passwords that allow her to enter the magical world of Centopia. The land is full of winged elves (fairies), pans (goat-like creatures), unicorns, dragons (which do not breathe fire), etc. When in Centopia, Mia is a winged, fairy-like elf girl. Mia is very special because she can talk to unicorns, and no one else has that ability. Mia and a unicorn, Lyria, using the oracles from the magic book, must find all the pieces of the Trumptus (a magic horn), which was stolen, broken into 20 pieces, and scattered throughout Centopia by order of the evil queen. The evil queen ordered this because the Trumptus is the one thing that can destroy evil creatures.

REFERENCES

American Academy of Pediatrics. (2011). Policy statement: Media use by children younger than 2 years. *Pediatrics, 128*(5), 1–7. Retrieved from http://pediatrics .aappublications.org/content/early/2011/10/12/peds.2011-1753

Bruner, J. (1983). Play, thought, and language. *Peabody Journal of Education, 60*, 60–69.

Bruner, J. (1986). *Actual minds, possibly worlds.* Cambridge, MA: Harvard University Press.

Canadian Paediatric Society. (2017). Screen time and young children: Promoting health and development in a digital world. *Paediatrics & Child Health, 22*(8), 461–468. doi: 10.1093/pch/pxx123

Davidson, C. (2009). Young children's engagement with digital texts and literacies in the home: Pressing matters for the teaching of English in the early years of schooling. *English Teaching: Practice and Critique, 8*(3), 36–54. Retrieved from http://education.waikato.ac.nz/research/files/etpc/files/2009v8n3art3.pdf

Davidson, C. (2010). "Click on the big red car": The social accomplishment of playing a Wiggles computer game. *Convergence: The International Journal of Research into New Media Technologies, 16*(4), 375–394. doi: 10.1177/1354856510375526

Edwards, S. (2011). Lessons from "a really useful engine"™: Using Thomas the Tank Engine™ to examine the relationship between play as a leading activity, imagination and reality in children's contemporary play worlds. *Cambridge Journal of Education, 41*(2), 195–210. doi:10.1080/0305764X.2011.572867

Edwards, S. (2013). Post-industrial play: Understanding the relationship between traditional and converged forms of play in the early years. In A. Burke & J. Marsh (Eds.), *Children's virtual play worlds: Culture, learning and participation* (pp. 10–26). New York, NY: Peter Lang.

Finch, B., & Arrow, A. (2017). Digital technologies in the literate lives of young children. In C. McLachlan & A. Arrow (Eds.), *Literacy in the early years: Reflections on international research and practice* (pp. 221–238). Singapore: Springer Science + Business Media.

Friedrich, N., Teichert, L., & Devadas, Z. (2017). The techno-literacy practices of children from diverse backgrounds. *Language & Literacy, 19*(3), 21–34.

Geist, E. A. (2012). A qualitative examination of two-year-olds' interaction with tablet based interactive technology. [Report]. *Journal of Instructional Psychology, 39*(1), 26–35.

Gillen, J., Aliagas, C., Bar-lev, Y., Flewitt, R., Jorge, A., Kumpulainen, K., … Tomé, V. (2018). *A day in the digital lives of children aged 0–3.* Summary report by DigiLitEY ISCH COST Action IS1410 Working Group 1: Digital Literacy in Homes and Communities.

Government of British Columbia. (2008). *British Columbia early learning framework.* Victoria, BC: Ministry of Health and the Ministry of Children and Family Development.

Government of British Columbia. (2018). *Revised British Columbia early learning framework.* Victoria, BC: Ministry of Education.

Harwood, D., Bajovic, M., Woloshyn, V., Di Cesare, D. M., Lane, L., & Scott, K. (2015). Intersecting spaces in early childhood education: Inquiry-based pedagogy and tablets. *The International Journal of Holistic Early Learning and Development, 1,* 53–67.

Hughes, B. (2002). *A playworker's taxonomy of play types* (2nd ed.). London, UK: PlayLink.

Huh, Y. J. (2015). Making sense of gender from digital game play in three-year-old children's everyday lives: An ethnographic case study. *Journal of Comparative Research in Anthropology and Sociology, 6*(1), 155–170.

Jewitt, C. (2008). Multimodality and literacy in school classrooms. *Review of Research in Education, 32,* 241–267. doi: 10.3102/0091732X07310586

Kabali, H., Irigoyen, M., Nunez-Davis, R., Budacki, J., Mohanty, S., Leister, K., & Bonner, R. (2015). Exposure and use of mobile media devices by young children. *Pediatrics, 136*(6), 1044– 1050. doi: 10.1542/peds.2015-2151

Kress, G. (2000). Multimodality. In B. Cope & M. Kalantzis (Eds.), *Multiliteracies: Literacy learning and the design of social futures* (pp. 182–202). New York, NY: Routledge.

Kress, G., & Van Leeuwen, T. (2001). *Multimodal discourse: The modes and media of contemporary communication.* London, UK: Arnold.

Kucirkova, N., Littleton, K., & Kyparissiadis, A. (2018). The influence of children's gender and age on children's use of digital media at home. *British Journal of Educational Technology, 49*(3), 545–559. doi: 10.1111/bjet.12543

Kucirkova, N., Snow, C., Grover, V., & McBride-Chang, C. (Eds.). (2018). *The Rout-ledge international handbook of early literacy education*. New York, NY: Routledge.

Laidlaw, L., & Wong, S. (2016). Literacy and complexity: On using technology within emergent learning structures with young learners. *Complicity: An International Journal of Complexity and Education, 13*(1), 30–42.

Levy, R. (2009). "You have to understand words … but not read them": Young chil-dren becoming readers in a digital age. *Journal of Research in Reading, 32*(1), 75–91. doi: 10.1111/j.1467-9817.2008.01382.x

Marsh, J. (2004). The techno-literacy practices of young children. *Journal of Early Childhood Research, 2*(1), 51–66.

Marsh, J., Brooks, G., Hughes, J., Ritchie, L., Roberts, S., & Wright, K. (2005). *Digital beginnings: Young children's use of popular culture, media and new technologies*. Sheffield, UK: University of Sheffield. Retrieved from www.digitalbeginnings. shef.ac.uk

Marsh, J., Hannon, P., Lewis, M., & Ritchie, L. (2017). Young children's initiation into family literacy practices in the digital age. *Journal of Early Childhood Research, 15*(1), 47–60. doi: 10.1177/1476718X15582095

Marsh, J., Plowman, L., Yamada-Rice, D., Bishop, J., & Scott, F. (2016). Digital play: A new classification. *Early Years, 36*(3), 242–253. doi:10.1080/09575146.2016 .1167675

McGlynn-Stewart, M., MacKay, T., Gouweleeuw, B., Hobman, L., Maguire, N., Mogyorodi, E., & Ni, V. (2017). Toys or tools? Educators' use of tablet applications to empower young students through open-ended literacy learning. In M. Mills & D. Wake (Eds.), *Empowering learners with open-access learning initiatives* (pp. 101–123). Heshey, PA: IGI Global.

McLean, K. (2017). Literacy, technology and early years education: Building sus-tainable practice. In C. McLachlan & A. Arrow (Eds.), *Literacy in the early years: Reflections on international research and practice* (pp. 239–257). Singapore: Springer Science + Business Media.

McPake, J., Plowman, L., & Stephen, C. (2013). Pre-school children creating and communicating with digital technologies in the home. *British Journal of Educa-tional Technology, 44*(3), 421–431. doi:10.1111/j.1467-8535.2012.01323.x

McPake, J., Stephen, C., Plowman, L., Sime, D., & Downey, S. (2005). Already at a disadvantage? ICT in the home and children's preparation for primary school. (ICT Research Bursaries 2004 Final Report). Retrieved from http://www.york .ac.uk/res/e-society/projects/3/already_disadvantage.pdf.

McTavish, M., Anderson, J., Anderson, A., Laidlaw, L., & Wong, S. (2017, July). *Accessing, using and understanding digital technologies and media across communities, contexts and social demographics: Cases of young children, youth, families, and teachers.* Paper presented at the 20th European Conference on Literacy, Madrid, Spain.

Northrop, L., & Killeen, E. (2013). A framework for using iPads to build early literacy skills. *The Reading Teacher, 66*(7), 531–537. http://www.jstor.org/stable/41853102

O'Hara, M. (2011). Young children's ICT experiences in the home: Some parental perspectives. *Journal of Early Childhood Research, 9*(3), 220–231. doi: 10.1177/1476718X10389145

Ontario Ministry of Education. (2016). *The kindergarten program.* Toronto, ON: Queen's Printer for Ontario.

Perry, K. (2012). What is literacy? A critical overview of sociocultural perspectives. *Journal of Language & Literacy Education, 8*(1), 50–71. http://jolle.coe.uga.edu/wp-content/uploads/2012/06/What-is-Literacy_KPerry.pdf

Plowman, L., & McPake, J. (2013). Seven myths about young children and technology. *Childhood Education, 89*(1), 27–33. doi: 10.1080/00094056.2013.757490

Plowman, L., McPake, J., & Stephen, C. (2008). Just picking it up? Young children learning with technology at home. *Cambridge Journal of Education, 38*(3), 303–319. doi:10.1080/03057640802287564

Plowman, L., McPake, J., & Stephen, C. (2013). Pre-school children creating and communicating with digital technologies in the home. *British Journal of Educational Technology, 44*(3), 421–431. doi: 10.1111/j.1467-8535.2012.01323.x

Plowman, L., & Stevenson, O. (2012). Using mobile phone diaries to explore children's everyday lives. *Childhood, 19*(4), 539–553.

Plowman, L., Stevenson, O., Stephen, C., & McPake, J. (2012). Preschool children's learning with technology at home. *Computers & Education, 59*, 30–37. doi:10.1016/j.compedu.2011.11.014

Rideout, V. J. (2011). *Zero to eight: Children's media use in America.* Retrieved from www.commonsensemedia.org/research/zeroeight-childrens-media-use-america.

Rideout, V. J. (2013). *Zero to eight: Children's media use in America 2013: A Common Sense Media research study.* Retrieved from www.commonsensemedia.org/research/zero-to-eight-childrensmedia-use-in-america-2013#.

Rideout, V. J., Vandewater, E. A., & Wartella, E. A. (2003). *Zero to six: Electronic media in the lives of infants, toddlers and preschoolers.* Washington, DC: Kaiser Foundation.

Roberts-Holmes, G. (2014). Playful and creative ICT pedagogical framing: A nursery school case study. *Early Child Development and Care, 184*(1), 1–14. doi: 10.1080/03004430.2013.772991

Rowsell, J., & Harwood, D. (2015). "Let it go": Exploring the image of the child as a producer, consumer, and inventor. *Theory into Practice, 54*(2), 136–146. doi: 10.1080/00405841.2015.1010847

Rvachew, S. (2016). Technology in early childhood education. In *Encyclopedia on Early Childhood Development* (pp. 3–4). Montreal, QC: Social Sciences and Humanities Research Council of Canada and Ruth Ratner Miller Foundation.

Spink, A., Danby, S., Mallan, K., & Butler, C. (2010). Exploring children's web searching and technoliteracy. *Journal of Documentation, 66*(2), 191–206. doi:10.1108/00220411011023616

Stephen, C., McPake, J., Plowman, L., & Berch-Heyman, S. (2008). Learning from the children: Exploring preschool children's encounters with ICT at home. *Journal of Early Childhood Research, 6*(2) 99–117. doi: 10.1177/1476718X08088673

Stephen, C., Stevenson, O., & Adey, C. (2013). Young children engaging with technologies at home: The influence of family context. *Journal of Early Childhood Research, 11*(2), 149–164. doi: 10.1177/1476718X12466215

Suhor, C. (1984). Towards a semiotic-based curriculum. *Journal of Curriculum Studies, 16*(3), 247–257.

Vygotsky, L. (1978). *Mind in society: The development of higher psychological processes.* Cambridge, MA: Harvard University Press.

Wohlwend, K. (2009). Early adopters: Playing new literacies and pretending new technologies in print-centric classrooms. *Journal of Early Childhood Literacy, 9*(2), 117–140. doi: 10.1177/1468798409105583

Wohlwend, K. (2010). A is for avatar: Young children in literacy 2.0 worlds and literacy 1.0 schools. *Language Arts, 88*(2), 144–152.

Wohlwend, K. (2013). *Literacy playshop: New literacies, popular media, and play in the early childhood classroom.* New York, NY: Teachers College Press.

Wohlwend, K. (2015). One screen, many fingers: Young children's collaborative literacy play with digital puppetry apps and touchscreen technologies. *Theory into Practice, 54*(2), 154–162. doi: 10.1080/00405841.2015.1010837

Wolfe, S., & Flewitt, R. (2010). New technologies, new multimodal literacy practices and young children's metacognitive development. *Cambridge Journal of Education, 40*(4), 387–399. doi: 10.1080/0305764X.2010.526589

Wong, S. (2015). Mobile digital devices and preschoolers' home multiliteracy practices. *Language and Literacy, 17*(2), 75–90.

CONTRIBUTOR BIOGRAPHIES

Zuhra Abawi is a contract lecturer at the School of Early Childhood Studies at Ryerson University. Zuhra holds a doctorate in education from OISE/University of Toronto and is an Ontario Certified Teacher and Registered Early Childhood Educator. Zuhra has worked as an early childhood educator and elementary teacher at the Peel District School Board and has taught teacher education at the University of Western Ontario and Niagara University. Zuhra's research interests are race and identity constructions in early learning.

Jessica Ball is a professor in the School of Child and Youth Care at the University of Victoria, Canada. She has written and taught countless courses on child and youth health and development, including teaching in universities in Canada, the United States, Malaysia, Singapore, and Bangladesh. At UVic, she was a founding faculty member in UVic's Early Childhood Development Virtual University, teaching initial cohorts of leaders in Africa and the Middle East. She teaches upper-level undergraduate courses on mental health and addictive behaviours and graduate courses on social determinants of child development. Her program of research includes a range of projects centring on cultural and policy contexts of child wellness, early learning, and development. She is the author or co-author of three books and more than 120 journal articles, monographs, and book chapters. She has presented at more than 300 conferences, symposia, policy roundtables, and workshops in Canada and internationally. Her achievements have been recognized by awards for teaching, knowledge mobilization, contributions to Indigenous children's well-being, and research in service of communities.

Rachel Berman is an associate professor in the School of Early Childhood Studies at Ryerson University and the director of the MA program. She is the editor of the book *Corridor Talk: Canadian Feminist Scholars Share Stories of Research Partnerships*, published by Inanna Publications in 2014. She is currently the principal investigator of the Social Sciences and Humanities funded research project entitled "Can We Talk about Race? Confronting Colour-Blindness in Early Childhood Settings," which examines ways to foster conversations about "race" in early childhood settings.

Aurelia Di Santo is an associate professor in the School of Early Childhood Studies at Ryerson University. Aurelia's main research interests are children's rights and their participation in their early learning programs and in research. Her current research includes how children's rights are integrated into curriculum for the early years and quality early childhood environments. Aurelia has extensive work experience in a variety of early childhood settings, which ranges from working directly with children to managing early learning and care centres. Internationally, Aurelia has worked in early childhood development projects in Brazil and Egypt. Her current work involves two projects in Bolivia: working with educators and families to construct low-cost custom adaptations for children with disabilities and supporting children to realize their right to play by providing them with a soccer program.

Enid Elliot is an early childhood educator who has been continually surprised, intrigued, and delighted by the babies, children, families, and early childhood educators with whom she has worked, played, and loved. Having experienced the influence of natural settings on young children over the years, she was involved in creating the Nature Kindergarten in the Sooke School District, which opened in September 2012. For the first four years of the program, she spent one day a week learning and listening with the children and educators outside and spent the past year gathering the educators' stories. Her current questions concern the pedagogy that emerges as educators and children explore/engage deeply with all the layers of the natural/material landscape found outside school walls. She is currently on faculty at Camosun College and is an adjunct professor at University of Victoria.

Lovisa Fung is a doctoral candidate at the University of Toronto and a teacher educator who specializes in research on transformative teaching and learning, teachers' life narratives, and preservice teacher development. She is a contract lecturer at Ryerson University and continues research through her doctoral studies and public speaking.

Susan Jagger is an assistant professor in the School of Early Childhood Studies at Ryerson University. Her research interests include environmental education, learning gardens, community mapping, poststructuralism and deconstruction, informal learning, science education, children's participation, participatory research, and arts-based research approaches. Currently, she is working with and in an urban elementary school community to explore the strengths and challenges of urban school gardening, map children's evolving environmental attitudes and actions, and engage children as researchers of their own school garden experience.

Noah Kenneally is a childhood researcher, a doctoral candidate in Social Justice Education at the Ontario Institute for Studies in Education at the University of Toronto, and a contract lecturer in the Ryerson University School of Early Childhood Studies. He uses relational approaches and arts-based methods to research with and alongside children to explore their perspectives of social worlds.

Randa Khattar has been teaching in andragogical contexts for the past 15 years. She is an adjunct assistant professor at Western University and executive director for the Centre of Excellence for Early Years and Child Care. Prior to that, she was an assistant professor at Charles Sturt University, where she continues to serve as adjunct professor in the School of Teacher Education. She has published and presented internationally and serves in elected positions as the Ontario provincial director for the Canadian Association for Young Children (CAYC) and vice-president on the board of the Ontario Reggio Association. She is the co-editor of the *Journal of Childhood Studies*, a peer-reviewed international journal. Her research, anchored within an interdisciplinary constellation of post-foundational, complexity, and eco-feminist theories, and located within the Common Worlds Research Collective, uses creative paradigms to problematize developmental childhood discourses. She is curious about the multiple ways we can co-exist in a more-than-human world.

Patrick J. Lewis is a professor of early childhood education with the Faculty of Education at the University of Regina since 2004. Prior to that, he was a primary teacher in the Gulf Islands of BC for 14 years and an elementary teaching vice-principal for three years in the Victoria, BC, school district. He has published articles, book chapters, and books on education, play, story, narrative, treaty education, and indigenization.

Margaret MacDonald is an associate professor in the Faculty of Education at Simon Fraser University in Burnaby, British Columbia, Canada. Her research focuses on pedagogical documentation and responsive, generative curriculum practices in early childhood education.

Meagan Montpetit is a doctoral candidate at the Faculty of Education at Western University. Meagan's doctoral research extends on her work as a pedagogical facilitator in London, Ontario, and engages with child/more-than-human assemblages. Thinking with posthuman feminism, Meagan's research highlights the sometimes messy tensions that emerge in the nuanced spaces she explores with children.

Veronica Pacini-Ketchabaw is a professor of early childhood education in the Faculty of Education at Western University in Ontario, Canada. Her current research, within the Common Worlds Research Collective, traces the common world relations of children with places, materials, and other species.

Bethany Robichaud is a doctoral student in the Faculty of Education at the University of Prince Edward Island. Her experience as an early childhood educator ranges from working directly with and for children and families in early learning centres to facilitating school- and community-based early childhood programming. Bethany's research interests include children's rights broadly, rights-based education, and children's rights and climate change.

Laura Teichert is a professor in the Department of Special Education and Literacy Studies at Western Michigan University. Her research interests focus largely on early literacy and early digital literacy in both home and school contexts. Laura previously worked at Pear Tree Elementary, a private K–7 school in Vancouver, and as an early literacy specialist with EarlyON.

Kristy Timmons is an assistant professor in the Faculty of Education at Queen's University. Kristy's teaching experience spans the early years, elementary, undergraduate, and graduate levels. Her research interests centre on the processes that influence young children's learning, engagement, and self-regulation. Within this broad focus, she has carried out research with children, families, and pre- and in-service educators. These studies include the implementation and impact of full-day kindergarten in Ontario, family literacy intervention programs, pre-service early childhood educators' beliefs about children's learning, and the influence of expectations on learning outcomes. More specifically, Kristy's current research explores the influence of educator and child expectations on kindergarten children's early reading, vocabulary, and self-regulation outcomes.

Peter Pericles Trifonas is a professor at the Ontario Institute for Studies in Education/University of Toronto. His areas of interest include ethics, philosophy of education, cultural studies, and technology. Among his books are the following: *Deconstructing the Machine* (with Jacques Derrida); *Converging Literacies*; *International Handbook of Semiotics*; *International Handbook of Research and Pedagogy in Heritage Language Education*; *CounterTexts: Reading Culture*; *Revolutionary Pedagogies: Cultural Politics, Education, and the Discourse of Theory*; *The Ethics of Writing: Derrida, Deconstruction, and Pedagogy*; *Institutions, Education, and the Right to Philosophy* (with Jacques Derrida); *Roland Barthes and the Empire of Signs*; *Umberto Eco & Football*; and *Pedagogies of Difference*.

Kathryn Underwood is a professor at Ryerson University. Her research interests are in human rights and education practice, particularly with regard to disability rights and inclusive education. As a postdoctoral fellow at the Faculty of Education, York University, and as a faculty member in the School of Early Childhood Studies, her research projects have spanned work in family-school relationships, special education policy, and early childhood education and care policy, both in Canada and internationally. She has been involved with over 20 research projects, with funding from government, the not-for-profit sector, and private foundations.

Angelina Weenie is a Plains Cree educator from Sweetgrass First Nation, Saskatchewan, Canada. Her research interests include resilience, language and culture, and land-based education. She teaches in the areas of early childhood education, Indigenous educational professional studies, and Indigenous pedagogy. Angelina completed her Master of Education degree in 2002 from the University of Saskatchewan. Her research topic was Resilience and First Nations Postsecondary First Nations Students. She received her doctoral degree from the University of Regina, in curriculum and instruction, in October 2010. Her doctoral dissertation is titled "Self-Study: The InBetween Space of an Aboriginal Academic." She currently serves as the Indigenous Education program coordinator at the First Nations University of Canada, Regina, Saskatchewan.